The Absent Voice

The Absent Voice

NARRATIVE COMPREHENSION IN THE THEATER

Stanton B. Garner, Jr.

UNIVERSITY OF ILLINOIS PRESS
Urbana and Chicago

Publication of this work was supported in part by a grant from the Horace H. Rackham School of Graduate Studies at the University of Michigan.

This book is printed on acid-free paper.

Library of Congress Cataloging-in-Publication Data

Garner, Stanton B., 1955–
    The absent voice : narrative comprehension in the theater /
Stanton B. Garner, Jr.
        p.   cm.
    Bibliography: p.
    Includes index.
    ISBN 0-252-01607-6 (alk. paper)
    1. English drama—History and criticism.   2. Plots (Drama, novel,
etc.)   3. Narration (Rhetoric)   4. Theater audiences.   5. Cognition
in literature.   I. Title.
PR635.P5G37 1989
822'.009—dc19   88-28727
                                                                        CIP

Contents

Acknowledgments

As a study of theatrical comprehension and its manipulation within specific dramatic texts, this book owes a variety of debts: to theorists within theater and literary studies, to critics of individual authors and texts, to theater practitioners, and to writers and researchers within cognitive psychology. I hope that I have made these often considerable debts clear within individual chapters, and within the notes that follow them. I would like to thank those of my colleagues at the University of Michigan and elsewhere who have read sections of this book in articles or in manuscript, and who have incurred my admiration and gratitude through their responses: Normand Berlin, Laurence Danson, James Gindin, William F. Matchett, Michael C. Schoenfeldt, Debora K. Shuger, J. L. Styan, and Herbert F. Tucker. My special thanks to Michael Goldman and Enoch Brater for more extensive response and for more frequently solicited support over the years, and to Sidney Homan, whose shrewd comments proved invaluable during the manuscript's final revisions. My gratitude extends, of course, to my family and friends, whose unfailing interest and concern helped sustain this project and its author. Among these, David M. Azen has been a source of inspiration from the book's beginnings, while Deborah R. Geis has been unceasingly generous with her time, interest, intelligence, and love. Mentor as well as friend, Joseph G. Price will always be in my debt for encouraging my interest in the theater and introducing me to the performance world within dramatic texts.

I would also like to express my gratitude to G. E. Bentley and family, the Princeton University English Department, the former University and College Theatre Association, the Horace H. Rackham Graduate School of the University of Michigan, and the

American Council of Learned Societies for acknowledgment and support of various kinds while this project was in its development. Finally, the editors of *Studies in Philology*, *Modern Language Quarterly*, and *Modern Drama* have graciously offered their permission for my use here of material that appeared, in earlier form, within their pages.

Introduction

To explore narrative and cognition in the theater is to become aware of a recurrent bias against these subjects, a bias that manifests itself in fields as antithetical as contemporary theater practice and traditional dramatic criticism. Much contemporary theater, displaying an Ibsenesque ambivalence toward its nineteenth-century inheritance, has set itself in strident opposition to the hegemony of plot in conventional drama and to the obsession with audience comprehension evident in a remark like William Gillette's (in 1916): "A play is a device—an invention—a carefully adjusted series of more or less ingenious traps."[1] The spectator conceptualized by Eugène Scribe, Francisque Sarcey, and William Archer as a locus of comprehension and curiosity has been branded naive by theorists as diverse as Brecht and Grotowski, and dramatic explorations of indeterminacy and disruption reflect an age whose scientific, literary, artistic, and philosophical currents have confronted traditional notions of time and sequence with profound skepticism. At its heart, this movement within twentieth-century theater has precipitated not only the rejection of certain forms of narrative structure, but a broader dismissal of narrativity itself, a distinctively modern sense that "plot" is irreconcilable with the essential (and myriad) energies of performance. The operations of narrative, and the narrative orientations of audience to play, have seemed incidental to the theatrical worlds of Tristan Tzara's *The Gas Heart*, Peter Handke's *Sprechstücke*, and contemporary performance art, and to a theoretical arena in which Artaud has denounced "story-telling psychology" in favor of a theater that "puts itself whenever possible in communion with pure forces."[2]

Somewhat paradoxically, the avant-garde split between narrative and performance, and the attendant relegation of narrative to a kind of bloodless abstraction, finds a parallel in the Aristotelianism that continues to influence the academic study of dramatic texts. As a consequence of Aristotle's abstract and analytic mode of inquiry in *The Poetics*, whereby tragedy (and *poesis* itself) is divided into its component "elements" or "aspects," "plot" has been accorded a preeminent, but lonely, autonomy, theoretically severed from other dramatic elements with which it interacts in performance and from the theatrical moment in which it is realized. Aristotle makes concessions to performance in *The Poetics*—providing cursory mention of "spectacle," for instance, and urging the dramatist to visualize the play's dramatic incidents—but the treatise displays a more profound antitheatricalism, standing in uneasy relation to the stage it addresses. In his remarks on acting, for instance, Aristotle deplores performances in which acting calls attention to itself, displaying suspicion toward the actor's histrionic art and a broader aversion toward any moment when the stage asserts its own theatrical presence. That Aristotle's conception of plot draws upon this antitheatricalism is evident in his claim that "tragedy even without action achieves its function just as epic does; for its character is apparent through reading." [3] According to this conception, plot reveals itself on the mind's interior stage, its structural features pure in their conceptual abstraction, the dramatic world uncontaminated by the performative. Denied its theatrical embodiment in this way, it is small wonder that narrative has been relegated to drama's second order, that academic discussions of plot have, for the most part, remained lifeless and formulaic, and that a critic like John van Druten might long for "a play that was all atmosphere with no plot at all." [4] If contemporary theater artists have marginalized narrative by celebrating the stage, Aristotle's dramatic legacy has achieved a comparable effect by paring the stage away.

Abstracting narrative from its conditions in performance involves stripping comprehension of its place within the totality of audience response: physiological, sensory, emotional, visceral. Complex though this response is in a medium so various in its stimuli, difficult though it remains to isolate and define, it remains central to the spectator's experience of the theatrical medium, a medium characterized by its phenomenal immediacy. This immediacy, and its attendant modes of address, constitute a crucial difference between dramatic performance and the printed text. A book, of course, is also "present" to us, and the experience of reading represents, in part, the reader's attempts to overcome the physical resistances it presents. But these resistances are, in the end, slight; with occasional exceptions such as *Tristram Shandy* and *Finnegans Wake,* the printed text is largely "transparent" as a medium,[5] indicating an imaginative world from which the book itself recedes during the reading process. The pace of reading is generally within our control, and because the printed text offers relatively little sensory address, it tends not to assert the kind of refractory immediacy that might form part of its aesthetic effect.

The stage, of course, is different in this regard, for the materials of performance constitute the materials of its fictional world. Whereas the linguistic world of a book points beyond itself to the conceptual, the objects, actors, sounds, and lights of the theater evoke the imaginative realm of fiction by pointing at themselves in an inescapable self-focus. Lacking the written text's mediations, the stage "stands in" for its represented world, and because its physicality represents the very condition by which the play is created, it never fully effaces itself in this transformation.[6] A book—even the printed version of a play—contains words that may describe the battlements of Elsinore, but the stage provides boards that constitute these battlements. The audience imagines more than those boards, imagines extensions of them in space and time, even imagines that they are other than boards, but they remain boards nonetheless, insistent in their physical and perceptual immediacy. To quote Bert O. States, "theater—unlike fiction, painting, sculpture, and film—is really a language whose words consist to an unusual degree of things that *are* what they seem to be. In theater, image and object, pretense and pretender, sign-vehicle and content, draw unusually close."[7] As Pirandello understood so well, one of drama's many paradoxes lies in this very point: that for the dramatic text to receive life in the theater, it must surrender itself to the medium of performance, a medium that intrudes its own opacity upon the imaginative material of fiction. Uncomfortable with the theater's myriad constraints, Émile Zola wrote: "How much more independent are we in the novel! And that's why, when the glamour of the footlights makes the blood dance, we prefer to exercise it by keeping aloof and to remain the absolute masters of our works. In the theatre we are asked to submit to too much." [8]

Zola's remark suggests a related reason why even narratologists have tended to shy away from dramatic narrative. From Ben Jonson's anger at Inigo Jones' elaborate stagings of his court masques to the literary intrusions of George Bernard Shaw and Eugene O'Neill into the texts of their plays, dramatists have displayed consistent uneasiness with one of drama's central features as a narrative form: the unique absence of the dramatist from the play in performance. As Shaw wrote (in defense of his distinctively "literary" presentation of playtexts), "since he [the dramatist] could not act the play singlehanded even if he were a trained actor, he must fall back on his powers of literary expression, as other poets and fictionalists do." [9] Events are told to us in a novel, selected for us by a guiding camera in film, but events on stage display the illusion of life itself in their apparent freedom from the originating writer's mediating perspective. "In the theatre we are not aware of the intervening storyteller," Thornton Wilder wrote in 1941. "The speeches arise from the characters in an apparent pure spontaneity." [10] Despite all the representatives of theatrical creation who take the stage of *Six Characters in Search of an Author,* the play's performance is precipitated by one who does not: the author, who has banished his creation from the womblike enclosure of his literary imagination and who now stands apart from the story to which he has given birth. Through this device, Pirandello foregrounds an absence central to the theater, both condition and consequence of its material autonomy. In theatrical performance, the authorship of writing is supplanted by the very different authorship of production, the collaborative effort of director, designer, technician, and actor. A dramatist like Shaw may exercise a strong hand in production, but the actual performance takes place with him, at best, in the wings, his powerlessness a result of the theater's material independence.

This "apparent pure spontaneity" has profound implications for dramatic narrative, for it releases a play's temporal meanings from the guidance of a narrational voice, which (in the novel, for instance) guides comprehension of events through its presentation of incidents and provides a kind of coherence through its textual mediations. While few contemporary novelists appropriate the omniscient voice of *Tom Jones,* vocalized within that novel as authorizing source of its design, a guiding narrator of some form still characterizes most novels, interposing a mediating consciousness between reader and event. Even when this ruling voice displays imperfect reliability, its presence constitutes a point of reference against which the novel's events can be verified or, if necessary, revised. While imperfect narrators may complicate the channels between reader and narrative, they nevertheless stand in relation to both, clarifying events through an essentially focalizing indirection. In Malcolm Bradbury's words, the novel's "main structural characteristic lies in a developing action about characters and events conducted in a closed—that is to say, an authorially conditioned—world containing principles, values and attitudes by which we may evaluate those events." [11] Experimental novelists, rejecting the univocal narrator, have undermined the presence of even the imperfect narrator, fragmenting their fictional worlds through disjunctions of voice and discourse. But even here—in the gaps and indeterminacies, the question about "who" is addressing us, the radical dislocations of time and place—the novel still presents us with an organizing presence: the primary linguistic source, what Todorov terms "the subject of the speech-act," [12] inscribed in the text's very words. Behind the narrator of *Tom Jones,* behind Faulkner's Benji, behind even the fragmentary voice of Beckett's *Molloy* and the French *nouveau roman,* lie discursive sources that serve as points of reference, subjects of organization and arrangement, the *sine qua non* of the novel's events because the *sine qua non* of its words. The novel is limited to linguistic presentation by the very nature of its medium, and because language contains implicit points of origination, this form of presentation inscribes the authorial "subject" within the work in a number of ways. We read a novel, as we do all exclusively textual literary forms, as something articulated, and our creation of an imaginary present happens against the completion of a written past. To a certain extent, a novel is over before we ever begin to read it, its events selected and transcribed against the retrospect of a completed utterance. Despite the varying degrees of narrative indeterminacy within this utterance, and despite the necessary creativity of the reading process, comprehending a novel involves locating its elements within a temporal whole that already exists in prenarrative potential. The very form of the book, with its printed pages enclosed between covers, reinforces our experience of what we read as something both authorially conditioned and linguistically complete, and this sense of a virtual whole is facilitated by what the book allows: flipping back, reading ahead, glancing at a table of contents.

This cursory discussion, to be sure, risks oversimplifying what is a complex and problematic process, the subject of many of literary theory's chief interests. But it does suggest the abstraction inherent in the reading process, and the formal characteristic by which this process is conditioned: a textual mediation, inscribed at various levels within the literary text, which facilitates the apprehension of a narrative whole as well as the construction of detail within it. The play in performance lacks this controlling mediation. Plays bear their authors' stamps, recognizable in patterns of dialogue and action, and one can always tell a Jonsonian from a Shakespearean play on the stage, by differences of language, characterization, and action. But such "signatures" are features of style, and they are often recognized and appreciated only as peripheral features of audience response. On the more fundamental levels of perception and cognition, and in terms of narrational function, the author's presence is *not* felt in the theater as it is felt in so many ways within the printed text. The movement from script to performance liberates the play from its exclusively linguistic embodiment: language becomes speech, directions become *mise-en-scène,* implied presence becomes performance reality. Production realizes the play as something outside the printed text, and as such it stands on its own, shaped only invisibly by the text it seeks to embody. The play may suggest its author's touch, allude to this author metadramatically, even—as in Beaumont, Jonson, and Pirandello—bring "him" or a representative on stage, but compared to the novelist's ruling control, the playwright's voice is an absent one, resounding in its narrational silences.

Like readers, the theater audience must engage in a complex process of construction, building a coherent framework—beginning, middle, and end—out of the material with which it is provided. Unlike readers, though, the audience must do so without the mediating presence of a narrator, and without the embracing control of linguistic voice. Instead, the audience of dramatic narrative faces a stage that exists on its own terms, and it must build an understanding of events out of the immediacy with which it is confronted and in which it participates. The process underlying this construction is at once straightforward and complex, and it involves activities and responses different in degree and kind from those engaged by the novel.

As the above remarks suggest, this study attempts to view narrative, and the cognitive operations that it occasions, within the environment of performance. At its heart are the following premises: that drama is a species of theater art, and that the moment of performance constitutes its formal realization. This study accordingly seeks to locate dramatic narrative within that moment, and to investigate the ways in which performance constitutes and infuses the dramatic object. It considers one of drama's central paradoxes: that the author's narrational absence from the play in performance makes possible certain modes of presence, and that presence constitutes the theater's primary gift to drama. Dramatic narrative, the following chapters will suggest, is bound to the theatrical moment in a fundamental reciprocity, through which the movements of narrative are intricately linked to the movements of performance, and the elements of fiction are finally inseparable from the elements of the stage. To speak of dramatic narrative is, of necessity, to speak of the performative world that embodies it, that world from which it emerges and to which it continually reverts.

This study will focus on cognition and on the "drama of comprehension" as it is occasioned by and within dramatic texts. In its attempt to understand dramatic narrative in performance, this study will focus on those members of the theatrical interaction most frequently neglected in discussions of drama: the audience. The audience, after all, occupies a position of particular centrality to dramatic narrative, and to the theater event in general.[13] As the target of the play's operations and final processor of its meanings, the audience represents a privileged point of closure within the theatrical interaction as a whole. Peter Brook has written: "I can take any empty space and call it a bare stage. A man walks across this empty space whilst someone else is watching him, and this is all that is needed for an act of theater to be engaged."[14] Pared

down to its essentials, stage narrative is possible without a director, without designers, even without a dramatist; it requires only
the circuitry linking performer and spectator. To modify Brook's
illustration, a man walks across this empty space *for* someone
who watches him, and it is in this watching—guided (of course)
by the arts of acting, directing, and playwriting—that narrative
arises in the theater. In the absence of authorial voice, the audience
bears an increased burden for drawing connections and establishing outlines. In performance—as the first fifteenth-century pageant wagon stands decorated, as the curtain rises on a provincial
Russian manor, as Coriolanus strides across the Globe platform—
the audience must face the stage in all its concreteness and begin
the cognitive activities involved in drawing significance out of
what it experiences. By virtue of its attention to the moment, and
its efforts to give this moment fictional shape, the audience serves
as a locus of the transformations and constructions that characterize theatrical narrative. It is no accident that the missing author in
Six Characters is replaced by a Chinese box of spectators—audience watching Manager watching actors watching characters
watching themselves—all involved in the quintessentially theatrical process of making sense out of what they see. Of all the participants in theatrical performance, it is through the audience, and
its efforts of comprehension that order (or fail to order) what
takes place on stage, that a play's events receive preceptual and
cognitive shape.[15]

Dramatic narrativity situates the student of audience response within particularly rich theatrical territory, one permitting
(indeed, demanding) multiple angles of vision. As a narrative form
compelling various modes of intellection, drama offers grist for the
student of cognitive process, foregrounding the play of incident
and idea as they are actualized through the play of mind. At the
same time, as a performance form addressing the spectator within
an experiential field, drama also makes itself uniquely available to
more immediate phenomenological insights. If it is true that the
phenomenological basis of art "rests finally in the immediacy of
perception's encounter with a world," then the performance
worlds of dramatic art have much to tell us about the parameters
of theatrical experience, the *gestalten* of audience response, and
the particular ways in which the theater's spectators inhabit fields

of perceptual, even physiological, activity.[16] That these fields have been theoretically severed from the realm of cognition represents an unnatural (and unnecessary) division of an experiential totality—especially in the theater, where the body is allowed its modes of intelligence and mind is distinctly bodied. Seeking to overcome the Aristotelian and avant-garde divisions between narrative and performance, this study attempts to bridge the cognitive and the perceptual, setting both within the broader continuum of theatrical response.

Chapter 1 investigates the cognitive activities engaged by dramatic narrative within the conditioning environment of the theater. In this investigation, two distinct pressures emerge, a dialectic of construction and resistance that determines the audience's processing of performance signals. From a performance's opening moments, the audience engages in a conceptual process designed to transform the stage and its activities into structured fiction, drawing upon the cognitive processes for ordering time that it employs outside the theater as well. On the other hand, while the theatrical medium encourages such comprehension, it also threatens it, since comprehension must continually struggle against the stage's nonconceptual immediacy, a performance present which is, in many ways, irreducibly nonnarrative. Even with the most tightly narrative drama, performance confronts an audience with the limits of its structuring abilities and with a spectrum of noncognitive responses to the stage's sensory address. Chapter 2 considers the play of this dialectic within dramatic texts and the opportunities for interpretation presented by dramatic narrative's unique rhythms of conceptual and nonconceptual effects. Extending this perspective on cognition into the play's own world, the chapter suggests that the stage's physical representations of time and space often confront dramatic characters with problems of comprehension similar to those it poses its audience—the relationship of the immediate present to its conceptual contexts of past and future, problems of reliability in the face of conflicting narrative possibilities, general problems of memory and anticipation—thereby establishing cognitive correlations between dramatic action and theatrical response.

Chapters 3 through 7 investigate the implications of cognitive analysis for the study of individual plays, chosen to illustrate a range of experimentation with narrative comprehension: *Everyman* and *Mankind, The Winter's Tale, Volpone, Major Barbara* and *Heartbreak House*, and Samuel Beckett's recent plays *Not I* and *Footfalls*. The heart of this study, these readings will extend and particularize the investigation begun in the earlier chapters, tracing—in varying dramatic contexts—the development and disruption of cognition.

A word or two about texts: given the abundance of dramatic material available to a study like this, selection of plays is a logistical inevitability. I make little attempt at historical or international inclusiveness: this study focuses primarily on British drama, and only with the advent of modern drama does it venture far abroad. That the sequence of plays chosen for Chapters 3 through 7 itself traces a kind of dramaturgical narrative—with developments and shifts, amplifications and contrasts—should not obscure the fact that other plays might equally well have been chosen, and other stories told. Moreover, in its use of dramatic material, this study accords relatively little weight to the conventional division of drama into tragedy and comedy. Expectations connected with these two dramatic modes do, of course, influence narrative response: an audience anticipates Othello's death and the marriage of Rosalind and Orlando for reasons that are, in part, generic. Yet the distinction between tragedy and comedy, like so many such distinctions, has grown to obscure at least as much as it clarifies, since its generic labels do little to illuminate specific features of audience response. That many of the plays chosen for close analysis have pronounced comic elements is no accident, since it is often in those plays labeled "comedies" that cognitive activity is most vigorously engaged and its conflicts with the stage most frequent. George Meredith defined comedy as "the humour of the mind," and the specific location of this conceptual play is suggested by Fergusson's observations that "comedy in any period assumes the presence of an audience."[17] But tragedy is also capable of intense cognitive address: one thinks, for instance, of the equivocation that opens *Macbeth* or the grotesque plot distortions of Websterian drama. As with all structural models, once the fundamental processes of narrative response are investigated, and the often complex ways of manipulating them detailed, we may be able to return to distinctions like "tragedy" and "comedy" with a more accurate understanding of their theatrical pertinence.

The fact remains that, despite the work of recent theorists, we still know remarkably little about temporality in drama, how it draws upon the theatrical, and how it is cognitively and perceptually structured.[18] As Bernard Beckerman notes, "In an art that is temporal as well as spatial, we have hardly any terms for designating the sequential features of a play, let alone the subtle interactions of the presentation itself. Our vocabulary is inadequate, our descriptions of the theatrical process imprecise, and our definitions of what constitutes the art of drama virtually nonexistent."[19] Beckerman's own theoretical work stands among a number of contemporary studies exploring drama in performance: studies addressing the disciplinary and conceptual boundaries that have long separated drama from theater, form from medium, text from performance. Overcoming such boundaries is the greatest challenge facing those who would understand the operations and modes of theatrical address that govern audience response. In that moment when an actor lurches across Brook's "empty space" in the role of Richard, the hunchbacked Duke of Gloucester—as his opening words "Now is the winter of our discontent / Made glorious summer by this son of York" begin to locate this theatrical world within the historical milieu of fifteenth-century England, and detail it—the arts of drama and theater draw imperceptibly close.[20] To understand the operations of narrative cognition, we must embrace this moment in all its complexity, discern its performative rhythms, and follow its dialectic of transformation and presence.

CHAPTER ONE

Narrative, Cognition, and Performance

Narrative Comprehension in the Theater

Since *narrative* (as we are using the term) designates the temporal dimension of drama's fictional world, this study will consider a range of material not often included within the narrower term *plot*. In Ibsen's *Hedda Gabler*, for instance, narrative includes not only the stage events that take place in the Tesman household, but also those that antedate them in the play's "past" and those projected beyond the play's concluding present. To speak of a play's narrative is to consider the outlines of this temporal whole, and how it is created, detailed, and sustained out of the materials of theatrical performance. Drama's narrational uniqueness lies, in part, in the sheer multiplicity of these materials, and in the variety of performance elements that replace the printed word as the medium for narrative creation: stage structures, props, light, sound, bodies.

The density of this performance present has obvious consequences for narrative extension and range, consequences that suggest some of the constraints imposed by the conditions of theatrical representation. In terms of narrative's "inner realm," for instance, the novel permits linguistic figurations of consciousness, in all its subjective particularity, while drama must suggest the "subtext" of thought and feeling indirectly, presenting subjective events through actions, gestures, and overt self-articulation. The two forms display similar differences concerning fiction's temporal and spatial dimensions. Susanne Langer's characterization of "literature proper" as "the mode typified by memory"[1] is useful, for the novel's handling of space and time can imitate memory's freedom from geographical boundaries and its broad, richly associative awareness of time. Not only does novelistic action extend into a past and future well beyond the main point of narrative focus, it is also characterized by a fluid arrangement of the central narrative events themselves: the temporal switches of *Portrait of a Lady,* for instance, and the complex fragmentation and scattering of events in *Ulysses, Absalom, Absalom!,* and *Malone Dies.* Such temporal and spatial range is formally unavailable to the dramatist, who is bound by the "real" time and space of theatrical performance. Lacking the novelist's point of view, which can omnisciently include a wide range of events and which can hold together these fragments of time and space in complex patterns of nontemporal order, the dramatist must create a stage sequence of several hours' length, its only narrators the characters/actors within it, its scope and duration constrained by the cognitive capacities of an audience that cannot turn back to an earlier page. Time is necessarily more concentrated in drama, past and future more insistently drawn toward the present. Even in a play as engaged with memory as Ibsen's *Ghosts,* anteriority has neither the breadth nor the detail of Proust's novelistic retrospect. Space, too, is bound to the stage, drawn almost magnetically within its physical boundaries. Beside the resonantly imaginative journeys across and beyond the Thames in the introductory paragraphs of Conrad's *Heart of Darkness,* and the geographical movement across Ireland at the close of Joyce's "The Dead," stand the contrasting evocations of offstage locales in drama, extensions necessarily more compressed because limited to the stage and to the characters who evoke them. When vaster scenes of action require more extensive offstage geography, it is often cast in sharp counterpoint to the present, as in Antony's lines to Cleopatra—"Let Rome in Tiber melt, and the wide arch / Of the rang'd empire fall! Here is my space" (*Antony and Cleopatra,* I.i.33–34)—the longing allusions to Moscow throughout *The Three Sisters,* and Nell's recollection of Lake Como, which form part of *Endgame*'s incongruous nostalgia.

It is easy to smile at the neoclassic obsession with the "dramatic unities" and to read with gratitude Samuel Johnson's rejoinder that "It is false, that any representation is mistaken for reality; that any dramatick fable in its materiality was ever credible, or, for a single moment, was ever credited."[2] The stage—especially the modern stage—has shown a persistent willingness to violate the naturalism insisted upon so rigorously by the neoclassic strictures on time and place. Yet the principle of the unities does reflect a naturalistic conservatism belonging to the stage, a conservatism that makes even the most experimental contemporary play more focused and coherent, spatially and temporally, than most literary narratives. In spite of the important role of exposition and the "past" in drama, Pinter's *Betrayal* is one of the few plays to move sequentially backward in its representation of events; when past events are represented onstage, as they are in *Death of a Salesman*, they are generally set within the context of a forward-moving present.[3] Such naturalistic tendencies suggest that the unities of time and place, so alien to modes of literary narrative, are more faithful to the theatrical medium than we have grown to think.

But the formal constraints imposed by performance mask a complex network of cognitive and perceptual activity, marshaled into action by the myriad exigencies of theatrical seeing. In order to explore the implications of this theatrical moment for narrative structure, and for the "narrative comprehension" that underlies the audience's engagement with performance, we will shift our attention to Chekhov's *The Three Sisters* and focus on the opening moments in which its narrative field is both received and evoked. Our discussion will begin, in short, where narrative in the theater begins, with a bare stage prepared to signal its dramatic world. It is at the levels of perception and cognition that drama reveals most fully its differences from literary narrative forms and that the dialectical activity particular to narrative response in the theater becomes apparent.

Evoking a naturalism different from the scenic bareness of the Elizabethan and Jacobean stage, Chekhov's directions detail the performance image as it appears during the play's opening moments:

> *In the* PROZOROVS' *house. A drawing room with columns, beyond which a large reception room is visible. Midday: it is bright and sunny outside. In the reception room a table is being set for lunch.* OLGA, *in the dark blue uniform of a girls' high-school teacher, is*

correcting exercise books, standing or walking about as she does
so; MASHA, in a black dress, her hat on her lap, sits reading a book;
IRINA, in a white dress, stands lost in thought.[4]

As with all such directions, these lines require imaginative effort if
we are to recreate the moment and what it represents to an audience intent on comprehending it. For *The Three Sisters'* audience
at once knows more and less than these directions provide. On
one hand, the spectator sees the stage in its totality, its particularity of detail unified by its visual continuity. On the other hand,
much of the information presented within these stage directions is
absent from the stage as the audience confronts it during the performance's opening moments. Most obviously, neither the house
nor the figures who first appear in it are named; they stand in
momentary anonymity, a set not fully transformed into setting,
actors not completely integrated into the play as characters. Like
the accompanying list of "Characters in the Play," the printed
stage directions assume a retrospective familiarity with the play's
world, a familiarity that emerges, in the theater, only during the
course of performance. But even more than this, the whole given
of a dramatic world as it is implied by these directions subtly misrepresents the theatrical moment as the audience initially experiences it, for the stage's prenarrative physicality precedes the establishment of a dramatic world. The Prozorovs' house, with its
columned drawing room and decorated reception room, is no
house at all, but an arrangement of stage materials meant to represent a house, just as the bright sun of midday is a calculated
illusion of stage lights. That the stage is quickly recognized to be
the representation of a Russian manor attests both to the mimetic
foundations of Chekhov's stage practice and to the audience's willingness to participate in the illusion, to credit the stage's imaginative reality. But the rapidity with which this process occurs should
not obscure the imaginative transformation that underlies it, or
the audience's crucial role in the process by which a medium arti-
ficial in its materials is transformed into the "then" and "there"
of dramatic fiction.

Even before the characters begin to speak, therefore, the audience has been challenged to create a dramatic world with its
own autonomy, a "now" at once the present of performance and

story, the outcome of a fictionalizing transformation. As the play progresses, this world will be given a temporal and geographic structure to match its visual basis, and its characters and events will be linked in a web of relationships that will constitute it in space and extend it forward and backward in time. The initial stage setting encourages this process: its decor locates the play historically, as do the costumes of the three actresses; the sunlit "outside" evokes not only an environmental extension, but also the seasons of spring or early summer; and the set table anticipates the more immediate affair of dinner. As in most drama, though, more intricate narrative identifications and extensions begin only with the play's dialogue, when Chekhov's characters begin to cast time's outlines:

> OLGA: Father died just a year ago today, on the fifth of May—your name day, Irina. It was snowing then, and very cold. I felt as though I should never live through it, and you lay in a dead faint. But now, a year has gone by, and we think of it calmly; you're already wearing white, and your face is radiant. [*The clock strikes.*] The clock was striking then, too. [*Pause*] I remember there was music when Father was carried out, and they fired a salute at the cemetery. He was a general, in command of a brigade, yet there were very few people walking behind his coffin. But then, it was raining. Heavy rain and snow.
>
> IRINA: Why recall it?
>
> [BARON TUZENBACH, CHEBUTYKIN, *and* SOLYONY *appear behind the columns near the table in the reception room.*]
>
> OLGA: It's so warm today we can keep the windows wide open, but the birches are not yet in leaf. . . . Father was given a brigade and left Moscow eleven years ago, and I remember perfectly that by this time, at the beginning of May in Moscow, everything was in bloom, it was warm, all bathed in sunshine. Eleven years have passed, but I remember it all as though we had left there yesterday. Oh, God! This morning I woke up, I saw this flood of sunlight, saw the spring, and joy stirred in my soul, I had a passionate longing to go home again.
>
> CHEBUTYKIN: Like hell he did!
>
> TUZENBACH: Of course, that's nonsense.
>
> [MASHA, *absorbed in her book, softly whistles a tune.*]

OLGA: Don't whistle, Masha. How can you! [*Pause*] Being in
school every day, then giving lessons till evening, my head aches
continually, and I'm beginning to think like an old woman. In fact,
these four years that I've been teaching in the high school, day by
day I feel my youth and strength draining out of me. Only one
dream keeps growing stronger and stronger . . .
IRINA: To go to Moscow. To sell the house, make an end of everything here, and go to Moscow. . . .
OLGA: Yes! To go to Moscow as soon as possible.
[CHEBUTYKIN *and* TUZENBACH *laugh*.] (pp. 235–36)

Little has happened on stage: characters have moved through
and around a stage occupied by objects and other characters; three
characters have entered unacknowledged by the others; four characters have spoken and one whistled. Yet during this sequence the
dramatic world has acquired a temporal outline already intricate
in its levels and its details. The stage present is further identified as
a May afternoon, its sunny atmosphere edged with weariness and
ennui. This present is shown in its relation to a past that stretches
imaginatively beyond its stage borders, a past telescoping backward through identifying points and stages: Father's death (one
year ago), Olga's years as a schoolteacher (the past four), the move
to the provinces (eleven years earlier), and—most resonant of all
as a counterpoint to these later times of sadness—the early years
in Moscow, with their springs "all bathed in sunshine," to which
the present occasions an imaginative return. Indeed, so pronounced is the memory of this former time, so strong the longing
that it evokes on the part of Olga and Irina, that its recapture
constitutes the future that the two project: "To go to Moscow as
soon as possible." Subsequent disclosure and action will add further detail to this narrative framework, and they will occasion revision of its outlines, but they will do so within and against the
temporal world that this opening scene has introduced. As *The
Three Sisters* develops, present, past, and future will stand in increasingly complex relationship, the contours of each dependent
on the details of the others, their outlines standing in intricate patterns of support and irony. These outlines will be further complicated by the provisional: past moments temporarily clouded by
the unknown, a dramatic present unclear in the relationships it

offers, a future whose actual form stands precariously balanced on the uncertainties of longing, whim, and inertia. In each case, these lines and outlines, images and shadings, represent imaginative constructions facilitated by the arts of acting, direction, and design, imposed by a collaborating audience on a stage that, prior to such imaginings, constitutes itself alone.

Dramatic narrative, in other words, hinges upon the imaginative transformation of theatrical space into dramatic space, of a physical here and now into an imaginative here and now. Theater is comprised of boards, lights, objects, actors gesturing, speaking, of movements counterpointed by stillness, sounds counterpointed by silence. Drama represents these things, but more: it also evokes a realm within which these elements have fictional meaning. Elder Olson observes that dramatists affect their audiences primarily through sensation and only secondarily through the imagination,[5] but it might be more accurate to say that dramatists affect their audiences imaginatively through (and only through) sensory address. The materials of performance retain their autonomous status, but they are endowed with a virtuality by which they exist simultaneously on the plane of dramatic fiction. This characteristic suggests the extent to which dramatic narrative displays the "twinness" that marks dramatic performance as a whole, the theater's peculiar coordination of actual and other. As fictional time, dramatic narrative forms only one of a set of temporal relationships activated by performance, including (most immediately) performance time itself, with its own sequence and duration. The neoclassic unity of time represented an attempt to bring these two temporal dimensions into closer proximity to each other, but the very effort reveals the usual tension that exists between performance and the world it designates, a tension foregrounded in the temporally sprawling Elizabethan drama that Sidney decried. Such discontinuity is inescapable given the essentially constructive nature of dramatic narrative, and the fact that performance time stands as pretext for fictional time. Narrative does not inhere in the materials of performance any more than it inheres in the words on a page; it constitutes an imaginative formulation, imposed upon the stage and its activities by actor, director, designer, and (most crucially) by the audience that assents to the fictionality of the dramatic world and constructs this world's temporal outlines.

That the forms of this imposition are usually conventional, and thereby taken for granted, should not obscure the fact they remain impositions, applied from outside on materials that retain their own autonomy: in the theater, "make-believe" retains its literal meaning of "making belief." It is this imaginative process, and the intense conceptual building underlying it, that the Chorus in *Henry V* describes in order to justify his presence on stage:

> Piece out our imperfections with your thoughts;
> Into a thousand parts divide one man,
> And make imaginary puissance;
> Think, when we talk of horses, that you see them
> Printing their proud hoofs i' th' receiving earth;
> For 'tis your thoughts that now must deck our kings,
> Carry them here and there, jumping o'er times,
> Turning th' accomplishment of many years
> Into an hour-glass: for the which supply,
> Admit me Chorus to this history. . . .
>
> (Prologue, ll. 23–32)

The Globe's wooden platform becomes the battlefields of France through imaginative projection alone, and this dramatic world acquires its history, its development, and its possible futures through similar activity. But such imaginative transformation is never complete, for the world of England and Agincourt, with its broad temporal span, remains nothing more than this platform and its simple materials: actors, props, and a figure who reminds the audience of what his stage alone cannot signify.

The audience's role in the transformation of theatrical space into dramatic space undermines the traditional image of the passive spectator, who "attends" upon performance and upon a dramatic representation shaped for his or her reception. While the theater's reliance on signals transmitted to an audience during performance renders it a "reactive art,"[6] play-watching is (from another standpoint) highly active, creative, a means of transforming the stage into the environment of fiction and incorporating its multiple percepts into patterns of comprehensibility. From this perspective, it is clear that the audience uses performance, processes it in a number of highly active ways, and that narrative constitutes one of the fundamental conceptual uses that the audience makes of the stage. In its attempts to construct and detail the frameworks of narrative, the audience engages in intricate cognitive activity, exercising comprehension upon the signals it receives during performance, what J. L. Styan terms the stage's "sequence of impressions."[7] As expected in a medium so dependent on the spoken word, many of these signals are verbal, embodied in the characters' own recollections and anticipations; as Keir Elam has noted, "in the absence of narratorial guides, providing external description and 'world-creating' propositions, the dramatic world has to be specified *from within* by means of references made to it by the very individuals who constitute it."[8] But they emerge as well from the stage's other resources, the other signifying elements that constitute theatrical performance. From a performance's opening moments, spectators engage in the process of scanning the stage and its activities, looking for material from which they can elaborate a narrative framework, corroborating this data with their expectations and what they have already formulated. Olga's opening line—"Father died just a year ago today, on the fifth of May—your name day, Irina"—is examined in terms of the stage and the characters who people it, and its information is located within a developing framework: spring, Father's death, Irina's birthday. Moreover, the suggestion of relationship is corroborated with the information suggested by the title, and by the stage trio Chekhov arranges almost in tableau. As the opening scene progresses, facts link with facts, and this interplay of information enables comprehension to construct a network of events and relationships that, five minutes into *The Three Sisters,* is already complex.

Experimental psychology confirms what is evident to observation: that the patterning activities of human consciousness are rendered particularly difficult during perception's initial encounters with an aesthetic object.[9] At this point, the audience establishes the dramatic world as a fictional construct with conceptually independent status, and works vigorously to discern the fiction's opening points and possible directions. Conventional dramaturgy has addressed this cognitive exigency by assigning to a play's opening sequence the role of exposition, easing the demands of audience induction through straightforward narrative presentation ("I thought the King had more affected the Duke of Albany than Cornwall" [*King Lear,* I.i.1–2]). But the difficulties of narrative comprehension in its initial encounters with performance and the dramatic world are perhaps more clearly evident in those plays that tax the audience's attempts to discern events and their connections, that force the audience to sift more actively among dramatic signals. Stephen Booth's celebrated essay on *Hamlet* explores that play's opening scene as part of a broader investigation of *Hamlet* as a "succession of actions upon the understanding of an audience." Booth demonstrates Shakespeare's simultaneous raising and frustrating of expectations in the battlement scene, his systematic assault on the audience's efforts to become "intellectually comfortable": the sentries fail to establish consistent contexts for their appearance on the castle walls, withhold information expected by the audience, and discuss questions gratuitously irrelevant to the actual narrative matters at hand. As Booth concludes: "Scene one is set in the dark, and it leaves the audience in the dark." [10]

The difficulties and ambiguities structuring *Hamlet*'s introductory scene exert such a profound influence on audience response precisely because comprehension depends so heavily upon performance and its signals. Though the audience bears the final burden of narrative construction, it generates these constructions largely from material internal to the theatrical and dramatic worlds themselves. Contemporary approaches to audience response such as the German *Rezeptiongeschichte* have stressed the role of audience expectations in the reception of dramatic narrative, just as traditional dramatic theory has privileged an audience's familiarity with the play's story. Both approaches highlight the audience's preparation for performance, and the outlines that it imposes upon the play before, and while, it unfolds. In such a model, audience expectation becomes a kind of template against which the novelties and originalities of individual dramatic performances are measured, or a kind of frame wherein dramatic action is given clearly recognizable context. To be sure, the theater engages a wide range of generic, formal, social, literary, and ideological expectations: these are historically, culturally, and individually determined, and performance often hinges upon the interaction of these expectations with the stage in varying relationships of corroboration and conflict. At the same time, though drama has always drawn upon such preexistent narrative contexts, the expectations thereby generated do not frame the play's action to the extent often assumed, as if the structures of performance derived exclusively from interpretive structures held firmly and consciously within the extradramatic world of its spectators. Audience cognition must still enact its transformations of the stage into a dramatic space, must still piece together a dramatic world out of the materials it is given. Though the audience's response to the theatrical moment is conditioned by its "horizon of expectations,"[11] it is far less mediated by this prior conditioning than is often claimed. The evidence for this is suggested, in part, by the dramatic texts themselves, which often demonstate uneasiness with the reliability of certain audience mental sets by explicitly reinforcing them within the play itself. Similar theoretical tentativeness must be applied to the "story familiarity" so often assumed to rule a play's reception by its audience—that narrative preparation said to distinguish Greek, Medieval, and Elizabethan drama, in which audience response supposedly hinged upon the representation of popular stories, from more recent (and less narratively familiar) drama. The choice of a known story is clearly significant for the medieval cycle dramatist who dramatized the story of Abraham and Isaac, as well as for John Osborne as he set Martin Luther on the twentieth-century stage. But story familiarity rarely determines response to the exclusion of performance itself and the powerfully immediate demands that the moment of performance exacts on attention and the comprehension of incident. These demands tend to subvert audience familiarity with a play's story, even the familiarity that results from knowing or having seen the play, and encourage uncertainty and suspense. Indeed, as Eric Bentley and Erving Goffman both point out, an audience is often brought to share the uncertainties of the dramatic world and identify mimetically with the ignorance of the characters onstage, surrendering itself to a kind of sympathetic unknowing. Goffman writes: "Being part of an audience in the theater obliges us to act as if our own knowledge, as well as that of some of the characters, is partial."[12] Even when a spectator enters the theater with a play's narrative outlines available to memory, in other words, he or she is still cognitively subject to the materials of performance and stands much closer to the naive spectator than we have traditionally recognized.[13]

For any model of theatrical response to account fully for the performance moment, it must avoid the temptation to excessively privilege what Jackson Barry calls "retrospective structures" of audience response over "improvisational structure," that engagement with time as "the eternally changing, eternally present 'becoming.'"[14] Performance is, before all else, a sensory medium, and the chain of responses that it occasions derive from specific theatrical signals. That the reception of these signals is inescapably influenced by prior cognitive and conceptual patternings should not obscure comprehension's fundamental dependency on the moment of performance, and the interface between performance and drama it must continually negotiate.[15]

Narrative comprehension looks to performance for its outlines and details. But though the narrative information that performance provides may be scattered and discontinuous, the framework within which comprehension achieves its organization is not. From its earliest, most tentative formulations, dramatic narrative structures past, present, and future into provisional wholes. When the Chorus in *Henry V* speaks of his audience's thoughts "turning th' accomplishment of many years / Into an hour-glass," he designates (among other things) the integrative tendencies of narrative comprehension, its insistent attempts to order the play's events into a temporal whole—like his "hour-glass"—containing time's three domains in continuous relationship to each other. Engaging this tendency, the stage draws upon activities that characterize perception outside the theater as well. There, too, the perceiving subject insists that events in time demonstrate coherence and unity and imposes personal orderings to ensure that they do. Coming upon a street scene—an argument, for instance—a spectator seeks to explain its abruptness, speculates as to antecedent events, projects resolutions or future conflicts, in short, participates in a process formulated by psychologists under the label of "temporal integration." As L. S. Hearnshaw explains, "Temporal integration cuts across faculty boundaries. It implies perception of the present, memory of the past, and expectation of the future . . . integrated into a common organization."[16] This essentially narrative operation of consciousness takes place on different levels, from the minute perception of two successive sensory stimuli up to an individual's perception of his or her life as a whole. The classic description of "temporal integration" in terms of the reading process is Augustine's introspective account, in the *Confessions,* of the mental operations involved in reciting a psalm:

> I am about to repeat a psalm that I know. Before I begin, my expectation alone reaches itself over the whole: but so soon as I shall have once begun, how much so ever of it I shall take off into the past, over so much my memory also reaches: thus the life of this action of mine is extended both ways: into my memory, so far as concerns that part which I have repeated already, and into my expectation too, in respect of what I am about to repeat now; but all this while is my marking faculty present at hand, through which, that which was future, is conveyed over, that it may become past: which how much the more diligently it is done over and over again, so much more the expectation being shortened, is the memory enlarged; till the whole expectation be at length vanished quite away, when namely, that whole action being ended, shall be absolutely passed into the memory.

Augustine extends the implications of this activity beyond the act of reading, into the nonliterary "wholes" of life and history:

> What is now done in this whole psalm, the same is done also in every part of it, yea and in every syllable of it; the same order holds in a longer action too, whereof perchance this psalm is but a part; this holds too throughout the whole course of man's life, the parts whereof be all the actions of the man; it holds also throughout the whole age of the sons of men, the parts whereof be the whole lives of men.[17]

The "action" of Augustine's reading extends "both ways"— into a past and future that balance upon the present's fulcrum— and it draws its material from the words at hand. But the psalm Augustine contemplates, and which his reading succeeds in appropriating, exists as a potential "whole" well before its elements are gathered and the reading process completed. Temporal integration, as described by Augustine and theorized by Hearnshaw, is the structuring of incident within a *gestalt* whose temporal realms exist *in potentia* from the start. Though (as we have seen) the reading process is characterized by its own interactive parameters, what we might call "narrative integration" in the theater shares much with the "temporal integration" of Augustine's account; indeed, the connection between Augustine's speculations concerning "longer actions" to dramatic action is intensified by the fact that his Latin *actio* also denotes a "dramatic incident." Drama unfolds in the moment, and in so doing it engages the cognitive impulse to organize the discrete immediacies of time into consistent patterns. Like Augustine's psalm, though, the dramatic world is an artifact, and it accordingly heightens the provisional continuity that cognitive integration proposes. Dramatic time is, by its aesthetic nature, "meaningful time," and our attempt to discern its temporal outlines and continuities is reinforced by our expectation that we will find them, by our sense that the play's narrative dimension will reveal itself to be a totality, complete in promise even before its detail has been fully articulated.

This process suggests that Aristotle's definition of dramatic unity—"To be a whole is to have a beginning and a middle and an end"[18]—also describes the structure of comprehension as audience confronts play in performance. As we have seen in the case of *The Three Sisters,* the audience responds to a play's opening moments by creating a narrative *gestalt,* one that generates beginning, middle, and end within the forms of past, present, and future. From its initial construction and elaboration, this construction constitutes a "potential narrative space," and (as such) its temporal realms exist in coherent relationship to each other, even before the details of past, present, and future have been fully provided. One of the audience's fundamental activities throughout performance is to set the narrative details it extracts from performance within this temporal whole, projecting backward into the dramatic past and forward into the future, drawing upon the faculties of memory and anticipation to place what it has been given within a cognitive framework. This narrative *gestalt* is subject to continual elaboration and to frequent revision, but such revisions and elaborations constitute modifications of a framework that, from the start of performance, has outline and provisional completeness. We may not know the past, may be uncertain as to future developments and outcomes, but we struggle to comprehend the dramatic world as one that indeed has a past and a future—a world that exists complete in time, the gaps of which stand ready to be filled. We work to know this world as it unfolds in time, to interpret its signals about itself, to make our best guesses better. It is to these ends, and within such frameworks, that narrative comprehension processes the materials of performance, seeking to bring the events they signal within its grasp.

Pressures of the Stage

So far, our discussion of cognitive reception has been an account of successful negotiation. We have considered the ways by which the audience seeks to "naturalize" the stage as dramatic world, subject its otherness to frameworks of comprehension, and thereby contextualize the moment of performance within the temporal structures of fiction. This account has stressed detachment, omniscience, and a kind of control: the control that derives from labeling and from fixing perceptual experience within cognitive boundaries. In so doing, it offers a portrait of theatrical cognition similar to that underlying traditional theories of audience response. From Aristotle to the present, such theory has always stressed the triumphs of comprehension—the dominance of dramatic illusion over the materials of the stage and the containment of dramatic time within fictional outlines. Privileging the coherence of temporal outline, this tradition has upheld clarity and abstraction as dominant dramatic values, implictly agreeing with Thornton Wilder's claim that the goal of dramatic narration is to present "a unifying idea stronger than its mere collection of happenings." [19] In their analyses of individual plays, critics within this tradition have historically stressed the text over the stage, the whole over its parts, clarity over confusion.

Even the most conservative of theorists, of course, have acknowledged the theatrical necessity of teasing comprehension and maintaining interest, activities that involve the suspension of certainties. According to William Archer, the playwright's business is to "play upon the collective mind of his audience as upon a keyboard—to arouse just the right order and measure of anticipation, and fulfil it, or outdo it, in just the right way at just the right time." [20] In theory, such recognition acknowledges the theater audience's intense conceptual activity as it pieces together the story, forming and reforming its memories and anticipations as knowledge confronts the unknown. In practice, though, this activity and the accompanying uncertainty have traditionally been valued only when they operate within a framework of coherence, when "intrigue" unravels within broadly anticipated boundaries, and when a spectator who remains in intellectual control of the events on stage is able to absorb details and comprehend how they fit. Although Archer rejects the playwriting wisdom that bars a dramatist from withholding information from the audience, for instance, he nevertheless considers the practice undesirable "inasmuch as it diminishes tension, and deprives the audience of that superior knowledge in which lies the irony of drama," and more severely condemns dramatic secrets when they actually jolt anticipation: "when a reasonable expectation is aroused, it can be baffled only at the author's peril."[21] Clayton Hamilton, casting his objections to dramatic surprise within a striking metaphor of omniscience, suggests that "the theatre-going public enjoys much more keenly the experience of pretending to be surprised than it can possibly enjoy the experience of actually being surprised; for this latter experience violates the age-old tradition of the Olympian spectator and disturbs the God-like point of view."[22]

Rhetorical excesses aside, pronouncements such as these reflect a *comprehension bias* that continues to infuse the analysis of dramatic texts, even those studies (like Richard Levin's *The Multiple Plot in English Renaissance Drama*) that describe narrative structures of considerable intricacy.[23] While the approaches that have resulted from this bias have provided often powerful readings of abstract structure, they risk misrepresenting the twinness of theatrical performance and the obstructions presented by the stage as narrative medium. In its independence from authorial mediation, the stage offers resistance to audience comprehension, undermining the construction of narrative outline in often insistent ways. From this perspective, narrative response necessarily involves failure, compromise, and incompleteness, and the audience that works to naturalize the stage must continually abandon its claims to cognitive mastery.

This suggests a necessary corollary to the preceding discussion of narrative cognition in the theater: that comprehension is limited in its operations in the theater, uniquely pressured by the very performance immediacy that it seeks to transform. Performance undermines comprehension's temporalizing efforts in a number of ways. Most apparently, it constrains them by its relentlessly forward-moving development, a movement especially pronounced for an audience with no control over the pace at which it receives and must process performance's signals. We have considered the impulses by which comprehension seeks to abstract narrative clues from performance—clues that signal temporal relationship and development within the play's dramatic world—and by which it integrates these clues into a framework of dramatic time, clarifying and arranging the information it receives. This clarification, however, remains necessarily provisional until the play's final moments, subject to uncertainty and to intrusions of the unknown. William James employs a tellingly theatrical metaphor when discussing the tentativeness that the mind experiences as it confronts uncertainties and the careful effort it makes to resolve them: "We see that the mind is at every stage a theatre of simultaneous possibilities. Consciousness consists in the comparison of these with each other, the selection of some, and the suppression of the rest by the reinforcing and inhibiting agency of attention." [24] As a play like Tourneur's *Revenger's Tragedy* underscores, drama compounds this multiplicity through the presence of different "futures" in the minds of individual characters, which establish complicated outcomes as conflicting possibilities jockey with the force of hope and foreboding. So uncertain is the future hinging upon *The Revenger's Tragedy*'s dramatic moments, with intrigues colliding and reforming within the play's own narrative, that the central characters themselves hardly dare predict its course. Like these characters, the audience of *The Revenger's Tragedy* struggles against confusion, holding in precarious balance the possible combinations of characters and incidents, rapidly readjusting its sense of the unfolding story as new incidents arise.

Tourneur's "multiple plotting" represents an extreme example of narrative confusion, but the tentativeness that he exercises with such anarchic effect derives from a more general feature of theatrical narrative. Like all dramatic elements, narrative in the theater is largely "emergent" in its meaning,[25] stretching forward into a future which it anticipates in uncertain and often conflicting ways. Central to the experience of *The Three Sisters,* for example, is the uneasy interplay between the projected return "to Moscow!" and the audience's steadily deepening realization of its unlikelihood and the futility of its attendant longing. For every event realized in the course of a play's development, there are significantly more potential outcomes it raises and others, of variable status, it banishes. Drama complicates mental activity through its continual presentation of possible narrative orders, and the frequent clashing of these hypothetical futures offers multiple and conflicting clues.[26] This narrative uncertainty is deepened by the continual threat of the unexpected, of that which lies outside patterns of anticipation, for surprise is a structural inevitability in a medium where events "happen," and where characters arrive with the ease and suddenness of a stage entrance. "Always great with things to come," [27] drama verges on the unknown, confronting its audience with phenomenal developments always slightly outside comprehension's grasp. At times, of course, the actual future contradicts those expectations the audience has been encouraged to form, an equivalent in audience response to the *peripeteia* that afflicts Aristotle's protagonist: Lear enters with the dead Cordelia in his arms, and anticipation collapses, confronted with the moment's piercing unexpectedness.

Less apparently, perhaps, the dramatic past is also subject to uncertainty and revision. *Long Day's Journey into Night,* for instance, a play that unifies itself around a shared journey into memory, reveals its past selectively, through suggestion and incomplete allusion. Mary's addiction, Edmund's illness, Jamie's disreputable life, Tyrone's childhood—all these emerge gradually, reveal their outlines slowly, as if stepping out of the fog that serves as backdrop to this play's dramatic world. The prevalence of exposition notwithstanding, the dramatic past stands open in many plays, and its modifications frequently shift the outlines the audience has projected; indeed, revision of the past is often radical, as it is in Ibsen's drama, where provisional frameworks of a dramatic past are repeatedly shattered in light of the present's revelations. Nora's business dealings with Krogstad and Osvald's disease both constitute revocations of audience comprehension and the understanding of the past it has been led to form, and the subtle anticipations of these secrets that Ibsen includes in his plays only mildly lessen their disruptive force. A play such as *Ghosts,* where little happens on the level of overt stage action, is fiercely active in its formulations and reformulations of the dramatic past, and this continual revision of unstable narrative frameworks occasions the play's cognitive disorientations. Revising a past potentially explosive in its revelations is a fundamental action of Ibsen's drama on its audience, and the dramaturgical complexity of this revision exposes comprehension's intrinsic instability.

Since narrative is structured as an integrated whole, instability within one temporal realm bears implications for the others. Revision of the past, for instance, often destabilizes the future, since this past often stands in constraining relationship to character hopes and projections. Ibsen's dramatic past, for example, represents the burden of "debt" or "inheritance" (in Ibsen's own metaphors) that weighs down the aspirations of characters—and audience—bent on denying confinement, and each disclosure further strips the future of possibility. Mrs. Alving's dream in the opening scene of *Ghosts*—"After tomorrow, it will really seem as if the dead had never lived in this house"—collapses, through the past's revelation, into the constraints of heredity and disease. Similarly, revisions of both past and future adjust comprehension of the dramatic present. Located at the center of a temporal construct extending backward and forward in time, the "present" the audience imposes upon the stage is partly contextual in meaning: it stands as an "outcome" of the projected past as well as a "promise" of possible developments. To revise either end of this contextual framework is accordingly to revise a fundamental means by which the present is apprehended and understood. The revelations that occur throughout *Ghosts,* for instance, shift audience comprehension of the dramatic present as they do comprehension of the future, fixing the moment as a deterministically recurring version of the past: "the sins of the father are visited upon the children."[28] Likewise, disclosure of the past in *Long Day's Journey* modifies perception of present relationships—complicating them, deepening their rich and painful ambivalence.

As an autonomously forward-moving medium, then, performance renders provisional the narrative outlines that an audience seeks to impose upon it, subjecting these conceptual frameworks to continual modification and revision. The security of narrative outlines is further compromised by the audience's cognitive faculties themselves, which operate within limits not often acknowledged in discussions of dramatic plot. In their investigations of cognitive capacity, psychologists have long affirmed that memory is a faculty structurally constrained in its ability to process and retrieve the information it receives. Their descriptive models offer insights pertinent to comprehension as it is engaged within the theater. Seeking to describe the mind's reception and storage of information from the external world, cognitive psychologists have generally distinguished three memory levels: sensory memory, in which visual and other sensory impressions are briefly retained in pre-categorical form; short-term (or primary) memory, in which attention appropriates this immediate information for temporary retention and further processing; and long-term (or extended) memory, in which some of this processed material is stored for more extensive periods of time. At each level, traces are held for longer stretches (sensory memory retains traces for, at most, only a matter of seconds, and short-term memory is limited to fifteen to thirty seconds), but it is also true that retrieval from each of the latter levels (or remembering) is unequal: material stored in long-term memory is less readily available, and accordingly harder to "bring to mind," than material stored in short-term memory.[29] Moreover, the path from sensory memory to long-term memory is not without its interruptions: short-term memory "bottlenecks" the appropriation of information because of its limited processing capacity, a fact demonstrated by George A. Miller's famous study setting the limit of short-term memory at roughly seven serial items. As Miller notes, "the span of immediate memory impose[s] severe limitations on the amount of information that we are able to receive, process, and remember."[30] Finally, attention—the activity of consciousness that draws material into memory's latter stages—is itself structurally limited, such that attending to one set of signals and concerns necessarily involves "disattending" to others.[31]

Models drawn from psychology should not be applied to the theatrical experience without qualification, and this is true for models of cognitive processes. The theater is a markedly different environment from the laboratory, and in important ways it allows comprehension a broader range. As we have already noted, the aesthetic nature of this environment supports audience efforts to generate and retain narrative outlines by the security with which coherence is expected, and the focused nature of the performance environment allows attention maximum powers of concentration.[32] But this support and focus by no means overcome the limitations and unreliability of audience cognitive processes, and the pressures that the unmediated stage exerts on the audience's attempts to structure its action. Comprehension remains constrained by the intrinsic limits of memory, by the fact that the mind cannot absorb and retrieve all that it is given. In a medium characterized by multiple and conflicting signals, complexity taxes the ability of attention and memory to appropriate narrative material, and the length of performance risks banishing what material is retained to the less available domain of extended memory. Despite the popular conception of plot as overview, narrative is never present to mind with summary completeness; its details are submerged, forgotten, and hastily recalled in complex rhythms of forgetting, surprise, and recovery. Indeed, in light of short-term memory's relative vividness, and the limited span of its retention, it is likely that a spectator's awareness of dramatic events at any given point focuses barely on the moment's most immediate antecedents. Beyond this immediacy, as research into the structures of memory suggests, the material that comprises comprehension's broader framework is more difficult to retrieve, and often fragmentary at that.

Comprehension, then, is limited when it seeks to generate narrative outlines in the theater by the provisionalness of its constructions, and by its own cognitive limitations. In these respects, audience finds kinship with reader, for the reading process, too, is subject to tentativeness and incompleteness. As Stanley Fish has suggested through his analysis of the reading process, the reader is subject to continual "misreading," liable to fall into traps within the text that implicate him or her, in various ways, within the text's uncertainties. Like the experience of play-watching, the activity of reading is cumulative and constructive, a process by which "a mind asked to order a succession of rapidly given bits of detail . . . seizes on the simplest scheme of organization which offers itself";[33] as in the theatrical experience, these constructions are vulnerable to the sheer amount of detail that the reader is asked to structure, and to the revisions forced by new material. Effects of tentativeness and disruption are the shared property of both literary and theatrical narrative, playing (as they do) upon the development and deflections of time.

But although the reader, too, is subject to the pressing of cognitive limits and to the revocation of narrative outlines and details, literary narrative lacks performance's phenomenal presence, which undermines comprehension through its nonconceptual actuality. For the very duality of the stage—its simultaneous status as theatrical environment and dramatic world—works to impede the transformation into fictional abstraction that comprehension seeks to effect. As we have suggested, dramatic illusion is never total, never loses its temporal basis in the moment of performance or its physical foundation in the materials of the stage. Beckerman discusses this duality of theatrical illusion in terms of "opacity" and "transparency," distinguishing between "the degree that we are aware of [the dramatic object's] sensuous surface" and "the degree that we see through the phenomenal object to the fictional content."[34] Despite the audience's attempts to subjugate performance to drama—to create a fictional world with its own autonomy—the stage, its props, and its actors never lose their fundamental status as performance elements. No matter how successful a play's evocation of its dramatic world, performance always addresses us on its own terms, as something intractably nonnarrative; it always resists, to some extent, our attempts to make it other than it is. During dramatic presentation, the stage is always, in varying mixtures, "translucent," intruding itself upon the fictional realm with a sensory dimension outside narrativity. In drama, as Patrice Pavis notes, "The fiction . . . is always at the mercy of . . . the enactment."[35]

The immediacy of performance foregrounds "the present" more radically than more strictly literary narrative, where present shades imperceptibly into past and future, its links stengthened by that unifying presence of authorial voice. Grounded in performance, the moment in drama asserts its autonomy from the pasts and futures drawn to contain it, and in so doing, it always threatens to dissolve these frameworks within the riveting immediacy it displays, drawing attention toward itself at the expense of its surrounding temporal contexts. It intrudes itself as dramatic present, a fictional now apprehended almost existentially on its own terms, autonomous in respect to past and future. This present, cut from its temporal moorings, looms large within the dramatic worlds of

Samuel Beckett, Harold Pinter, and other contemporary dramatists: as Jerry says to Emma in Pinter's *Betrayal*, "Nothing has ever
happened. Nothing. This is the only thing that has ever happened."[36] But, by intruding itself this way, the stage also asserts
itself as theatrical present, that performance moment infusing the
dramatic present and providing its actuality and force. Through
this intrusion, comprehension must compete with the other dimensions of audience response, dimensions that extend well beyond the cognitive and that derive from drama's grounding in actuality—in what Jean-Louis Barrault has called that "physical
state . . . outside of all comprehension."[37] For the theater is an
ensemble of languages that address the perceiving subject on a
number of levels in addition to the cognitive: sensory, emotional,
empathic, visceral. The audience's efforts of comprehension inevitably confront those components of the stage that make different
claims on attention and threaten to bypass the channels of
thought. This nonconceptual address has subversive effects for the
autonomy of comprehension within the theater, and for the stability of its construction, effecting a complex of responses often
independent of the strictly cognitive. By highlighting the dramatic
present and drawing attention from narrative outlines to the moment, the stage also foregrounds itself, activating responses outside cognition, asserting a presence that is only partly—and often
secondarily—narrative.

Drama's grounding in the actuality of performance, in other
words, makes itself felt in the continual pressure of the stage and
its materials on dramatic narrative's fictional "otherness," a form
of intrusion more fundamental than the strokes of "metadrama"
by which the stage's assertion of itself is more frequently recognized. Despite the audience's attempt to transform *The Three Sisters'* stage into a Russian countryhouse, it remains a stage, constructed out of boards and props, a presence, not only in the
dramatic present, but in the here and now of performance. Indeed,
through Chekhov's dramaturgy, this stage is made to signal itself
in a variety of ways. Within the opening sequence, Masha's
whistling, unmotivated and apparently discontinuous with the
main dramatic action, draws attention to itself, not only as dramatic act, but as stage sound—as does the background laughter
that punctuates Olga's aspiration. Like all Chekhovian drama,
The Three Sisters is filled with music, with erratic stage movement,

and with a variety of stage objects that often seem merely to occupy the stage. Such material intrusions underscore the play's
striking counterpoint between the projections with which characters seek to escape the confinements of the present's inescapable
immediacy and an attention to *mise-en-scène* that often dominates
the stage action. In Chekhov's hands, this stage presence becomes
luminously ambiguous, modulating between static immobility and
an almost balletic formal grace.

To speak of the stage's presence is to speak of its "theatricality"—not its ostentatiousness, as the word often connotes, but the
basic level at which it asserts itself as stage, and the awareness that
it enforces of its intrinsic actuality. The stage asserts its theatricality in music, movement, sound, objects—in all the various forms
that performance reality assumes. It asserts itself when Hamlet
holds Yorick's skull at arm's length, and when Sir Fopling displays
his French coat to the general admiration ("It makes me show
long-waisted, and I think slender"),[38] each drawing attention to
an item as both dramatic object and theatrical prop. It asserts itself
when Stoppard's Jumpers perform their acrobatics, testing their
abilities as actors against the stage's gravity, providing performance equivalents to George Moore's intellectual tumblings. It asserts itself, tragically, in Lear's opening words when he enters the
stage with Cordelia's body—"Howl, howl, howl!" (V.iii.258)—
for each repetition further strips the word of rational meaning,
reducing speech to the bestial harshness of sound, the sensory
foundation of all language within the theater as without it. Shakespeare's stagecraft here is bold: in its harshness, the moment is
allowed to collapse into itself, and the stage draws close to what,
in this moment, it really is: a group of figures—at once actors and
characters—standing mute, witnessing and enacting a suffering
beyond comprehension. *King Lear* contrasts the fragility of human creation with the existential barrenness of such moments,
and Shakespeare's stagecraft extends this contrast to the audience,
reducing the imaginative flights of drama to their origins in the
inert stage.

In the end, dramatic narrative also yields ground to the very
individuals who create it, individuals who retain their identity independent of dramatic illusion. Throughout performance, the audience maintains its awareness of the actor, whose art of enact-

ment is the vehicle of fictional transformation but who takes the stage with a personal identity never effaced by the dramatic role. "The fact that the actor is, inescapably, alive," Michael Goldman notes, "means that there is always extra reality thrusting to break into the convention, and this gives added intensity to our natural awareness of unaccommodated reality thrusting and threatening to break into the play-world in which we are absorbed."[39] The full complexity of the original audience's experience of Jonson's *The Alchemist,* and the multiple claims made on its attention, are comprehensible not only in light of the histrionic demands placed on its performers (in this play that draws so heavily upon the art of acting), but also in light of the fact that the 1610 King's Men production featured a number of the age's most prominent actors: we must try to imagine the impact on its Jacobean audience, for instance, of Drugger's entrance in IV.vii, when Robert Armin walked onto a stage already held by Richard Burbage, John Hemings, and Henry Condel as Face, Subtle, and Surly, each bringing to his impersonation a pronounced artistic personality and a history of previous roles.[40] Nor is such theatricality restricted to the actors, for the audience likewise maintains awareness of itself as participants in a specific performance bound to a specific moment in real time. This self-awareness has been ignored by modern illusionistic theater, which has sought to relegate the audience to the anonymity of darkness, but even here the audience fails to efface itself within the theatrical medium, retaining (instead) its communal consciousness of itself and affirming—with its shared attention, its rustlings, and its applause—its kinship with the jostling crowds below the Globe stage and the boisterous Restoration audiences memorialized by Samuel Pepys. Rejecting the theatrical suppressions attempted by illusionism, dramatists such as Brecht, Pirandello, and Genet have returned the audience to its place in the theater and, in so doing, called attention to a presence that asserts itself within all dramatic representation. In one of the theater's paradoxes, the spectators observe a performance field of which they are a part.

Newly awakened on the edge of Oberon's forest, her memory of the night's events "out of joint" with the reality before her, Shakespeare's Hermia offers a remark resonantly suggestive of the-

atrical perception: "Methinks I see these things with parted eye, /
When every thing seems double" (*A Midsummer Night's Dream,*
V.i.189–90). Caught between the demands of cognition and the
intransigence of performance, between a world of fictional outline
and the actual unfolding of a stage present that renders such outlines provisional and precarious, the theater audience is often similarly divided, forced into a dialectic of attention. This division,
the "parted eye" of audience response, is overtly and extensively
dramatized by the onstage figures who "frame" Thomas Kyd's
The Spanish Tragedy: Revenge and Don Andrea's Ghost. Both
stand outside the play's events, witnessing the unfolding action
from the security of their invisibility to others. At the same time,
the two are carefully distinguished in their relationship to what
they observe, embodying with the force of emblem the doubleness
of theatrical vision. Revenge asserts authority over the play's actions, both the authority of having designed it and the more
strictly cognitive authority of knowing its outcomes:

> Then know, Andrea, that thou art arriv'd
> Where thou shalt see the author of thy death,
> Don Balthazar the Prince of Portingale,
> Depriv'd of life by Bel-imperia.
> Here sit we down to see the mystery,
> And serve for Chorus in this tragedy.
> (I.i.86–91)[41]

Revenge's omniscience stands secure, for in the play's ironic levels
of "authorship" he occupies the outermost point, Dramatist as
well as Chorus: "though I sleep, / Yet is my mood soliciting their
souls" (III.xv.18–19). This assurance, unshakable by the appearances of the moment, is borne out by the play's action, which follows Revenge's script to its grimly inexorable conclusion.

Andrea, on the other hand, lacks Revenge's cognitive mastery
and assurance; in contrast to his companion, he loses himself in
the dramatic moment, forgetting the outcomes that he has been
promised. A naive spectator on the play's scale of knowing, he
succumbs to the immediacy of the stage present and forces Revenge to respond with the assurances of a broader narrative
scheme, conceived in a clear Aristotelian relationship of beginning,
middle, and end. In the drama that animates this frame, the drama

of Andrea's education as spectator, the former soldier and lover must be repeatedly drawn back from emotional engagement with the dramatic action, returned to comprehension's broader outlines and the laws that they reveal:

> *Andrea.* Brought'st thou me hither to increase my pain?
> I look'd that Balthazar should have been slain;
> But 'tis my friend Horatio that is slain,
> And they abuse fair Bel-imperia,
> On whom I doted more than all the world,
> Because she lov'd me more than all the world.
> *Revenge.* Thou talkest of harvest, when the corn is green;
> The end is crown of every work well done;
> The sickle comes not till the corn be ripe.
> Be still; and ere I lead thee from this place,
> I'll show thee Balthazar in heavy case.
>
> (II, vi, 1–11)

In this play so often remarked for its sensationalism, Kyd displays a sophisticated awareness of the pulls of audience response. His characters render this tension explicit: Revenge and Don Andrea engage in the struggle between involvement in the moment and awareness of the whole that characterizes audience narrative response, mirroring and externalizing the cognitive operations that their play occasions.

Understanding the cognitive interactions of audience and stage allows us, at last, to begin to reintegrate the cognitive operations occasioned by dramatic plot with theatrical "spectacle" in its broadest sense, so multiple in its modes of address. Narrative cognition forms part of a complex of responses engaged by performance: sensory response to the sights, sounds, touches, and smells of performance; interpersonal responses to the actor's physical proximity, and to that of fellow spectators; physiological responses to Barrault's "mystery of Presence"; individual and communal responses to Artaud's "pure forces"; the psychic traces of Brook's "scorching" event.[42] Cognition interrelates with these other activities and responses in ways that we do not yet fully understand—abstracting from them, competing with them, defending against them. Its cognitive operations seek to order theatrical experience in all its nonconceptual forms and to affirm the boundaries between internal and external upon which the cognitive "self" depends. But the theater's irreducible presence asserts internal and external environments resistant to the mind's orderings, demonstrating (in the end) that comprehension is more richly tied to the body's experiences, to the psyche's less conscious regions, and to the world with which they interact than labels such as *mind* and *body, self* and *other,* allow. Indeed, awareness of performance's complex effects—its simultaneous engagement of the conceptual and the physiological, its exploration of the interface between the dramatic world and what lies outside it—suggests that it is precisely the unsure lines between such realms that constitute the theater's primary, and most deeply registered, domain. To trace the fortunes of audience comprehension, its failures as well as its triumphs, is to confront these lines and to begin to reintegrate the detachment of observation with the vulnerability of participation.

Narrative in the theater faces us with the theatrical paradox as a whole. On one hand, the stage makes possible the transformation that characterizes all of the narrative arts: it allows the audience to create a fictional otherness, a world represented, in part, within the temporal outlines of past, present, and future. On the other hand, the immediacy of performance that allows this world of make-believe its dramatic presence also undermines the processes by which it is constructed and perceived. Tentative in its formulations, limited in what it can process and hold in mind, narrative comprehension depends on a medium that exposes fiction and its narrative outlines as the conceptual constructions they are and that asserts its own non-narrative claims on attention and response. Comprehension and presence constitute the twin poles of dramatic narrative, and it is the richness of their interplay that lends drama its powerful cognitive and theatrical complexity. To strip drama of the theater is to rob it of its distinctive rhythms, and the effects made possible within a medium that stands slightly beyond narrative's reach.

CHAPTER TWO

Narrative Analysis and Interpretation

Implicit throughout this study is a notion of dramatic meaning that departs in important ways from dramatic criticism as it has traditionally been practiced. Such criticism has concerned itself, as a rule, with elements intrinsic to the dramatic world: with character and its fortunes, action and its patterns, language and its uses as dramatic speech. Above all, it has focused on issues of thematic interest: the interrelationship of pattern and the individual act in Sophocles' Theban trilogy, the disruptions and reconstitutions of society in Shakespearean tragedy, action and aspiration in Chekhov, Ionesco's *Bald Soprano* and the deconstruction of language. By working within the dramatic world as it is given, on stage or within the printed text, thematic criticism has tended to consider a play's intellectual dimension as something autonomous and self-contained, thereby conceiving meaning as something independent of those performance dimensions seemingly extrinsic to the dramatic world and its concerns.

By focusing on the theatrical interaction between audience and performance, this study proposes a different conception of a play's meaning, one that approaches the dramatic and its various elements in terms of their theatrical embodiment. From this perspective, meaning is no longer something given to audience or reader, it is created within the structure of response occasioned by the play in performance. "In the theater," Patrice Pavis reminds us, "meaning *is the use made of the stage*"[1]—at that fundamental level where the audience is no longer passive spectator, but active participant in the creation of the dramatic artifact and guarantor of its effects. Comprehension and its more sensory foundations are not subordinate to the performance, but rather constitute the primary ground of dramatic activity, the domain within which more abstract narrative and ideational content generates, shifts, and changes. From this perspective, the audience's creation of the dramatic world out of the materials of performance—its cognitive efforts to transform the materials of performance into something narratively meaningful and the interaction of these efforts with other responses occasioned by the stage—become as important as the meanings thereby constituted. Performance no longer points beyond itself to an autonomous world of actions and issues; it is itself such a world, shaping action and issues through the reponses it occasions.

Focusing upon anterior levels of audience response by no means precludes the thematic; indeed, locating the dramatic world within its medium serves to ground the thematic within this reponse, complicating and enriching a play's intrinsic issues with insights concerning their generation within the theatrical environment. The twin challenge facing the student of narrative comprehension is to analyze the response that a play's temporal dimension occasions, and to suggest the interpenetrations of this response, its governing rhythms and conflicts, with the issues represented and developed within the world of the play. If one understands the "theatrical relationship" as "concretely, the position of the spectator facing the stage and, arbitrarily, his effort to constitute meaning by his act of reception," [2] then the study of dramatic narrative within its performance context promises to touch the very heart not only of dramatic form in its autonomous dimensions, but of the creation of form through theatrical activity.

The theatrical tension between frameworks of comprehension and their undermining by stage actuality carries profound implications for the dramatic text and its resulting performance(s). Since the dramatic text (or playscript) is, as Richard Hornby notes, "something *having spatial and temporal elements implicit in it,* to be projected into performance," [3] it carries inscribed within it the structures of comprehension that its performance will both evoke and frustrate. Narrative strategy, therefore, involves a dramaturgical orchestration of comprehension and the pressures it confronts. To read a dramatic text in these terms is to read through it to the theatrical duality that it conditions and by which it is conditioned.

Bernard Beckerman has stressed a distinction, within dramatic theory, between analysis and interpretation,[4] underscoring the difference between the act of describing dramatic elements and effects and that of applying them to broader issues of meaning. This distinction is particularly important in relationship to structural dimensions such as narrative. Narrative forms patterns within a play, and these patterns underlie more abstract interpretive structures. But such structures are themselves grounded in dramaturgical decisions concerning the disposition of specific devices of cognitive manipulation. The devices and techniques by which dramatists address the audience's cognitive efforts reveal conflicting narrative strategies, opposing stances toward the dialectic of comprehension and its failure. At times, dramatists manipulate the elements of stage and play in order to activate and support the structuring operations of cognition. In order to "articulate" narrative outline, such a strategy must overcome the scattering diffuseness of time and facilitate the processes involved in narrative integration; it must stimulate an awareness of broader narrative outline against which the shifting moments of stage activity may be set. Drawing upon the stage and its supports, dramatists often avail themselves of the corollary fact of theatrical representation: that drama is also a phenomenon in space and that, somewhat paradoxically, the physical reality of the stage that undermines the dramatist's narrative presence also serves as a potential, indeed inevitable, element of narrative control. Through a variety of means, dramatists inscribe the stage and its supports within the dramatic text. Most obvious are the varied setting specifications that have increasingly characterized plays, from the elaborate scene descriptions of Shaw and O'Neill to the spare opening of Ionesco's *Macbett* ("A field"). Such descriptions specify narrative signals, locating the stage moment and often constraining its development. Drawing further upon the theater arts, dramatists also specify character movement and costume—each serving to draw further upon the stage's resources and clarify fictional meaning—as well as stage props, specific theatrical objects that extend and counterpoint character aspiration and narrative development in an often complex relationship of signification. Props circumscribe the projections expressed in the dramatic worlds of Ibsen and Chekhov; Miss Julie's frenzied plans ("And then we'll get a hotel . . . There's life for you!") are shaped by the continual visual presence of the Count's boots and the speaking tube, which constitute an ominous reminder of his presence "behind the scene," his imminent return, and the rigid structure of roles and relationships that his authority maintains; and the hopes of Synge's Aran Islanders in *Riders to the Sea* are confronted with the grim inevitability of defeat symbolized by the "new boards standing by the wall."[5] In view of the wagon that Mother Courage must pull around in order to survive—a wagon that becomes steadily harder to pull as her children are lost—and the mound that surrounds Winnie in *Happy Days,* it is clear that modern dramatists often use stage props for severe narrative control and that this control involves an increasingly ironic relationship between the narrative projections of the characters and the constraints symbolized by their stage environment.

Dramatists, of course, also shape the dramatic text itself, its action and its inhabitants, to achieve control over the stage action, to simplify its potential for disruption and confusion, and to render performance more available to the outlines that the audience attempts to impose upon it. This is a domain of traditional dramaturgy, and a brief inventory of some of its devices and techniques ring familiar in the history of dramatic texts:

1. "Extradramatic" figures, who stand outside the principal action and represent its outlines through often explicit anticipation and summary (the Prologue figures in *Romeo and Juliet* and *Troilus and Cressida,* Gay's Beggar, the Vexillators who read the Banns summarizing the N Town cycle);

2. Central or focal characters, who constitute a privileged presence within the dramatic world and whose fortunes serve as a central line within the play's shifting action (Antigone, Tamburlaine, Schweyk);

3. Long-range action, motivational "spines," and other streamlining projections around which memory and anticipation can cluster (Orestes' pursuit of vengeance, Richard III's ascent to the throne, the Six Characters' search for life through authorship);

4. Temporal and spatial patterning of dramatic action (the historical cycle of mystery drama; the polyphonic counterpoint of locales and plot lines in *1 Henry IV,* the dialectic opposition of time and place in Caryl Churchill's *Cloud Nine*);

5. Devices, such as the dumb show and play-within-a-play, that foreground—through analogy and condensation—the play's broader outlines (the dumb shows in *Gorboduc,* Hamlet's "mousetrap," Stoppard's *The Real Thing*);

6. Narrative symbols and motifs, which encapsulate the actual and potential development of incidents (sea gull, wild duck, streetcar named Desire);

7. The heightening of a play's "storiness"—and, thereby, an audience's awareness of narrative patterning—through metafictional, metahistorical, and metadramatic reference (*Pericles, Deirdre, Saint Joan*).[6]

On more pervasive levels of "tactics," as opposed to "strategy" (to borrow Pinero's distinction between "the art of . . . conveying information to the audience," among other things, and "the general laying out of a play"),[7] one enters the narratively fluid world of character statement, the sphere of intrinsic information—expository and projective—upon which audience comprehension depends so keenly and within which its formulations must negotiate. Within this sphere, narrative inference confronts a scale of reliability, from the extradramatic commentator (like Wilder's Stage Manager or Williams' Tom Wingfield) whose knowledge of events is cast in explicit counterpart to the limited understanding within the dramatic world, through the *raisonneurs* and other figures of authority (often endowed with quasi-supernatural prescience concerning events), down to the level of less privileged character understanding. The characters in individual plays position themselves along a similar scale, a hierarchy of awareness and power that ranges from the most to the least knowing.

Through all of these devices and techniques, dramatists underscore the patterning of events, directing attention beyond stage activity to the ways in which this activity is shaped, making performance more available to comprehension's ordering frameworks. The strength of this narrativity varies over the course of a play: in addition to the differing availability of narrative information and the accumulating strength of narrative structures as this information is made available, moments or sequences of moments can be set off from the rest by a kind of "local" cognitive heightening, allowing us to speak of specific narrative "points" within a play. Extradramatic figures, for instance, establish particular narrative impact at the points of their appearance, abstracting the action retrospectively or prospectively, counterpointing stage activity with often sudden outline. Other narrative devices, including those instances when characters within the dramatic world rise to moments of prediction and summary, provide similar underscoring, moments when the perception of immediacy modulates into the more detached awareness of pattern. While such devices modify perception of the action as it unfolds, in other words, they also provide momentary heightenings of special force, "crowning" narrative points. As Shakespeare demonstrates in *The Winter's Tale,* the culminating reunions of which are given a narrative prominence unusual even for a play so richly charged with such heightening, dramatists frequently give their plays a sense of resolution and closure through an increased narrative emphasis in their closing moments. *Romeo and Juliet* ends with the explicit distancing of stage action into story—"For never was a story of more woe / Than this of Juliet and her Romeo" (V.iii.309–10)—and Shakespeare's characters often conclude the action in which they have participated by casting it as narrative: Othello (V.ii.338–44), Cleopatra (V.ii.214–21), and Gonzalo (V.i.206–13). Nor are such effects restricted to the Shakespearean canon: even so naturalistic a play as O'Neill's *Long Day's Journey into Night* ends with storylike retrospective outlines: Tyrone's tortured memory of his childhood, Edmund's account of his experience at sea, and—most resonantly—Mary's final reverie: "That was in the winter of senior year. Then in the spring something happened to me. Yes, I remember. I fell in love with James Tyrone and was so happy for a time. [*She stares before her in a sad dream. Tyrone stirs in his chair. Edmund and Jamie remain motionless*]." The play's repeated attempts to disclose the past break through to broader memory, and the final clarity of its outlines, fixed within the despair of inevitability and the calm of acceptance, belongs not only to the characters, but to the audience as well.[8]

The heightening of narrativity effected by these techniques and devices, though, represents only one strategy through which dramatists address the theatrical tension between comprehension and its theatrical material. For dramatists, aware of the medium for which they write, have always manipulated the dualism of narrative and presence in order to undermine comprehension and liberate the dramatic and theatrical present, and they have done so even within the most consciously narrative drama. This "antinarrative" strategy is obvious within modern and contemporary drama, in its rejection of the values of classical narrative, and within the justification of such drama by theorists as opposed as Brecht and Artaud, who—despite their different theatrical aims— share the dramaturgical belief that "Stories we understand are just badly told."[9] But the contemporary rejection of narrative coherence draws upon a dramaturgical impulse deeply embedded within the dramatic tradition, one that seeks to undercut, in different ways and to varying extents, the processes of comprehension upon which narrative depends, and to oppose the effort toward narrativity with other responses to the stage's immediacy. *The Comedy of Errors* subjects characters and audience alike to confusions of incident and identity, while the opening scenes of *Macbeth* reject clear exposition in favor of obscurity, equivocation, and incantation. If dramatic form involves, as Kenneth Burke has suggested, "the creation of an appetite in the mind of the auditor, and the adequate satisfying of that appetite,"[10] drama has always worked, in part, to heighten the stage's indigestibility and frustrate the appetites of cognition.

Dramatists reveal the strategic undermining of narrative frameworks in a number of ways. Often, they work to subvert devices of explicit narrative control, intensifying the stage's pressure on these devices and drawing them within the activity they seek to structure, foregrounding the local and the particular over the geographical and the abstract. In terms of character reliability, for instance, the spectator who attempts an awareness of temporal outline and direction confronts the stage's inescapable multiplicity and relativism. Those framing figures who stand, extradramatically, above the play's action are subject to the movement of stage time and to the democratic nature of theatrical space, which they must share with other figures and voices. The discontinuous onstage presence that usually characterizes such figures often gives them a more tenuous control over events, and their pronouncements and predictions often recede in awareness during their absence. Similarly undermined by this spatial relativizing, character authority within the dramatic action finds its privileged position concerning events further undermined by the distortions and biases of character individuality, as even omniscience becomes involved in the world it seeks to describe. The satirist figure of English Renaissance drama stands as an example of this undermining: as Alvin Kernan has argued, the moral superiority of a satirist such as Jonson's Macillente, based upon an objectivity and clarity of perception within the dramatic world, is often tainted by envy and malice, which psychologically "motivates" his bitter judgments of the world around him but also implicates him within that world and its self-absorption.[11] Sharing this moral ambiguity, the intriguer of Jacobean tragedy (such as Tourneur's Vindice), who initially moves with such clarity through the world around him, often succumbs to the blindness of that world through his participation, relinquishing both his objectivity and his ability to see. As with Strindberg's Captain, Pirandello's Henry, and O'Neill's Hickey in later drama, this subversion of omniscience has profound implications for an audience attempting to use these figures as fixed points of narrative certainty.

Since it is comprehension's function to contextualize dramatic space within a framework of present, past, and future, the dramaturgical subversion of narrative often exploits devices that undermine the comprehensibility of one or more of these realms, thereby frustrating the clear construction of narrative outline. Actually, given performance's constant pressuring of such outlines, anti-narrative devices often constitute little more than the absence of devices and techniques that otherwise facilitate temporal integration. Within the dramatic present, for instance, narrative comprehension is rendered difficult when streamlining gives way to complication, when the absence of guiding devices of dramaturgy and stagecraft releases stage activity to proliferate with its own apparent autonomy and comprehension is left on its own. The claims of outline and outcome on stage activity loosen when organizing principles are removed: when focal characters recede into the background or are replaced by multiple focal characters (*Friar Bacon and Friar Bungay*, *The School for Scandal*, *The Cherry Orchard*); when clearly delineated narrative lines, and the character groupings that often underlie them, dissolve or fail to establish themselves (*Bartholomew Fair*, *The Ghost Sonata*, *The Balcony*); when long-term objective and action are replaced by the short-range and the provisional (*The Duchess of Malfi, The Man of Mode, Baal*); when entrances, exits, and other stage activities occur without devices of anticipation (*The Alchemist, The Bald Soprano, Jumpers*); or when devices of liaison are absent or inadequate to the gaps between acts and scenes (*A Chaste Maid in Cheapside, Woyceck, Plenty*). In general, explicit outline loosens whenever a dramatist forgoes the organizing devices mentioned earlier and compounds the stage's demands on comprehension, through number, complexity, and the unexpected. Overarching action gives way to the momentary and the episodic, the provisional undermines the extended, and multiplicity heightens the discontinuity of dramatic incident.

Dramatists also work to resist the very transformation into narrative that comprehension works to effect. This subversion often manifests itself in a stage present that resists localization in space and time and becomes a kind of dramatic Noplace, severed from exact connection with the surrounding action. Nonspecific settings are traditional within much earlier drama—morality drama, for instance, differs from the symbolic narrative settings of the Mystery pagaents through its locations generalized to represent "everywhere"; the staging of medieval drama as a whole featured nonlocalized acting areas (*plateas*);[12] and nonlocalized setting is frequent in the Renaissance. In the context of naturalistic drama, however, where the contours of time and space are established with a specificity unknown to Shakespeare and his predecessors, such nonlocalization creates cognitive indeterminacy, evident in the ambiguous present of much contemporary drama: the starkly bare settings of *Waiting for Godot* and the rest of the Beckett canon, the unspecified stage present that opens Stoppard's *Rosencrantz and Guildenstern Are Dead* ("Two ELIZABETHANS passing the time in a place without any visible character"),[13] the indeterminate spaces of Pinter's *Landscape* and *Silence*. As part of this broader subversion of the stage's fictional identifiability, one can note the opacity of stage props in much twentieth-century drama, props that resist narrative connection with the dramatic world and its action: the hyacinths and the statue of Buddha in Strindberg's *The Ghost Sonata* and the random stage objects in Cocteau's *Wedding on the Eiffel Tower*. Increasingly assertive, props on the modern stage often acquire intrusive singularity: Ionesco's chairs; Beckett's carrots, urns, and rocking chair; Shepard's artichokes and corn husks; and the dense clutter of Mamet's *American Buffalo* and Pinter's *The Caretaker*.

Scenic indeterminacy works to impede the audience's cognitive movement from one level of apprehension to the other, from a perception of theatrical immediacy to a more abstract perception of dramatic fiction, and to fragment temporal and spatial continuums. Dramatists, particularly more recent ones, further obstruct this movement by breaking down the lines between the theatrical and the dramatic, rendering problematic the distinction, and the movement, between them. This kind of confusion lies at the heart of Pirandellian drama, with its continual awareness of itself as staged drama and its giddying dislocations of theatrical reality, and the theater of Brecht, forthright in its presentation of its theatrical foundations. With a metatheatrical gesture preempting narrative entirely, Handke's speakers "offend" the audience by locating them in the actual moment of performance and stripping this moment of all dramatic constructs: "This is no drama. No action that has occurred elsewhere is reenacted here. Only a now and a now and a now exist here." By foregrounding audience expectations their presentation will fail to meet, Handke's speakers liberate performance from comprehension's usual transformations; by stripping the stage present of its claims to fictional "otherness," they force the audience out of modes of comprehension by which this otherness is conventionally structured and understood. "We are not acting out a plot. Therefore we are not playing time. Time is for real here, it expires from one word to the next. . . . The time here is *your* time." [14] As theatrical time subsumes performance, the very possibility of dramatic/fictional time collapses, and performance appropriates a field that is at once actual and metatheatrical.

If the fictional present, the unfolding center of a play's narrative structure, can be deliberately subverted, the same is true for the temporal projections that enclose this present: past and future. The past, for instance, that groundwork upon which the action of the present so frequently builds, is often presented with an obscurity antithetical to the clarity of conventional "exposition." Dramatists occasionally achieve this obscurity by multiplying the network of relationships among characters and complicating antecedent facts beyond the capacities of theatrical cognition. *The*

Way of the World, for example, features a relational tree perplexed even beyond the intricate norm of Restoration comedy; emerging sporadically, the play's dynastic ties and inheritance lines, and its history of romantic intrigues, expose a past elliptical and over-wrought in outline, the ornaments and incidentals of which con-stitute an almost Baroque background to the present's action. Sim-ilarly, the "troublous and extravagant details" of *The Duchess of Malfi,*[15] many of them only half-suggested by the play's characters, share the tortuous intricacy of *The White Devil, The Maid's Trag-edy,* and *'Tis Pity She's a Whore,* where overlapping relationships of obligation, loyalty, betrayal, violation, and incest reveal them-selves within both the dramatic present and its inherited past. Dramatists also subvert the narrational foundations of the past by rendering its details conflicting, subjective, problematic, a victim of memory or a casualty of negotiation; in *The Master Builder, Death of a Salesman,* and *Old Times,* for instance, characters sub-merge the past within incompletely articulated subtexts of guilt and fantasy, desire and evasion. Finally, of course, the dramatic past can be rendered indeterminate by the bare absence of impor-tant narrative material, especially material that would provide context or motivation for elements of the present. As with all de-cisions affecting the contours of the dramatic past, the absence of such information has decided implications for the present and how it is apprehended, leaving it (as in Strindberg's *Ghost Sonata*) strangely unmotivated, adrift from its temporal contexts, often alien and uncanny.

Indeterminacy and disorientation also threaten the future, formulated throughout the dramatic action and generally clarify-ing itself to provide the final stage moments with projective com-pletion. Even in its final formulation, when action has ceased and narrative reaches beyond the boundaries of stage activity, the dra-matic future is subject to gaps and instabilities, and this indeter-minacy bears consequences for narrative closure. The striking ta-bleaux at the ends of *Happy Days, The Homecoming,* and *Buried Child* block projection of any future that might serve as an escape from the present; and the conclusion of *Six Characters in Search of an Author* draws any conceivable dramatic future into the vor-tex of reality and illusion. William Butler Yeats makes similar use of thwarted projection in *Purgatory.* Believing that he has ended his dead mother's torment by murdering his son ("But you are in the light because I finished all that consequence"), the Old Man hears the hoofbeats of his father's horse and realizes that no atonement has been made, that the future is consigned to be nothing more than a repetition of the past: "Twice a murderer and all for nothing. / And she must animate that dead night / Not once but many times!" [16] With the hoofbeats actualized as stage sound, the play ends with past and future both devolving into the present as narrative sequence surrenders itself to a recurrent moment of purgatorial suffering.

Narrative comprehension works to abstract temporal frameworks from the moment of performance, and to enclose the moment within such contexts. What we have been calling antinarrative techniques frustrate this abstraction, and this contextualizing effort, forcing audience attention more fully onto the moment itself, both the dramatic present and the moment of performance that infuses it and gives the fictional moment its scenic immediacy. From this perspective, cognitive frameworks risk subversion whenever dramatists draw upon the stage's innate theatricality, heightening the dramatic and theatrical moment and giving it temporary predominance over its narrative contexts. Dramatists evoke this theatricality in a number of ways, and one can only begin to suggest their range and outline. They evoke it, most obviously, through characters who represent "theatricality" in its conventional meaning, riveting attention onto themselves through strategies of self-display. Mak, Falstaff, the Knight of the Burning Pestle, Ursula the Pig-Woman, Tony Lumpkin, Pirandello's Liolà, Brecht's Azdak, Genet's "Blacks," the stage performers of Dario Fo—these figures are joined across the dramatic canon by their assertive vitality, and by an often flamboyant presence, grounded in the actor's stage life. But theatricality also manifests itself in subtler forms, as a more universal quality of dramatic activity, apparent in those gestures by which even less histrionic characters focus attention on themselves and their surroundings. Richard II gazes into a mirror held at arm's length; Wilde's trivially earnest Algernon tastes phrases with the same palate he treats to cucumber sandwiches, savoring the elegance of sound over their truth; Stoppard's Guildenstern watches his coin spin through the space in front of him. In such moments, characters direct attention away from abstract contexts and onto the immediate and the physical, the momentary and the particular.

Theatricality is heightened, too, by the *mise-en-scène* itself, for the visual, kinetic, spatial, and aural components of theater compel response on their own terms. This assertiveness reveals itself in stage configurations; effects of lighting, stage movement, and sound; moments when characters are isolated within a large acting space. Shakespearean narrative temporarily dissolves within the dances and festive activities that fill the stage, and the conclusion of Pinter's *Homecoming* suspends narrative sequence through an opaque visual tableau. Similarly, the Welsh song of Mortimer's wife in *1 Henry IV*, the operatic interludes of Gay's *Beggar's Opera*, and the rock ballads of Shepard's *Tooth of Crime* establish a strong nonnarrative presence, often causing broader narrative lines to be suspended while its more directly physiological effects are felt. The charming power of music upon the characters who roam Prospero's island is only an exaggerated image of its more general theatrical power to seduce comprehension, to distract the senses away from narrative's "clearer reason" (V.i.68). In one of the paradoxes of theatrical signification, the elements frequently harnessed to aid narrative, to articulate the stage for comprehension's benefit, also assert a nonconceptual presence of their own.

Finally, dramatists manipulate the cognitive resistances of that dramatic element most consistently undervalued in discussions of plays: silence. Nothing is more crucial to the generation of dramatic narrative than language, shaped to the play's world as dramatic speech. The fundamental tool for "world-making," language grounds the fictional "otherness" of dramatic illusion in its own signifying activity, imposing a virtual world onto the materials of performance as it evokes patterns of meaning out of bare sound. Accordingly, few effects more effectively suspend narrative outlines, and pressure the dramatic with the theatrical, than those moments when speech stops, and the stage exists, if temporarily, without the word's abstracting pressure. At such points—when Viola and Sebastian stand gazing at each other, Nora walks numbly across the empty living room, and Mother Courage looks impassively at Eilif's dead body—the moment looms with its immediacy and presence, freed from language's conceptual activities, and from the temporal projections that characters and audience impose upon it. Temporality wavers within such silence, momentarily releasing the present from its hold.

Considering techniques of narrative heightening and subversion, and exploring their various effects upon audience response, provides an opening into broader features of dramatic form, into the manipulation of cognitive rhythm and sequence. In individual plays, such sequences may display the predominance of outline or its undermining—the narrative introductions of Japanese Noh drama or the Mozartian strains within "omnipresent nothing" that open Act III of Shaw's *Man and Superman*[17]—or they may delineate segments during which these impulses stand in a relationship of tension, as in the opening scene of *The Sea Gull*, where the introduction of narrative details is counterpointed by the distracting noise of the background stage-builders. Cognitive sequences display varying lengths, ranging from minute strokes of narrative outlines (messenger scenes in the middle of Shakespearean tragedies) or abrupt anti-narrative moments (the arrival of the Stranger in Act II of *The Cherry Orchard*) to segments comprising all or most of the play (the broad narrative sequences that comprise Racinian tragedy, the equally broad proliferations of stage activity in *Bartholomew Fair*). Since narrative sequences of any kind represent different orientations of audience to play, from the relative distance of intellectual comprehension to more immediate confrontations with performance, narrative analysis can uncover, in the borders between sequences, powerful shifts in audience response, moments when one mode of apprehension modulates into another, with often breathtaking effect. Dapper's cry from the privy in V.iii of *The Alchemist*, where he has been abandoned, and forgotten, for nearly two acts, plunges the provisional denouement that Face has patched together into blank confusion. With opposite effect, the appearance of the Angelus at the close of the Wakefield *Second Shepherds' Pageant* effects a sudden, and final, shift from the comic antics of Mak to the outlines of the Nativity story that stands as its metaphysical/historical backdrop: "Rise, hyrd-men heynd, for now is he borne / That shall take fro the feynd that Adam had lorne. . . ."[18]

Though cognitive rhythms and sequences pertain most directly to the drama of fictional worlds and plot lines, they also have implications for seemingly nonnarrative drama. Declarations to the contrary notwithstanding, and excepting the most radical of performance art, such moments often depend upon a background of narrative suggestion for their impact to be felt. Strindberg's *Ghost Sonata,* for instance, achieves its expressionistic effects against a narrative line, a story in which events and relationships are complicated with dreamlike distortion but one that remains, nonetheless, a story. In the first act, the Student speaks for an audience whose understanding of events is teased into the magical and the grotesque: "I don't understand any of this, but it's like a fairy story." [19] Even Artaud, despite his attacks on "a purely descriptive and narrative theater—storytelling psychology," had little intention of dispensing with narrative altogether in his Theater of Cruelty; in place of conventional dramatic plot, he demanded a theater based on "primitive Myths" and "Fables whose very atrocity and energy suffice to show their origin and continuity in essential principles." [20] Fairy stories and primitive myths may lack the conventional logic and coherence of the well-made play, but they nevertheless provide organizing narrative frameworks; as *The Ghost Sonata* and *Jet of Blood* both demonstrate, the responses that Strindberg and Artaud seek to compel clearly depend on such frameworks and the expectations of coherence that they occasion. Likewise, Tristan Tzara's seemingly nonsensical *Gas Heart* is in fact a carefully arranged pastiche of narrative motifs, each brilliant in its momentary evocation while teasing in the order it fails to provide: "Tangerine and white from Spain / I'm killing myself Madeleine Madeleine." [21] As Robert L. Caserio observes: "every attempt not to plot or tell a story is pervaded by a stubborn narrative impulse"; and although this observation is directed toward the novel, it applies equally to the theater, where the violation of comprehension paradoxically depends upon its deliberate engagement. [22]

From the devices and sequences that condition audience orientation to the stage and its activities, narrative analysis can attempt to describe a play's overall cognitive shape and the rhythms that this shape assumes in performance. Understanding the means by which the dramatic text signals audience response allows one to trace the shape of this response—to map out, as it were, the audience's cognitive orientation toward the unfolding dramatic activity and the oscillations between comprehension and modes of apprehension less strictly bound by the awareness of narrative outline. Such an understanding, and the analysis it permits, also allows one to discern the principles governing this overall shape and rhythm: the specific pulls, within the play, that draw the audience toward and away from narrative perception.

Analysis of Marlowe's *Doctor Faustus,* for instance, reveals a variety of narrative devices and techniques, organized into specific patterns according to equally specific principles. On the one hand, the play is characterized by a powerful narrative impulse, of the kind especially prominent within early- and mid-Elizabethan dramaturgy. A Chorus appears at four points: before the first, third, and fourth acts, and at the play's close. The middle appearances of this figure serve as a bridge between scenes, abstracting the play's narrative and calling attention to its shape. The Chorus' initial speech provides the background of Faustus' life and outlines the progress of his fortunes during the dramatic action, effectively containing this action within the moral progress of transgression and punishment which, Icarus-like, Faustus will enact: "Till swoll'n with cunning, of a self-conceit, / His waxen wings did mount above his reach / And melting, heavens conspired his overthrow!" (Prologue, ll. 19–21).[23] The specific outlines provided by the Chorus concerning Faustus' surrender to necromancy and the consequences thereof are reinforced throughout the first two acts by Faustus' own acknowledgment of his actions and where they will lead, and by the covenant that he signs with Mephostophilis, a document that anticipates the play's outlines in explicit form:

> I, John Faustus of Wittenberg, Doctor, by these presents, do give both body and soul to Lucifer, prince of the east, and his minister Mephostophilis, and furthermore grant unto them that, four and twenty years being expired, and these articles above written being inviolate, full power to fetch or carry the said John Faustus, body and soul, flesh, blood, or goods, into their habitation wheresoever. (II.i.108–16)

Rarely in drama is a play's action so directly projected, and its protagonist's assent to this development so forthcoming.

The narrative heightening provided by these outlines is most explicit during Acts I and II, when Faustus moves from his decision to make the infernal pact to the agreement itself. This initial heightening is reinforced by the extradramatic presence of Lucifer and four accompanying devils during Faustus' initial summons of Mephostophilis[24] and by the procession of the Seven Deadly Sins (II.ii.116–77), who underscore through allegorical signification the moral framework from which Faustus departs. The consequences that will inevitably follow from Faustus' bargain are represented in subsequent acts by the presence of Mephostophilis, who stands as a reminder of Lucifer's control over the play's outcome, and by Faustus' own moments of morbid remembrance, when an awareness of what he has lost pierces his gaiety. The domination of outlines is not fully reestablished, though, until the play's closing act, when the deferred consequences reassert themselves with an almost emblematic inevitability: Faustus must come to terms with his fate, and once this fate has been executed its lessons are made explicit in the Chorus' final speech, which recapitulates its opening summary: "Faustus is gone: regard his hellish fall, / Whose fiendful fortune may exhort the wise / Only to wonder at unlawful things" (Chorus after Act V, ll. 4–6).

At the play's beginning, then, and at its very end, Marlowe establishes a strong awareness of narrative outline—an awareness so underscored that it gives the play's action a quality of illustration, of moral exemplum—and this quality is evoked within the play's middle as well. But the play is complicated beyond this initial description, for Marlowe counterpoints this ruling narrative shape with devices and techniques that subvert, to varying extents, the abstract linearity of events and the hold of moral outline on action. For one thing, the rigorous anticipation of the Chorus' opening speech is counterpointed by the establishment of a rival narrative possibility, represented by the Good Angel, by the Old Man, and by Faustus' own theological training, that the bargain for damnation might be overturned by even a last-minute repentance. The fact that divine mercy overturns all consequence and is available to the most lost of sinners provides a structural insecurity in the ruling narrative anticipation, establishing a tension of outcome within the dominant irony and giving Faustus' vacillations genuine force in terms of the play's events. For another thing, the secondary plot involving Wagner and Robin, while it reinforces the main action through its parallel story of conjuring, nonetheless dissipates the rigorous outlines of this story through its comic tone and the stage diversions that its characters engage in. Wagner's parody of Faustus' scholastic logic (1.ii.1–30) dissolves argument into nonsense, and the conjuring games of I.iv and II.iii confront the gestures of necromancy with slapstick. The thematic connections of sequences such as these with the Faustus story are evident, but their power to draw attention in terms independent of the play's moral scheme is, theatrically, of equal significance.

More fundamentally, the dominance of outline over action, and the strict working of moral laws within which dramatic events are supposedly set as exempla, are subverted by a pronounced theatricality within the main action, a quality that derives from Faustus' "sinful" egocentrism but that gives his words and actions a stage vitality in part outside such moral designations. Faustus articulates his histrionic self-display, grounding his speech in the pronoun "I" (the speech in I.iii beginning "Had I as many souls as there be stars" contains seven instances of the first-person nominative in thirteen lines) and objectifying this "I" through narcissistic self-reference ("Settle thy studies Faustus, and begin / To sound the depth of that thou wilt profess," I.i.1–2). When applied to the external world, as in the famous address to Helen's image, his language is no less characterized by self-assertiveness, and its celebrated poetry ("In wanton Arethusa's azure arms . . .") displays a self-focusing richness of sound and image. When he acts, he focuses on the performance of the moment and the histrionic skill he exhibits in its execution: "Then in this show let me an actor be / That this proud Pope may Faustus' cunning see!" (III.i.76–77). So powerful is the theatrical in Faustus' actions, so marked his self-delight, that Mephostophilis himself is drawn into participation and play.

Driven by Faustus' drive to perform, his antics in the play's middle acts acquire an improvisatory quality, subject to the whim of the moment and the deflections of incident, a quality so subversive of the play's dominant tone and its ruling moral scheme that its structural relevance to the rest of the play has long been questioned. Matters of authorship aside, Acts III and IV form part of the larger tension within the play's narrative strategy as a whole, one rich with thematic consequence: the complication of moral argument by the sheer attractiveness (and eventual tedium) of the theatricality that the play's moral backdrop condemns. Ironic detachment from Faustus' actions is never broken, and moral guidelines finally triumph, but they do so in conjunction with a display of the self in its fundamental assertiveness, an assertiveness that draws upon the stage's theatricalized space and exerts an attractiveness partially belying the Chorus' stern judgment. In its broadest contours, the narrative of *Doctor Faustus* moves from a heightened narrativity, through the theatrical, and back again, and this development forces corresponding movements and conflicts in audience orientation toward the unfolding action, seemingly straightforward in its initial promises.

Narrative analysis offers different insights into Synge's *Playboy of the Western World,* a work characterized by disjunctions in both its dramatic representation and its interplay with the audience. Within the narrative sequences of this play, narrativity and disruption stand in continual confrontation, each rendering the other problematic as the audience works to disentangle the threads of narrative and stage action. On one hand, the play is filled with story and with language's storytelling capacities: its narrative background is woven from the material of ballads, songs, tales, and from the collective psyche of the west Irish as Synge portrays them. So pronounced is this "story" background that it dictates action, at that point when a stranger appears whose own tale captures and obsesses the narrative imagination of the Mayo villagers. Christy becomes the hero of Mayo, and the play's protagonist, because his tale of violence establishes him within a preexisting role elevated by admiration to a realm of heroic myth: "Drink a health to the wonders of the western world, the pirates, preachers, poteenmakers, with the jabbing jockies; parching peelers, and the juries fill their stomachs selling judgments of the English law."[25] Like Brecht's Macheath, Christy assumes his role within a world constructed by the narrative imagination, a world where boldness and transgression earn epic status: "A daring fellow is the jewel of the world" (p. 71). As the man of perceived valor and strength, Christy moves into the villagers' admiration, and discovers the rewards that his position assures him. That Christy is himself gifted in language and storytelling only heightens his standing: as Pegeen remarks, "I've heard all times it's the poets are your like, fine fiery fellows with great rages when their temper's roused" (p. 23).

This narrative activity within the dramatic world, and the glorification with which it crowns its Playboys, establishes expectations as to the possible development of the play's own narrative line. It does so, in large part, because stories, and Christy's in particular, exert such a powerful hold over the characters and their actions. Through language and gesture, the Mayo villagers reify the heroic, celebrating Christy as legend and themselves as vicarious witnesses. On Christy's part, all he must do is choose the image he sees in the mirror (p. 31) and claim the laurels; his triumph in the Homeric games of Act III represents his movement into this narrative elevation. To the hero goes the spoils: the play's first act explores the government of action by this kind of heroic law, with its elevation of individual transgression. The very power of this law in the popular imagination gives its outlines determining power: for Pegeen and Christy, as well as for the other villagers, action seems swept along by the compelling force of story.

But the projective glory set into apparent motion by Christy's tale and its reception is undermined at every turn by the realities of this dramatic world, realities that counter the heroic and poetic transformations effected by language. The poverty and bareness of the setting stand in ironic relationship to the elevating flights of language, constituting a harsh parody of the "Western World" and its inhabitants. The effects of such discrepancies are twofold: the gap between story and stage throws emphasis on the transformations that language and narrative seek to effect, but it also renders the play's overall development unstable by presenting a constant potential for deflation. That deflation might assume conventional comic forms, its consequences muted, is suggested by the appearance of Old Mahon, a development initially charged with comic force. But the instability of the heroic code that the villagers impose upon Christy, and the play as a whole, is given a decidedly noncomic dimension by the language in which they articulate it, a language charged with latent violence. Pegeen Mike derides Shawn by evoking the ideal that he fails to meet: "Where now will you meet the like of Daneen Sullivan knocked the eye from a peeler, or Marcus Quin, God rest him, got six months for maiming ewes, and he a great warrant to tell stories of holy Ireland till he'd have the old women shedding down tears about their feet" (p. 9). As with other characters in the play, her language betrays a sadistic imagination, and its poetic cadences fail to hide the brutality of its imagery. Embedded throughout the play's dramatic language, this substratum further subverts the dominant narrative line and its implicit promise of heroic elevation or comic deflation.

By undermining the narrative world that his characters' stories and his own comic ironies present, Synge destabilizes the outlines that seem to govern the play's dramatic action. This instability erupts when reality fails the test of myth. In the play's central disclosure, the latent violence within the play's language breaks through with horrific starkness: Christy, frantic at the loss of his prestige, reenacts the murder that he thought he had accomplished, and the villagers express with savage cruelty both the betrayal they feel and their revulsion at actual murder. Disappointment issues, not in reconciliation, but in a stage inflamed with rage and bitterness, and Christy's final attempt to reenter the comforts of story only deepen the rejection to which he has already been exposed. The elevations and transformations of language give way to the ugliness of specific stage actions: squeezing a rope around a neck and pulling on it, biting, screaming, burning with a stick. In the play's final disruption, Old Mahon reappears a second time, but the romance and glory of the play's initial narrative promise have been violated for good, and the play ends in disillusionment, Christy and his father leaving in a harsh inversion of normal resolution. Such a conclusion stands as far outside the world of heroes and their rewards as the sadistic violence that preceded it.

Seeking to disown the mode of violence in which she is participating, Pegeen instructs Christy that "there's a great gap between a gallous story and a dirty deed" (p. 77). Through the instabilities of the story elevating Christy to the role of Playboy, and through the narrative disruptions that characterize the play's final half, Synge explores this gap, both in the play's dramatic action and in its theatrical effect. The play's audience participates in the structural insecurities of narrative, and in the inability of outlines, specifically evoked by the characters themselves, to guide the play's action. Narrative expectations shatter in an eruption of stage violence, and the audience is confronted with a stage terrifyingly stripped of narrative guides—a stage, at the same time, inflamed by the very stories designed to transform it. It is this stripping, savage in its rejection of story's masks, that gives the play its disruptive potential in the theater: narrative explodes from within, and—through Synge's manipulation of narrative outlines and the stage they are employed to enclose—the audience must suffer its detonation. Addressing Synge's stylistic and generic antinomies, Edward Hirsch concludes that "the play is problematic precisely because it insistently creates a way of responding to it which it then contradicts."[26] The 1907 riots at the Abbey Theater attest to the potential turbulence within the "great gap" this play explores, and the dissonance occasioned by its narrative instabilities and breakdowns.

For both *Doctor Faustus* and *Playboy of the Western World*, more particular analysis might focus on the interplays between outline and the moment within individual sequences: in the exchanges, for instance, between Faustus and Mephostophilis, or within individual recountings of Christy's story. Whatever the level of detail, such description offers a portrait of the dramatic work in performance, sketching the general features of action and response as they are imaged by the dramatic text and engaged within the theater. In the face of individual performances, with their different emphases and articulations, this kind of analysis offers broader models of "possible" response, seeking to isolate the spine of activity that runs through performance variations, as well as the range within which individual stage artists might establish interpretation. As Roger Gross has argued, the dramatic text is characterized by "parameters" and "tolerances"—lines that determine what must occur in performance and what must not[27]—and it is within such possibilities and proscriptions that dramaturgical analysis proposes its insights. If this analysis is truly representative of narrative's theatrical unfolding, its descriptions will provide solid interpretations within which individual differences of staging and response can be explored.

As we have suggested, analysis of a play's narrative devices, and the modes of response they occasion, leads naturally and inevitably into the play's own world, and into a convergence of audience response with issues of theme and idea within the dramatic world. This overlap is made possible by the fact that narrative, in its manipulations of the audience's cognitive engagement with the stage, draws upon processes and activities by which the human subject confronts the world at large. Many of drama's most recurrent thematic concerns (the nature of action and intention, for instance, or the ethics of imitation) raise experiential questions which coincide in significant ways with the audience's own structuring of time during performance, its engagement with levels of theatrical reality and illusion, its exploration of the relationship of cognitive frameworks to the movements of stage action, and its discovery of the limitation of these frameworks. Investigating narrative comprehension, therefore, provides insights into what we might call the "phenomenology of the thematic," its experiential basis in perception and cognition. Understanding Marlowe's counterpoint of narrative outline with theatricality in *Doctor Faustus,* for instance, uncovers the poles that organize the play's moral exploration, while careful analysis of Synge's dramaturgy in *Playboy*—his destabilization of narrative expectations—suggests a psychosociology of myth: its relation to the nonmythic, its personal and social uses, the individual and collective consequences of its disillusion.[28]

But this kind of narrative analysis leads even more deeply into the play's fictional world than the concept of "theme" allows. With its emphasis on individual cognitive processes, and on the construction of conceptual patterns as a means by which individuals orient themselves toward their environment, the study of narrative *effect* in the theater has clear relevance to the domain of *action* within the dramatic world—to the thrust of intentions and activities through which characters seek to interpret this world and manipulate it to their ends. Such narrative activity has been explored in much more depth with novelistic characters than it has within drama, in part because critics and theorists concerned with drama's self-consciousness have restricted themselves to the metadramatic study of acting, rendering narration a subgesture of the performative act. But overtly "theatrical" performance represents only one of the means by which dramatic characters give shape to events and structure action within temporal models. Drama's unsurpassed dependence on its characters for its narrative material makes them storytellers by necessity—recalling facts, drawing connections, anticipating developments, testing these frameworks against the world in which they act. The difficulties facing Hamlet, for instance, revolve around acts of comprehension and narration: from his first meeting with his father's Ghost, he is forced to verify the story of his father's murder and to initiate the action that will resolve it; he seeks narrative analogies in the experiences of others; and he ends his life by recasting it, specifically, as "story" (V.ii.349). Drama's energetic depictions of acting are generated through, and in conjunction with, a high degree of narrative activity on the part of its characters. By isolating this activity as a central component of dramatic action and exploring its correspondences to the activities of playwatching, one can discern the common threads linking Iago's insinuations, Rosmer's agonized probing of the past, the comedy of mistaken identity in *What the Butler Saw,* and the flight into history on the part of Pirandello's Henry. Although not all such activity constitutes action in the Stanislavskian sense of motivational objective, its formal inevitability in a medium where character voice replaces authorial voice, and where characters must define themselves in actual space, provides dramatists with an opportunity to make storytelling and other narrative gestures central dramatic activities. It allows them to probe, within their dramatic fictions, the pervasive and complex narrative activities of life outside the theater, what Barbara Hardy calls "that inner and outer storytelling that plays a major role in our sleeping and waking lives."[29]

If narrative lies at the heart of the dramatic character's confrontation with an external world, thereby establishing connections with the private activities of consciousness inside the theater and without, it also constitutes an important force in character interactions. Characters must formulate and reformulate narrative material in constant interaction with the other characters and objects around them, the act of retrospection bound up within performance's social field. Such interaction, and the energy that infuses it, are distinctively theatrical, characteristic of a medium where, as a rule, narrator physically confronts listener. Moreover, since dramatic time is shared time, and since the temporal constructions of performance space serve to configure and define the individuals who inhabit it, its outlines become a source of contest, and its details provide material for the various influences that

characters seek to exert upon one another. *The Alchemist's* opening scene suggests the potential ferocity of narrative negotiation:

> *Face.*   Why, who
> Am I, my mongrel? Who am I?
> *Subtle.*   I'll tell you,
> Since you know not yourself—
> *Face.*   Speak lower, rogue.
> *Subtle.* Yes. You were once (time's not long past) the good,
> Honest, plain, livery-three-pound-thrum, that kept
> Your master's worship's house, here, in the Friars,
> For the vacations—
> *Face.*   Will you be so loud?
> *Subtle.* Since, by my means, translated suburb-Captain.
> *Face.* By your means, Doctor Dog?
> *Subtle.*   Within man's memory,
> All this I speak of.
> *Face.*   Why, I pray you, have I
> Been countenanced by you, or you by me?
> Do but collect, sir, where I met you first.
> *Subtle.* I do not hear well. [*Cupping his ear.*]
> *Face.*   Not of this, I think it.
> But I shall put you in mind, sir: at Pie-corner,
> Taking your meal of steam in from cooks' stalls,
> Where, like the father of hunger, you did walk
> Piteously costive, with your pinched-horn nose,
> And your complexion of the Roman wash,
> Stuck full of black and melancholic worms,
> Like powder-corns shot at th'artillery-yard.
> *Subtle.* I wish you could advance your voice, a little.
>
>   (I.i.12–32)[30]

The competing "storytelling" of Face and Subtle forms a major
part of their broader struggle for domination, a struggle that
emerges in moments such as this and that otherwise remains submerged as a latent destabilizing force for the play's action as a
whole. As part of this broader interaction, their narrative moves
are shaped by the constant presence of a listener who receives the
blows of rejoinder and accusation, responds, and redirects the story's trajectory onto a new course. Subtle begins the narrative at-

tack, working to fashion an account of the past and its corresponding hierarchy of power, but he is abruptly overborne by Face
and must suffer a reversal of accusation until, later in the exchange, a detail allows him to regain his domination and momen-
tum. Each struggles to escape the other's narrative onslaught
through strategies of deflection: directing attention, for example,
from the storybuilding aspect of language onto the volume of the
utterance ("Speak lower, rogue"). Unlike stories within the novel,
which tend to efface questions of relationship among the characters assembled, the fierce action of story-control between Face and
Subtle animates and articulates dramatic confrontation, issuing
from the present relationship of speaker and listener, taking this
relationship as its narrative subject, and seeking (through move
and counter-move) to adjust it.[31]

"But I shall put you in mind, sir," threatens Face, following
Subtle's claim that his own account took place "within man's
memory." By no means tangential, these references to memory
underscore the extent to which the dramatic character, alone and
in his interactions with others, engages in the same cognitive strategies for comprehending incidents within the dramatic world as
the audience does in its efforts to structure the incidents of dramatic representation. Though these strategies are more insistent
within the play—characters, unlike the audience, must directly
participate in the activities surrounding them—they reflect similar
cognitive issues: the problem of reliability in accounts of events,
temporality and its relation to the present, the interpenetration of
fiction and nonfictionalized reality, the power and the limitations
of cognitive structures designed to organize the flux of incident.
Even when the line between the audience and the dramatic world
remains fixed, the processes of integrating time that the audience
brings to the theatrical experience are remarkably like those it encounters on stage.

The dynamics of comprehension, then, not only constitute
the heart of a play's narrative effect, they also influence dramatic
action—the pulse, frequently, behind an encounter, a scene, or an
entire play. Rarely do the two correspond exactly; indeed, they
often work in counterpoint, establishing discrepancies between
character and audience comprehension. Many plays that depict
imperfect comprehension, for instance, and the breakdown of

cognitive structures, simultaneously employ devices that heighten the audience's perception of narrative continuity, interposing a distance through which the performance moment is subject to the mediations of outline. Their effect lies within the tradition of classical irony, which hinges upon the audience's detachment from the misperceptions it witnesses and its awareness of temporal structures that the characters must struggle to discern. Exploring this discrepancy in Shakespearean comedy, Bertrand Evans has written, "Attention is centered for nearly two hours on persons whose vision is less complete than ours, whose sense of the facts of the situation most pertinent to themselves is either quite mistaken or quite lacking, and whose words and actions would be very different if the truth known to us were known to them."[32] Such a relationship between action and effect, between character audience comprehension, is exploited in Sheridan's *School for Scandal*. The play depicts a social setting where characters act against a background of gossip, innuendo, and deceit, where the surname "Surface" underscores the treacherousness of appearances, where cognitive surety is undermined by imperfect awareness. From the first scene, though, in which Lady Sneerwell and Joseph Surface confide in each other, the audience maintains a comparably untroubled understanding of events, aided by devices and techniques deigned to uphold this privileged vision. Deception, essential to the plays' action, is not practiced on the audience: the celebrated "screen" scene, for example, although certainly the play's most complicated and vigorous stage moment and an apex of character unknowing, nevertheless depends upon a high degree of audience comprehension for its ironies and delights, the "clear vision" that William Archer so strongly preferred to the "shock of surprise."

If plays such as *The School for Scandal* probe the limitations of comprehension within the dramatic world without manipulating corresponding effects in audience response, one finds instances where the reverse is true, where cognitive disruption is employed on the level of technique unaccompanied by equivalent characterological explorations. An extreme version of such discrepancy is obvious, of course, in the twentieth-century avant-garde, where vigorous anti-narrative dramaturgy is combined with a rejection of psychological action within the dramatic world. Artaud, for instance, expressed his contempt for such dramatized conceptual activity, for "this conception of theater, which consists of having people sit on a certain number of straight-backed or overstuffed chairs placed in a row and tell each other stories, however marvellous. . . ."[33] Even within less radical drama, though, versions of this discrepancy reveal themselves. *The Way of the World,* for instance, exploits a sophisticated program of narrative subversion without the vigorous storytelling activity evident in the earlier Jonson and the later Sheridan. While the play's characters deceive one another, implicating themselves within a world of perceptual convolution, their command of information generally exceeds that of the audience. In such moments, when the audience is placed in a position of inferior knowledge, the theater exploits an effect that constitutes the opposite of irony, a relationship of audience to action for which dramatic theory has no word and to which it has paid little attention. This "anti-irony" is a ruling mode of more recent plays such as *The Bald Soprano, The Balcony, The Birthday Party,* and *Who's Afraid of Virginia Woolf?,* where questions are not answered, motives not revealed, and where the audience's surrogate within the dramatic world (if there is one) is the character most bewildered by surrounding events.

Between these two extremes, and even at points within the plays just mentioned, lies a middle ground for interpenetration, where the efforts and failures of comprehension within the play touch those offstage, and where the audience witnesses a reflection of its own attempts to structure events. Such a reflection occurs in *Henry V,* where the Chorus' narrative gestures toward the audience find actional equivalents within the play. If the Chorus abstracts dramatic events by highlighting the outlines of "story" (V.i.i), Henry's speech to his soldiers before the field of Agincourt constitutes a similar effort to contextualize the present:

> Then shall our names,
> Familiar in his mouth as household words,
> Harry the King, Bedford and Exeter,
> Warwick and Talbot, Salisbury and Gloucester,
> Be in their flowing cups freshly rememb'red.
> This story shall the good man teach his son;
> And Crispin Crispian shall ne'er go by,
> From this day to the ending of the world,
> But we shall in it be remembered. . . .
>   (IV.iii.51–59)

This exercise of the historical imagination recalls both the Bishop of Ely's urging in the first act—"Awake remembrance of these valiant dead, / And with your puissant arm renew their feats" (I.ii.115–16)—and Henry's assent to the campaign:

> Either our history shall with full mouth
> Speak freely of our acts, or else our grave,
> Like Turkish mute, shall have a tongueless mouth,
> Not worshipp'd with a waxen epitaph.
>
> (I.ii.230–33)

Narrative sanctions the moment, as war evokes the contexts necessary to its execution; Henry's storytelling skill, his ability to set the present within the privileged narrative of historical legend, is essential to the French campaign and to the English success in its key battle. This mythologizing suggests a kinship of function and address between Henry and the Chorus, whose rhetoric he echoes, and the audience joins the onstage characters as targets of his narrative acts, responding both to the outlines that Henry's speeches offer as potential contexts for the surrounding dramatic action and to the rhetorical seduction that his words attempt. Through such correspondence, narrative memory and anticipation in the audience meet historical memory and anticipation onstage, and the intersections involve the spectator within the play's own exploration of historical recourse.[34]

Simultaneously grounded within theatrical and dramatic time, cognition bridges the worlds of audience and play, establishing intricate relationships of counterpoint and coincidence. Through such relationships, which ally perceiving subjects within the dramatic world with those subjects whose perception stands at the heart of the theatrical interaction, dramaturgical effect bears much more directly upon content than is generally acknowledged. If analysis describes the rhythms by which the audience constructs the stage world as a temporally structured dramatic universe, interpretation promises to trace this structuring into the dramatic world itself, considering audience and play as part of a larger continuum whereby the moment is signaled and shaped. For the two worlds draw upon each other with a richness and complexity particular to the theater, that medium that both dramatizes and engages cognitive formulation. The remaining chapters will consider a number of plays in which this continuum is manipulated with particular vigor, plays in which the interrelationship of audience and dramatic world becomes a primary subject of dramatic and theatrical exploration. As an audience struggles along with Face and Subtle to construct a past that might stabilize the present— applies, with Henry's Englishmen, the frameworks of history to the problematic exigencies of the moment—issues of theme and action extend themselves outside the dramatic world, to the anterior level of its construction and to the cognitive activity that it calls into play.

CHAPTER THREE

Moral Stages in
Everyman and *Mankind*

The fifteenth-century English morality play is a useful place to begin more detailed exploration of theatrical comprehension, not only because it stands at the opening of modern European drama, but also because, to an unusual extent, the structured allegory of morality drama seems to fit the conventional notion of dramatic narrative as an abstract story line clearly articulated and received. Called "the archetype of the theater of ideas in our western tradition of drama,"[1] the century's half-dozen or so extant moralities are peopled by characters with names like The King of Pride, World, Mercy, and Knowledge, who act within the narrative pattern of temptation, fall, and restoration that the majority of these plays share. Yearning, no doubt, for the variety and multiplicity of Elizabethan drama, subsequent ages have taken the redundancy and didacticism of this pattern as evidence (at best) of a historically bound primitivism or (at worst) of artistic and dramaturgical clumsiness. In a study otherwise seeking to locate morality drama within a tradition of theatrical reflexivity, for example, Anne Righter's characterization of the morality play as "a kind of sermon with illustrations"[2] comes revealingly close to the more popular sense of these plays as simple moral fables, their characteristic modes of audience address a reflection of rhetorical, not dramatic, force. Our own century's rediscovery of didacticism as a potential source of theatrical power has, in fact, done little to modify the general condescension toward the moralities as a group. When they are considered as drama, the moralities are commonly approached in terms of their ruling ideas and with the positing of an omniscient spectator who, occasionally addressed, follows these ideas to their dramatic completion—an approach which supports the opinion that these dramatic "sermons" are plays almost by accident.

The comparative neglect of morality drama in discussions of drama, as well as the literary response it so frequently occasions, result (in large part) from the paucity of evidence concerning how these plays actually were performed and from the relative infrequency with which (*Everyman* excepted) they have been produced since. But no matter how directly derived from sermons and tracts, no matter how similar to other, nondramatic forms of medieval allegory, these plays were written for and performed in the theater, as one discovers in the Macro manuscript's diagram for *The Castle of Perseverance*'s staging or in the theatrical antics preserved so elaborately in *Mankind*'s stage directions. According to the evidence marshaled by historians of the medieval theater, the performance of these plays was accomplished within a lively theatrical tradition and with considerable popular success.[3] As with all drama, this theatrical reality is indispensable to a play's universe of action: a sermon on mercy differs in kind and effect from the words and gestures of a character named Mercy who stands forward to address a theatrical audience, and a devil grinning from the margins of an illuminated manuscript engages very different response from one prancing about the edges of a Cambridgeshire platform.

As a theatrical reading of its texts reveals, morality drama is unusually aware of its existence in performance, drawing upon the stage in various and specific ways and presenting some of the most striking artistic and moral explorations of the theatrical environment in English drama. Approaching these plays with an understanding of narrative response in the theater and its relation to narrative activity onstage allows one to see how closely these supposedly primitive plays of ideas exploit the narrative and antinarrative possibilities of performance, and how directly issues of theatricality and comprehension bear upon the moral action onstage and its moral effect upon the audience. To illustrate this, and to establish the poles of austerity and abandon within which morality drama manipulates its stage and audience, we will consider the relentlessly stark *Everyman* (ca. 1495) and the lively *Mankind* (ca. 1465–70), tracing the different narrative experience each represents and evokes in its drama of the individual's moral life. In each of these plays, we will see, the stage constitutes not simply a dressing for literary or rhetorical content, but a fundamental condition of meaning.

The predominantly literary view of the moralities has been supported by the disproportionate attention paid by theorists and producers to *Everyman,* a play severe in narrative outline and moral point: Dethe comes, and all abandon Everyman save Good Dedes rejuvenated by Penaunce. Even the most cursory investigation of the fifteenth-century morality play reveals, though, how unique *Everyman* is among the moralities as a group. With its focus on mortality, it forgoes the central soul-struggle associated with the protagonist of the other plays, and it lacks the conflicts, choices, and *peripeteias* that more regularly characterize action within the morality universe. At first glance, *Everyman* appears nondramatic in structure and tone, its allegorical development more the function of illustration than of any kind of theatrical tension. But the play's allegorical clarity must not be seen as exclusively "literary," independent of the stage and its effects. A play about endings, its dominant mode is retrospect: the distractions of life flourish in the past, and are represented in the present only so that the play can dramatize their falling away. This ideology of relinquishment finds its equivalent in *Everyman*'s distinctive dramaturgy, a strategy of theatrical address that takes on the energies of performance in order to displace and suppress them. The very asceticism that isolates *Everyman* from the other moralities, precluding the histrionics of plays such as *Mankind* and *Wisdom* or the ornate staging in *The Castle of Perseverance,* results from a powerful antitheatricality, through which the stage's energies are ruthlessly subordinated to the outlines of story and idea.[4]

Everyman opens with the entrance of a Messenger, whose introductory address not only sounds the play's issues, but also establishes two important features that will characterize the play as a whole:

> I pray you all give your audience,
> And here this mater with reverence,
> By figure a morall playe:
> The *Somoninge of Everyman* called it is,

That of our lives and endinge shewes
How transitory we be all daye.
This mater is wonder[ou]s precious,
But the entent of it is more gracious,
And swete to bere awaye.
The story saith: Man, in the beginninge
Loke well, and take good heed to the endinge,
Be you never so gay!
Ye thinke sinne in the beginninge full swete,
Whiche in the ende causeth the soule to wepe
Whan the body lieth in claye.
Here shall you se how Falawship and Jolité,
Bothe Strengthe, Pleasure, and Beauté,
Will fade from the[e] as floure in Maye;
For ye shall here how our heven Kinge
Calleth Everyman to a general rekeninge.
Give audience, and here what he doth saye.

(ll. 1–21)[5]

For one thing, the interplay of "mater" and "entent" in this Prologue underscores the connection that we are tracing throughout this study: the mutual dependence of thematic subject and theatrical effect, and the interpenetration of the world represented with the world addressed. The generalized "our" and "we" in lines 5 and 6 dovetail with the almost accusatory specific "ye" of line 13 to establish a juncture characteristic of morality drama as a whole, whereby the audience joins the protagonist as the target of the play's moral instruction. The "Man" addressed by "the story" in line 10, in other words, is both subject and object, a universalized agent located on both sides of the stage.

Of equal dramaturgical consequence, the Prologue outlines the play's events, providing anticipatory summary of *Everyman*'s human and theological action. In so doing, it offers a perspective essential to its moral vision as well. Structuring the individual story of Everyman is the relationship of sin to its effects within the context of human temporality; the "entent" so "swete to bear away" is a perception of the unbroken and inevitable connection between "our lives and endinge," a connection obscured by the transitory vibrancy of "all dayes" but nonetheless issuing in a "rekeninge" at which the consequences mandated by life's actions are realized. The ensuing speech, spoken by God, sets the span of life within even broader outlines: the pattern of salvation history within which mankind receives the chance for redemption beyond death: "To gete them life I suffred to be deed" (l. 32). In the play's moral psychology, proper vision directs itself toward the abstract assurance of "things not seen" (Hebrews, 11:1),[6] while sin is conceived as an abandonment to the moment and its allure. Underscored at the beginning of *Everyman,* in other words, is a dualism, largely antagonistic, between time and the present, a dualism fundamental to morality drama as a whole. Like the other moralities, *Everyman* contrasts an abstract salvation scheme with the distracting presence of the here and now, and like them it exploits this tension in theatrical terms, manipulating that dualism of dramatic performance between the immediate and the abstract, between what an audience directly experiences and what it is made to signify. *Everyman*'s insistence on the seductiveness of "all dayes" and its repeated connections between beginnings and endings ("Man, in the beginninge / Loke well, and take good heed to the endinge") suggests that the action onstage and the impact of that action on the audience involve the issues of temporal comprehension so central to the theater, where the stage is localized within narrative and ideational patterns, and where the flux of performance risks "dis-tracting" attention from abstract patterns of meaning to the sensory realities of the moment. For *Everyman*'s audience, as well as its protagonist, moral struggle is conceived as a conflict between short-sightedness and broader temporal perception.

Everyman differs from the other moralities through its focus on abstraction, a focus achieved through specific dramaturgical means. For the audience, the play's "lenten austerity"[7] derives from an abundance of narrative devices, like the Messenger's Prologue, that establish and reassert the play's narrative and moral outlines and their dominating relation to stage activity. At least one critic has considered this Prologue "somewhat superfluous,"[8] but the effects of this introduction on the audience's experience of the dramatic action are central to the play as a whole. Actually, the main action of *Everyman* is introduced three times—by the Messenger, by God, and by Death—each introduction anticipat-

ing the shape of Everyman's reckoning. With their emphasis on
the journey motif, they underscore the plot's streamlined, teleological linearity, thereby providing the play with a rigorously arranged beginning, middle, and end. By establishing their outlines
with such firmness, these anticipations significantly adjust the audience's conceptual relationship to the unfolding action, shifting
its status from participants to observers, focusing its attention on
what the stage is being made to signify. This distancing strategy
continues throughout the play, as its characters—who all, at various points, serve the role of extradramatic commentators—sum-
marize the action that has taken place and speculate about future
outcomes. Abandoned by his kin, for instance, Everyman sums up
both the rejection and its lessons:

> A, Jesus, is all come hereto?
> Lo, faire wordes maketh fooles faine;
> They promise, and nothinge will do, certaine.
> My kinnesmen promised me faithfully
> For to abide with me stedfastly,
> And now fast awaye do they flee;
> Even so Felawship promised me.
>
> (ll. 378–84)

Everyman reflects upon what has happened, abstracting from his
experience those patterns that constitute its instructional significance, pressing the unmediated stage moment ever further into the
background.

Tightness and pattern pervade all aspects of *Everyman*'s dramaturgy, working to enhance the play's narrative and moral outline. The play features seventeen characters, but these characters
are carefully grouped within the action and on the stage, and they
make no attempts to disrupt these groupings: there are frequently
only two onstage at any moment, and when there are more, as
there are during Everyman's final approach to death, they generally address each other singly. Conceived within rigid allegorical
boundaries, these figures are emblematic in identity, characterized
far less by individuating traits than by broader signifying features.
Felawship's initial greeting to Everyman, for instance, is "well spoken, and lovingly" (l. 215), strictly appropriate to their past
friendship, while his preordained exit is in keeping with his spe-

cific role within Everyman's journey. Throughout the play, speeches suggest little or no gesture beyond that appropriate to explanation and illustration, and such gesture, when it is called for, draws attention toward spiritual action and its consequences, toward allegorical, not material, identity. Goodes, for instance, displays himself to Everyman and to the audience, but the spectators are concerned less with the actor displaying his body than with his abstract significance. Indeed, insofar as the actor playing Goodes represents the temptation of material wealth, it is precisely his physicality that is discredited as illusory. Character movements are similarly harnessed: when they cross the stage, they do so with an almost processional simplicity. With the exception of the Doctor, each character is announced, upon entering, by another—from the Messenger's reference to the "heven Kinge's" speech to Knowledge's introduction of the Angell: "Methinketh that I here aungelles singe" (l. 891). Befitting the play's narrative linearity and its theme of abandonment, what V. A. Kolve calls "that movementinto-aloneness generic to tragedy," no character who exits the stage of *Everyman* ever returns.[9] Finally, in keeping with the play's ascetic suppression of the physical, there are few props in *Everyman,* and those props that are dictated by the text—book of reckoning, scourge, garment of sorrow, rood—point through and beyond themselves; attention is drawn toward their sacramental quality, that divine reality which suffuses, and thereby transforms, the items' mere objectness.

From its opening moments, then, *Everyman* displays a range of devices and techniques designed to facilitate the audience's perception of narrative and moral pattern. Within the play's world, Everyman the character is less fortunate, entering the stage without benefit of the opening speeches, preoccupied with the moment's distractions and consequently unable to discern its broader outline of cause and consequence. Everyman encounters Dethe having forgotten the brevity of his life as well as the pattern of salvation history against which it exists and through which it finds the promise of redemption: as Dethe remarks, "Full litell he thinketh on my cominge; / His minde is on flesshely lustes and his tresure" (ll. 81–82). Dethe's reproaches for forgetfulness—"Hast thou thy Maker forgete?" (l. 86) and "Thoughe thou have forgete him here, / He thinketh on the[e] in the hevenly sp[h]ere" (ll. 94–

95)—situate him among those whom God earlier lamented for
forgetting his redemptive sacrifice (ll. 29–32, 58–59). Guided by
the introductory speeches and their stern warnings concerning
those things that fade "as floure in Maye," the audience recognizes
the futility of Everyman's approaches to Felawship, Kinrede, and
Goodes and appreciates the irony behind a remark like Felawship's: "For, in faith, and thou go to hell, / I will not forsake the[e]
by the waye" (ll. 232–33). The audience watches Everyman slowly
begin to understand the actuality of his past and its implications
for his future, acquiring a temporal vision that will finally match
its own.

At the same time, the play's narrative development qualifies
the audience's ironic perspective, with its risky detachment from
the human condition represented within the dramatic world. For
both character and audience, comprehension shifts when Everyman looks down and addresses Good Dedes, in dismay at her
weakened condition: "But, alas, she is so weke / That she can
nother go nor speke" (ll. 482–83). For Everyman, Good Dedes
represents the first character who actually knows his plight and
offers to accompany him: "And you do by me, that journay with
you will I take" (l. 495). For the audience, her reply constitutes
the beginning of an unanticipated movement within the broad
outline of Everyman's journey, since the introductory speeches
provided few clues, and little hope, that he would escape damnation at that journey's end. God's resolve to

> Have a rekeninge of every mannes persone;
> For, and I leve the people thus alone
> In their life and wicked tempestes,
> Verily they will become moche worse than beestes!
>
> (ll. 46–9)

suggests a pessimistic anger the tone of which approaches the bib-
lical God's judgments of mankind in Genesis. Likewise, although
Dethe acknowledges the salutory possibility of good works, these
words come, parenthetically, within his more vivid mention of
damnation:

> He that loveth richesse I will strike with my darte,
> His sight to blinde, and fro heven to departe—

Excepte that almes be his good frende—
In hell for to dwell, worlde without ende.

(ll. 76–79)

Dethe's brief suggestion of rescue provides no indication of the stages it might entail, nor is the hope that his remark occasions supported as the play develops. As Goodes' mocking reproach in lines 429–34 and the weakness of Good Dedes both attest, "almes" and Everyman have been, if at all, only slight acquaintances.

After the introductions to Everyman's journey, the play's action confirms the predictions that the things of the world prove transitory, but although the play's opening sequence has maintained its focus on Everyman's "endinge" and the accompanying "rekeninge," it has offered little suggestion as to how this reckoning might be made clear. In a dramaturgical sense, when Good Dedes speaks from the ground, she becomes the audience's guide, too, filling in salvation's details. The audience's narrative experience, still broadly comprehensive in its focus on outlines, shifts toward the suspense of not knowing, and the steps of Everyman's sanctification are anticipated and described by a series of characters invested with instructive narrative authority. Good Dedes introduces Everyman to Knowledge; Knowledge sends him to Confession; each step of his purification is carefully directed and explained: even Five Wittes provides an exposition on priesthood before Everyman receives the last sacrament. Attention stretches ahead, and the deepening interest that the audience experiences concerning Everyman's final moments attests to the anticipation that characterizes the play's ending as a whole. That the narrative authority which instructs and guides this anticipation is now in the hands of the characters surrounding Everyman explains the mild jolt when Beauté, Strength, Discrecion, and Five Wittes exit, for in the discoveries of the play's conclusion, they have led us as well.

If it is indeed true that "the problem which *Everyman* presents with such daring and subtlety is the effort of dying mankind to find a solution for death,"[10] then the audience participates in the clarification of the solution. Presented with the journey toward death, it witnesses the dropping away of illusion and the steps of sanctification that bring Everyman to good ending. By the play's close, Everyman has himself assumed a position of narrative authority, completing the process of clarification and understanding that has comprised his spiritual growth. At the start, his mind is clouded with forgetfulness, a forgetfulness expressed in images of darkness and obscurity: he tells Dethe "This blinde mater troubleth my witte" (l. 102), and his "rekeninge," the account of his life, is called "blotted and blinde" (l. 419). By the play's end, though, his "rekeninge," like his sight, is "crystall clere" (l. 898). Everyman has grown to comprehend the divine plan of salvation, with its temporal spans of human life and salvation history, and how action in the former determines participation in the latter. He assumes the "way of rightwisness" (l. 582), in which the individual surrenders particular identity to a pattern at once historical and eternal and thereby triumphs, in spite of personal vulnerability, over sin and death.[11] The *imitatio Christi* of Everyman's final words ("*In manus tuas . . . / commendo spiritum meum*, ll. 886–87) indicates how completely he has grown from blindness to participation in the broader salvation narrative presented in God's introductory speech.

The point of Everyman's education into comprehension is directed to the audience in the play's final moments, through a trio of recapitulations that mirror the triple introduction. Everyman, at last forsaken by his personal attributes, warns the audience to profit by what they have seen of his ending: "How they that I love[d] best do forsake me / Excepte my Good Dedes, that bideth truely" (ll. 868–69). Good Dedes herself summarizes the narrative in more detail:

> All erthly thinges is but vanité:
> Beauté, Strength, and Discrecion do man forsake,
> Folisshe frendes, and kinnesmen, that faire spake—
> All fleeth save Good Dedes, and that am I.
> (ll. 870–73)

And the story and its underlying moral pattern are stated a third and final time by the Doctor who delivers the play's epilogue, after Everyman has abandoned in death his transitory life and his invisible soul is greeted by an angel who visualizes its entrance into heaven, the reward of his sanctifying final actions. In theatrical terms, this stage exit and its triple explication represent the play's final triumph of abstraction over action, of narrative over performance. For the story, now freed from its embodiment on stage, is all that remains of Everyman the character and those he encountered on his journey toward death: this journey and its temporal and moral contexts, reiterated so often through reminder and anticipation, are now the property of Everyman the audience, now charged to live their "dayes" with an awareness of beginnings and endings, and an understanding that all are held accountable for the actions of the middle. "This morall men may have in minde" (l. 902): *Everyman* completes itself on the audience's inner stage of memory and judgment as action becomes lesson, pure in its conceptual autonomy. As this conclusion demonstrates, the triumph of the conceptual over the physical and the ephemeral is not only the "matere" of *Everyman,* it also constitutes the "entente," the play's challenge to its audience. Its wealth of narrative devices are designed to hold this "morall" forward from the flux of performance—to subordinate the experience of the senses, with its transitory distractions, to the experience of the "minde."

Much like the invisible liberation of Everyman's soul, *Everyman* demonstrates a dramaturgical impulse to attain the purity of conceptual truth, through its steady paring away of theatrical inessentials and its tight narrative controls. The play's dramaturgical center lies in its theatrical austerity and the insistence with which it works against its condition in performance, finally abandoning the things of the stage as it does those of the world in which the stage has its existence. In many ways, *Everyman* embodies a theatrical paradox. On one hand, its demonstrative force depends on its embodiment in performance, its "bodying forth" in props and actors, words and actions. Good Dedes owes her homiletic power, in large part, to the actress' material presence onstage and to the histrionic arts of declamation and presentation upon which she draws. At the same time, the play resists the distraction threatened by this embodiment, the tendency of all performance to undermine cognitive structures and to intrude itself on its own, nonconceptual terms. *Everyman*'s contemptus mundi tenor—its banishment of the world as part of a triumph of the spirit—is reflected in a profound antitheatricalism, unrivaled among the moralities (and among virtually all of English drama): a steady suppression of performance in favor of the spiritual pattern that stands as its referent. Like a tightly patterned dance, or like the ritualistically formal Japanese Noh,[12] the play's power lies in the insistence with which it keeps its energies under control, subordinating display to design, rendering inconceivable the theatrical extravagance of later and different drama. This tension gives *Everyman* its distinctive narrative power: simple, even severe, its activity luminous with the power of outline and abstraction.[13]

Everyman's tightness and austerity become even more pronounced in light of the earlier *Mankind,* a play characterized by different aims and correspondingly different narrative techniques. It begins similarly enough with the opening exhortations of Mercy, who serves as spokesperson for the play's morality of vigilance and theology of forgiveness. Representing the claims of the eternal on fallen humanity in the present, Mercy urges upon the audience an awareness of the broad patterns of salvation history:

> The very fownder and beginner of owr first creacion,
> Amonge us sinfull wrechys He oweth to be magnifiede,
> That for owr disobedienc[e] he hade non[e] indignacion
> To sende His own son to be torn and crucifiede.
>
> (ll. 1–4)

As in *Everyman*, this pattern is available to sinners through mercy and "goode werkys" (l. 25); and, like the blindness and forgetfulness of the other play, the main threat to this salvation is the "diversion" of a transitory world:

> Diverte not yowrsilffe in time of tem[p]tacion,
> That ye may be acceptable to Gode at yowr going hence.
>   . . . .
> O ye soverens that sitt, and ye brothern that stonde right uppe,
> Prike not yowr felicites in thingys transitorye!
> Beholde not the erth, but lifte yowr ey[e] uppe!
> Se how the hede the members daily do magnifye.
>
> (ll. 19–32)

Mercy's moral program is clear: humanity must interact with the things of the earth "with parted eye," recognizing the transitoriness of earthly things and mindfully directing attention toward the divine pattern that gives the present significance. Such an admonishment represents a further internalization of the spiritual scheme detailed within *Everyman*'s main action, for in *Mankind* the central fact of God's mercy is, more explicitly, a burden of memory. Memory is a cornerstone of the moralities, a means of detaching oneself from the moment and aligning oneself with the unchanging realities that stand behind it. As *Mankind*'s subsequent action makes clear, memory is a necessary precondition for mercy, since for God's forgiveness to be sought and received it must, before all else, be remembered. In the context of the play's own "diversions," it is with these issues in mind that "these[e] worschipp[f]ull men" (l. 309), Mankinde's counterparts in the audience, are made privy to Mercy's warnings.

Like *Everyman*, then, *Mankind* opens with explicit address to the audience, outlining the moral and theological contexts of the ensuing action. Unlike the Messenger and the other figures who introduce *Everyman*, though, Mercy's *authority* in relation to this action is tenuous. His opening speech provides few specific details of the play's stage activity: its only clues come in the general warning that "yowr gostly enmy will make his avaunte, / Yowr goode condicions if he may interrupte" (ll. 27–28) and in his reminder that spiritual recovery is available solely through forgiveness. Moreover, unlike the Messenger's speech in *Everyman*, Mercy's is a truncated prologue, compromised in its extradramatic relation to the play's action by the interruptions of Mischeffe, who mocks Mercy's moral and narrative authority and taunts him with the play's distractions. Forced to contend with other characters as a participant within the play's events, Mercy actually seems surprised by the arrival of the mischief figures, a far cry from the omniscience that marks so many of *Everyman*'s characters. Despite his protestations (l. 82), he is shortly surrounded by the dancing Nowadays, New-Guise, and Nought and (if we take Nought's boast at line 113 to indicate a stage direction) physically, as well as metaphorically, tripped up.

The undermining of narrative authority and outline evident in Mercy's opening appearance extend throughout *Mankind*, a play that forgoes or qualifies the narrative devices and techniques manipulated so deliberately in *Everyman*. It lacks, for instance, the narrative linearity of the journey toward death that provides the later play with such clearly anticipated direction. Although its story of the farmer Mankinde's seduction and rescue fits the morality paradigm, the play's emphasis is less on the overall narrative development than on its individual episodes. Instigated and propelled by the rogues who rule the play's middle third, its action is much more localized than the action of *Everyman* and the other moralities. Improvisationally disruptive, the mischief figures act as much in response to other actions as they do to any broader plan or strategy: beaten off by Mankinde, the three lesser rogues (Nowadays, New-Guise, and Nought) flee to Mischeffe, and, after a consultation, they call for Titivillus, who promises to revenge them. Often, as Mischeff's interruption of Mercy's introductory speech indicates, they act without apparent motive at all, engaging in a provisional set of projects and reversals closer to the stage activity of *The Alchemist* than to the relentlessly and purposefully direct *Everyman*.

Although *Mankind* has only seven characters, their onstage behavior is neither conceived nor managed with strict pattern in mind; indeed, these characters often subvert the controls of allegory. This is especially true, of course, for the mischief figures, whose antics tend to obscure specific connection to frameworks of narrative and idea. Several critics have expressed dissatisfaction with Mercy's relegation of the mischief figures to the categories of World, Devil, and Flesh, and although at least one critic has given scholarly defense of these categories,[14] they are hard, if not impossible, to defend as organizing categories in performance, since Mercy's classification occurs at lines 883–90, twenty lines from the play's end and after the rogues have exited for good. While they are onstage, their names provide scant means for distinguishing them from each other; indeed, Titivillus' name ("all vices") could easily apply to the mischief figures as a group. This deflection of clear allegorical identity is further highlighted by the frenetic, assaultive theatricality with which these figures seize control of performance. In contrast to Mercy, whose physical presence onstage is no doubt as stolid as his latinate verse, the mischief figures dance, prance, and tumble; they holler and sing. In short, they engage in the business of circus clowns, drawing attention through ostentatious self-display. They enter and move onstage with confusing randomness,[15] filling the stage less with clearly delineated moral abstractions than with a chaos of individual bodies. Significant in this regard is the frequency with which they call attention to particular body parts: face, neck, feet, anus, genitals. Titivillus, adorned (most likely) with an oversized head, announces himself (in one of the finest of all entrance lines) with this bodily focus: "I com, with my leggys under me!" (l. 454). Such references and the gestures that accompany them (New-Guise clutching his "jewllys," for instance, and later putting his head in a noose) suggest the extent to which the antics of these figures draw attention toward the particular, toward those components of performance most specific and inert. It is in keeping with this "objectifying" of the stage that much of the activity of the play's middle sequence centers on stage props, and that attention is repeatedly focused on the materiality of these items: a fake head's size, a shovel's weight, a board's thickness.

　　Their disruptiveness, and the pressure they place on an audience's attempt to abstract narrative and moral outlines from the theatrical moment, is equally evident in the mischief figures' use of language. Mercy's initial speech to the audience concludes with a warning about Judgment Day, that end of human time which will judge its course:

> For sekirly the[r] shall be strait examinacion:
> The corn shall be savyde, the chaffe shall be brente.
> I besech yow hertily, have this [in] premeditacion.
>
> 　　　　　　　　　　　　　　　　(ll. 42–44)

Mischeff enters, and launches his mimickry:

> I beseche yow hertily, leve yowr calc[ul]acion!
> Leve yowr chaffe, leve yowr corn, leve yowr daliacion!
> Yowr witt is lityll, yowr hede is mekyll, ye are full of predicacion.
> But, ser, I prey [you] this question to clarifye:
> Misse-masche, driff-draff,
> Sume was corn and sume was chaffe,
> My dame seyde my name was Raffe;
> On-schett yowr lokke and take an halpenye.
>
> 　　　　　　　　　　　　　　　　(ll. 45–52)

Parody is a powerful instrument of ridicule, and in his supple mimickry of Mercy's syntax and vocabulary, Mischeff accomplishes this end, moving from the "corn" and "chaffe" of Mercy's instruction to the "corn" and "chaffe" of nonsense verse. But behind his mockery is a more fundamental strategy, and the inversions that it effects are disruptive on a much deeper level. Mischeff attacks Mercy's language by pressing sense into literal "nonsense": mimickry and rhyme deflect attention away from the meaning of words onto more strictly phonetic characteristics, while doggerel breaks the logic of syntax on which comprehension depends, setting words loose in a nonreferential free-for-all. In the end, Mischeff subverts the claims of Mercy's language to intelligibility by reducing his words to the pure sound of stage chatter: "Misse-masche, driff-draff. . . ." This linguistic reductio ad absurdum recurs throughout the stage language of *Mankind*'s middle, as sound obliterates sense and the stage that Mercy tried so hard to dedicate to conceptual patterns becomes filled with noise. Words themselves acquire a near physicality that renders them verbal equivalents of stage props. New-Guise chirps:

> Hic, hic, hic, hic, hic, hic, hic, hic!
> That is to sey, here, here, here, ny dede in the cryke!
> If you will have him, goo and syke, syke, syke!
> Syke not over-long, for losinge of yowr minde.
>
> (ll. 775–78)

The phrase "losinge of yowr minde" is fitting, for the descent into babble represented by this speech constitutes a vocal manifestation of temptation's broader assault on higher meaning. In such moments, as a Latin word is stripped to the sound of hiccups, the stage loses its narrative translucence, unbounded by the conscience of signification, filled with the Dionysiac energy of itself alone. Mercy's words point beyond the stage; the words of vice and "temptacion" point "here, here, here. . . ."

Kathleen M. Ashley offers a perceptive reading of *Mankind* in terms of its exploration of language, and of the play's central opposition of "corn" and "chaffe." She considers Titivillus the center of "idle chatter" in the play, a center surrounded by the guiding presence of Mercy's doctrine: "Mercy's words frame the drama; the audience is not allowed to think what it will about the play because Mercy, mediating between audience and drama at two crucial points, sets up the governing interpretation of the action." [16] But such an assessment overestimates the power of any point of view to "frame" a play's action, and it underestimates the sheer disruption the mischief figures effect. As Robert Weimann notes, the morality Vice "stands for himself alone," [17] and the Vice figures of *Mankind* underscore this through strategies of self-display that draw attention away from broader outlines and rivet it onto themselves. *Everyman* avoids this distraction by relegating mischief to the past: Felawship alludes to past revelry (ll. 272–75), but his imaginative projection is counterpointed by the sparseness of the present, and its relative stillness. In *Mankind,* by contrast, the language and stage antics of the mischief figures create a world of theatrical play that stands, in its immediacy, in counterpoint to the abstractions proposed by the play's beginning; and for much of the play, this theatricality owns the stage. The struggle between Mercy and the mischief figures, then, is not simply a dramatic struggle for Mankinde's soul; it is a broader struggle over the stage and how it will be apprehended.

Not only, then, does *Mankind* lack *Everyman*'s controlling narrative devices, but its narrative technique actually involves, throughout much of the play, a deliberate disruption of comprehension that propels attention into the more immediate realm of performance. Against the familiar pattern of the morality plot occurs a continual stream of diversions, pitting moral comprehension against the distracting forces that threaten it, and despite Mercy's warnings against temptation, *Mankind*'s audience repeatedly succumbs, seduced by a theatricality irresistible in its stage vitality. As in *Everyman,* audience experience stands in significant relationship to the experience of the play's central character, for (like the audience) Mankinde the character undergoes a temptation the essence of which lies in distraction from the dictates of moral comprehension. Urging Mankinde to "Be stedefast in condicion; se ye be not variant" (l. 281), Mercy warns him that he will be assaulted (even naming the individual mischief figures), exhorts him to follow the example of Job, and reminds him that if he should succumb to temptation he must solicit God's mercy. Like the audience, then, and unlike Everyman, Mankinde begins the play with conceptual frameworks designed to make explicit the moral realities of temptation and salvation. To underscore the importance of these frameworks as guides for memory, Mankinde writes a reminder to himself of what he has been told and wears a cross for protection:

> To have remo[r]s and memory of mysylff thus wretyn it is,
> To defende me from all supersiti[o]us charmys:
> "*Memento, homo, quod cinis es, et in cinerem reverteris.*"
> [*He points to the cross depicted on his breast.*]
> Lo, I ber[e] on my bryst the bagge of min[e] armys.
>
> (ll. 319–22)

Mankinde's *memento,* and the spiritual understanding it emblematizes, are quickly put to the test, as the rogues who ridiculed Mercy's speech from offstage rush onstage with their derision and their antics. Mankinde beats them away, but his diligence and "memory of mysylffe" eventually collapse as a result of Titivillus' provocations—most completely, after the false dream about Mercy's suicide, a "wrong comprehension" that causes him to abandon Mercy's lesson concerning action and the moral hierarchy that structures it. The extant text provides no indication of what happens to the message and the cross, but the shortening of his coat between lines 678 and 718 no doubt represents their loss. The coat antics constitute part of the stage activity surrounding Mankinde's capitulation to the rogues: on stage and off, it is the play's most frenetic sequence, with the rogues engaging in a variety of antics on the stage and rushing to and from the audience. That Mankinde's moral self-abandonment involves a surrender to this diversion is evident when he greets the returning Mercy with similarly antic lines: "We shall goo forth together, to kepe my faders yer-day. / A tapster, a tapster! Stow, statt, stow!" (ll. 728–29).

Mercy returns to initiate the play's final movement, a recollection of the initial promise of mercy and salvation as well as the triumph of this promise over temptation and fall. From this point on, the stage belongs to Mercy and his admonitions. He exits briefly to search for Mankinde, but when the rogues reenter for their final stage antics, he chases them off, rescuing Mankinde from the ultimate forgetfulness, despair, while chastising him for his "oftyn mutabilité" (l. 746). But the giddying theatricality of the play's middle section has extended this "mutabilité" to the audience as well, which has reveled in its diversions and even participated in its antics. To an extent unusual even for the moralities,

Mankind has drawn its audience into its entertaining middle and implicated them in its action: Nowadays, New-Guise, and Nought have led the audience in the singing of the scatalogical "Cristemes songe" (ll. 331–43), pranced among them, and (in a striking inclusion) even made them pay to see the popular Titivillus (ll. 459–70). During another sequence (ll. 503–17), the mischief figures refer to individuals in, or familiar to, the play's original audience, a ploy that further implicates the audience within the particularized moment of performance. When Mercy laments "Man onkinde, wherever thou be!" (l. 742), in other words, he addresses (in part) an audience that has itself fallen, from the strictures of mindfulness to the distractions of performance in their amoral, and immoral, theatricality, an audience that has shown itself to be "convertible" as "the fane that turnith with the winde" (l. 749). This Mankinde will no doubt continue to succumb, abandoning the salvation narrative for the moments of the world, for "Mankend is wrechyd, he hath sufficient prove" (l. 911). In view of the moral division the play has illustrated, character and audience must seek salvation through the strictness of spiritual "examinacion" (l. 908) and vigilant remembrance of the world's vanity.

Everyman's Messenger warns the play's audience: "Ye thinke sinne in the beginninge full swete, / Whiche in the ende causeth the soule to wepe," and the difference between the two plays could be said to derive from the one's inclusion of sin's "beginninge" and the other's focus on its "ende." But this difference reflects a deeper difference in how each uses the stage on which it is presented. If *Everyman* works to contain its theatrical energies, *Mankind* dramatizes the conflict between world and spirit by drawing the audience into the entertainments of performance—engaging them in a medium that is not simply a vehicle for narrative and allegory but an actual, material presence—and thereby foregrounding its condition in performance as part of its broader moral exploration. The play embraces its theatricality and embroils its moral action within the sights, sounds, and movements of performance; it merges its conceptual effects with the other impressions sparked by its activities. "Beholde not the erth, but lifte yowr ey[e] uppe!": didacticism and the things of the spirit triumph, but they do so in concert with a brilliant display of the things of the world, and of the stage, its entertaining magnetism inextricably bound up with moral threat. Once we recognize that *Mankind*'s audience is implicated in its central dialectic, through the theatrical pull between comprehension and distraction, we can avoid the extremes of the play's critical reception: the view that the play's moral component lies exclusively within its sermonizing, and that the comic elements constitute evidence of the play's "degeneracy," as well as the view that the play stands as pure entertainment, demonstrating "how nominal the homiletic or conversional aim could become." [18] Diametric though these views appear, they share the assumption that the comic and serious in *Mankind* represent both a moral and a dramaturgical inconsistency. In light of the dynamics of theatrical comprehension, one can recognize how fully the play manipulates its theatricality and how it aligns its anti-narrative dimension with its conception of sin. As Richard Axton observes, the play counterpoints the modes of sermon and game,[19] and in so doing it achieves a dramatic mixture of moral comprehension and entertainment uniquely suited to the stage. This uniqueness is made possible, in part, by the play's recognition that temptation very often lies in the diversion of a dirty joke, the frustration of trying to dig through an underground board, and the insinuations of a bad dream—that distraction has the power of forgetfulness, and that temptation's defeat often begins in a moment of recollection. One does not preclude taking *Mankind* seriously, in other words, by taking much of it lightly, and by acknowledging its interplay with the stage.

Nor are *Mankind*'s dramaturgical principles artistically anomalous, for the play's theatrical style places it within the context of broader developments in oratory and the arts evident by the late middle ages, when "the calm, reflective statements of the romanesque era came steadily to be replaced by more forceful, demonstrative and individualistic forms of expression, emotional, theatrical, and often deliberately shocking"—the development suggested, for instance, by the proliferation of intricately realistic painting, and of popular, even comic elements in the medieval sermon.[20] What *Mankind* demonstrates is that this intrusion of the "demonstrative" bore particular fruit within the morality tradition, where the very medium of performance could be made an element of the didactic impulse and its typical narrative and moral patterns. Moreover, the success with which the theatricality of the stage, its props, and its actors were incorporated within morality drama's broader oppositions between soul and body, good and evil, virtue and vice, salvation and sin suggests a dramaturgical source, not only for the secular moralities that followed, but also for the great plays of the age of Elizabeth and James. Shorn of its didactic framework, the theatricality of *Mankind* and other moralities makes itself felt in the broader thematic frameworks of these plays, and it retains some of the structural features of the earlier drama: a tendency toward distraction and confusion; a pronounced awareness of the theatrical event itself; and a focus on the momentary and the particular, which often stands in direct contrast to broader, more abstract patterns of value. The influence of the Vice on English Renaissance drama has been well established, but the more general legacy of medieval theatricality itself has not been adequately acknowledged. Though participating in differing moral spheres, one can find versions of *Mankind*'s theatricality in *1 Henry IV, The Shoemakers' Holiday,* and *Every Man in His Humor,* as well as in the darker worlds of *Richard III, The Duchess of Malfi,* and *'Tis Pity She's a Whore.*

The contrast between these two plays, so near to each other historically, could not be more pronounced. Linking them, though, is a common concern with the possibilities of performance—its riveting presence as well as its availability to abstraction and outline. Dramatizing protagonists "of condicion contrarye," between whose body and soul is "grett division" (*Mankind*, ll. 194–96), *Everyman* and *Mankind* address an audience that is similarly conflicted, likewise subject to the competing pulls of mind and body. Through clear dramaturgical strategies, the two plays ground their explorations in the audience's theatrical interactions, transforming moral vision into moral experience. Considering narrative response and how it is shaped allows one to understand the didactic and theatrical sophistication of these "morall playes," in which morality is often diverting and entertainment uniquely moral, in which the struggles of the moral life find an aesthetic equivalent in the rich counterpoints of theatrical performance.

CHAPTER FOUR

"Grace and remembrance": *The Winter's Tale*

Literally as well as figuratively, Time stands at the center of *The Winter's Tale,* giving strikingly emblematic stage life to a theme that had occupied Shakespeare's imagination since the sonnets and the earliest plays, through the often turbulent drama of the playwright's middle years, and into the romances, those strangely fabulous works that play variations on what came before. The confusions of Syracuse and Illyria sort themselves out in the movements of time; Richard of Gloucester and Macbeth draw back to seize time's promise; an aging poet reminds his younger friend, still in time's graces, of time's quiet ravages: "That time of year thou mayst in me behold / When yellow leaves, or none, or few, do hang."[1] Though time constitutes an organizing motif in Shakespeare's nondramatic work, as this last example suggests, its presence is actionally more central to the world of the plays, where characters must confront dramatic time as it unfolds in the present and where actors must navigate through the temporal movement of performance. In drama, as we have seen, time is a theme by necessity, for in the medium of performance it stands as a structuring component of stage activity, and of the dramatic action that this activity bodies forth. In the sonnets, time makes its appearance through reflection, with the virtual atemporality characteristic of meditation and address; its movements and their consequences are presented within linguistic parameters, manifested through a poetic utterance that, textually fixed, itself eludes time. In the plays, time intrudes itself experientially, through the unmediated temporality of performance: moments happen in the theater and within the play, establishing time as a felt reality for characters and audience alike. Time lies at the heart of Shakespeare's dramatic interests, in large part, because of its centrality to the theater for which he wrote.

The Winter's Tale—with its memories fond and bitter, its plans and prophecies, its tales and ballads, and its striking leap of sixteen years—explores the experience of temporality with a prominence and self-consciousness unusual even for Shakespeare. As Inga-Stina Ewbank notes, "while in *The Winter's Tale* time has largely disappeared from the verbal imagery, it is all the more intensely present as a controlling and shaping figure behind the dramatic structure and technique."[2] In keeping with the other pairs that serve to organize this dramatic diptych—Sicilia and Bohemia, youth and age, Nature and Art, rosemary and rue—*The Winter's Tale* presents human engagement with time in terms of a duality edging into paradox. On one hand, humanity lives in the present, a moment so complete in its immediacy that it seems to escape time entirely. This experience of the Now, and its apparent eternity, infuses Polixenes' description of the childhood innocence that he and Leontes shared:

> We were, fair queen,
> Two lads that thought there was no more behind
> But such a day to-morrow as to-day,
> And to be boy eternal.
>
> (I.ii.62–65)

His lines undermine the very idea of time, for the word *today*, charged with the force of the "eternal," subsumes *behind* and *tomorrow* in such a way that temporal distinctions blend and dissolve. Past and future warp into the seemingly boundless expanse of the present, and sequence unravels into a moment of Wordsworthian innocence, experienced as a condition outside Time's hourglass.

For all its apparent timelessness, however, this Edenic state is a memory, telescoped into what Prospero calls "the dark backward and abysm of time" (*The Tempest*, I.ii.50) in part by the very tense through which it is articulated. The stage presence of Leontes and Polixenes, both adults, constitutes a visual reminder of temporality, in which the present is barely an instant, collapsed into recollection by inexorable change. As Time boasts,

> I witness to
> The times that brought them in; so shall I do
> To th' freshest things now reigning, and make stale
> The glistering of this present, as my tale
> Now seems to it.
>
> (IV.i.11–15)

These words recall the temporal world of the sonnets, where existence is subject to the ironies of mutability as it plays its movement from "glistering" to "staleness"—a world where "every thing that grows / Holds in perfection but a little moment." [3] From this vantage point, time confronts humanity with the inevitability of consequence, since action, in the temporal realm, always has outcomes, foreseen or unforeseen: "I, that please some, try all, both joy and terror / Of good and bad, that makes and unfolds error" (IV.i.1–2). The contrast is pronounced: if the present in *The Winter's Tale* is the realm of an almost prelapsarian joy, time is the province of memory and anticipation, nostalgia and longing, regret and foreboding. It is, in short, the province of narrative, public and private, that cognitive and social domain where the images of events assume a fixed relationship with each other.

That presence and temporality rule this play, halved as it is by its dramatic caesura between III.iii and IV.ii, comes as no surprise, for Shakespeare's dramaturgical break forces characters and audience alike to come to terms with time's changes and consequences. But the sixteen-year gap signaled by Time's appearance is only one of many instances in which temporal change dramatically and ironically counterpoints the present. Down to the level of individual lines, like those fondly spoken by Polixenes, the play displays a temporal intricacy rivaled, perhaps, only by Shakespeare's other romances. As a number of critics have noted, Shakespearean drama is characterized, as a rule, by relatively little antecedent action[4]: unlike the drama of Kyd or Tourneur, its action falls largely within a present that moves forward to its culmination. But the past bears on the present of *The Winter's Tale* through a number of subtler inclusions: the childhood of the two kings; the courtship of Hermione; the Old Shepherd's wife; the man who "Dwelt by a churchyard," frozen in Mamillius' "sad tale" (II.i.25–32); numerous moments of story and remembrance.

This layering of past on present and present on past becomes more pronounced as the very stage moment in which the characters move is set against the broader passage of years, and as these years in turn verge upon an ever-emerging present. As *The Winter's Tale* progresses, in other words, it acquires—like *Pericles*, *Cymbeline*, and *The Tempest*—a temporal double vision tonally reminiscent of the opening lines of a fourthcentury Chinese poem: "Swiftly the years, beyond recall. / Solemn the stillness of this fair morning."[5]

For the play's characters, double vision of this kind eventually bridges the gap between memory and the present, between the frozen image of the past and the often robust vitality of the moment. For the play's audience, such multiple perspective constitutes the experiential matrix against which the play's action unfolds. Like the characters, though at an aesthetic remove, the audience is faced during performance with a dramatic world subject to the laws of temporal relationship, and with a stage present that is actual, changing, always somewhat outside the structures of time created to enclose it. *The Winter's Tale*, then, Shakespeare's most explicit treatment of time, counterpoints the twin experiences of temporality and presence, not only in its dramatic action, but also in its narrative and theatrical effects. As elsewhere in his plays, Shakespeare grounds thematic issues within theatrical experience, and makes performance fundamental to dramatic meaning through the audience's cognitive engagement. In relation to both characters and audience, *The Winter's Tale* displays a profound concern with perception and its consequences, and with the personal and social challenges posed by temporality in life and in the theater. In this chapter, we will trace Shakespeare's broader dramaturgical balancing in *The Winter's Tale* of time's outlines with a dramatic and theatrical present that can never be fully "staled." In so doing, we will see that this strange but powerful Shakespearean play, like *Everyman* and *Mankind*, forges clear experiential links between the dramatic action on stage and the stage's "action" on its audience.[6]

When Time exits from the middle of *The Winter's Tale*, he leaves a world disrupted by his passage. For the play's characters, time's impact is concentrated in "that wide gap" (IV.i.7) between the dramatic present and the events of the first three acts, a tem-

poral fissure during which, as Time informs us, Leontes has continued to mourn "Th' effects of his fond jealousies" (l. 18) and
Perdita and Florizel have grown up. This span, though, bears dif-
ferently upon the various characters. Those who have lived
through it, the members of the now older generation, have hard-
ened themselves against time by maintaining a sharp remembrance
of its losses, a remembrance that they are nonetheless powerless
to erase. Camillo misses Sicilia and still feels bonds of loyalty to
Leontes, whose "sorrows" remain so tangible that Camillo calls
them "feeling" (IV.ii.7–8). Polixenes, too, lives in memory, burdened with a past that refuses to fade:

> Of that fatal country Sicilia, prithee speak no more, whose very
> naming punishes me with the remembrance of that penitent (as
> thou call'st him) and reconcil'd king, my brother, whose loss of
> his most precious queen and children are even now to be afresh
> lamented. (ll. 20–25)

Focused through trauma's inward gaze, time only underscores the
memory of what has been lost, and in its irrevocability the past
seems more real than the present that has taken its place.

Polixenes, however, has more recent concerns to temper his
bitterness: shifting from friend to father, he urges Camillo to accompany him on a mission to discover the cause of his son's dis-
appearance from court. The scene likewise shifts, and before the
two arrive at the Shepherd's cottage the stage is given to Perdita
and Florizel, who demonstrate a markedly different relationship
to time. Neither is burdened by the events at Sicilia, and both
show an attitude toward their more immediate pasts less rigorous
than that of their elders. Perdita says nothing of her early years as
a shepherdess, and Florizel hides the signs of his past by donning
rustic clothes. In response to Perdita's concern over his father's
disapproval of their match, he modulates between the languages
of present and future and affirms a love outside such threat:

> To this I am most constant,
> Though destiny say no. Be merry, gentle!
> Strangle such thoughts as these with any thing
> That you behold the while. Your guests are coming:
> Lift up your countenance, as it were the day

Of celebration of that nuptial, which
We two have sworn shall come.

                            (IV.iv.45–51)

Both are characterized by this forward-gazing anticipation, conceiving of the future as a never-ending continuation of the present, with "such a day tomorrow as to-day." In their innocence, free of time's psychic damages, they dwell on this present and on the sounds, objects, and gestures that constitute it. Florizel's description inscribes Perdita within the moment:

                    Each your doing
(So singular in each particular)
Crowns what you are doing in the present deeds,
That all your acts are queens.

                            (ll. 143–46)

Perdita, more the realist, nevertheless allows hope to "strangle such thoughts." "O Lady Fortune," she exclaims, "Stand you auspicious!" (ll. 51–52).

When Polixenes and Camillo enter disguised, then, and the sheep-shearing scene gets under way, the stage contains a mixture of attitudes toward time and its relationship to the present. On one hand, it offers the lovers, with their sense of the immediate and their vision of possibility; on the other, the king and counselor, aged by time and scarred by its memories, their awareness of consequence a potential threat to Perdita and Florizel. By this point in the play, though, the audience has had its own experience of dramatic time shifted and modulated, through the play's broader dramaturgical rhythms. Theatrical versions of immediacy and temporality are counterpointed throughout the play's development, often in sharp juxtaposition, as we can see if we review the audience's comprehension of dramatic time in the first three acts. There is, for instance, the play's beginning, in which the stage image of friendship between Polixenes and Leontes, the present's version of the past's innocence, is abruptly dispelled by the King's distorted jealousy. William H. Matchett points out sexual ambiguities in the lines between Polixenes and Hermione and claims that the audience is made to feel suspicious,[7] but these ambiguities are subliminal and largely recollected, if at all, in light of Leontes' misinterpretation of them. More pronounced is the audience's awareness of their "timeless" friendship, of which Archidamus has said "I think there is not in the world either malice or matter to alter it" (I.i.33–34) and of which Polixenes has described the childhood origins. The initial stage interaction between the characters does little to dispel these accounts: gracefulness and compliment characterize the scene's beginning, and the "gestural dialogue between hands" that Charles Frey discerns throughout the play here expresses bond and affection.[8] When Leontes' "*tremor cordis*" does appear, it constitutes an intrusion of dissonance into the scene's easiness, and the stage present becomes abruptly shadowed by the threat of disturbance: "I am angling now, / Though you perceive me not how I give line" (I.ii.180–81). The words *angling* and *line* are revealing, for it is the essence of Leontes' jealousy to form imaginary connections between people and between incidents, quickly generating a web of misperception and suspicion that includes even Mamillius and Camillo. As Leontes begins to act on these misperceptions, consequences multiply with rigorous inevitability, and the stage present becomes increasingly pressured by a network of events, imaginary as well as real.

One of the most remarkable features of the developing Sicilia sequence (I.i through III.ii) is its narrative tightness and autonomy; omitting Perdita's survival, it could stand by itself, brief but complete. Its incidents are relentlessly forward-moving and continuous. For one thing, the narrative line of Leontes' jealousy and its effects is, to an extent unusual even in Shakespearean tragedy, unrelieved by breaks. Hermione's exchange with Mamillius constitutes only thirty-two lines, and the scene in which Cleomines and Dion describe their visit to Delphos is shorter still (twenty-two lines). Far from serving as self-contained interruptions, both are themselves interrupted, and devoured, by the omnivorous main action: the former by Leontes' entrance, the latter by a reminder of the proclamations against Hermione. For another thing, incidents and details are introduced and linked with a high degree of narrative continuity. Shakespeare changed the source material of *Pandosto* to increase the "probability" of the story's incidents,[9] and he did so, in part, by tightening its plot connections: whereas Greene's young prince Garinter dies suddenly, for instance, Shakespeare's Mamillius sickens and dies specifically out of grief concerning his mother's predicament. This tight sense of antecedents and consequences focuses audience attention even more closely on the unfolding narrative sequence, on dramatic time in its actual and potential outlines.

The sequence concludes with a pronounced note of closure, heightened by the rapidity with which its final events take place. The oracle's tersely declarative pronouncements reveal the truth concerning the preceding actions, a truth the audience and all the characters save Leontes have known. Entering with news of Hermione's death, Paulina condemns his folly by outlining the consequences of his misconceived actions on Polixenes, Camillo, his abandoned daughter, Mamillius, and Hermione: "O, think what they have done, / And then run mad indeed—stark mad!" (III.ii.182–83). Her speech (ll. 175–214) rings with summary force, and—together with Leontes' heartbroken resolve to bury his wife and son in a single grave, to display an account of "the causes of their death" (l. 237), and to visit it every day for the rest of his life—it gives the sequence of the Sicilian first half what J. H. P. Pafford has called "a Miltonic close fitting for the end of a tragedy."[10]

"The King shall live without an heir, if that which is lost be not found" (III.ii.134–36). A strand remains incomplete—an opening, as it were, in the closed sequence of action and its consequence that the audience has followed for over two acts. With Antigonus' entrance in III.iii, the narrative sequence continues. But the audience's temporal comprehension of *The Winter's Tale*'s events and its orientation toward the stage and its actions shift in two important ways. First, attention no longer centers on the inevitable triumph of truth and the stripping away of a central character's delusion. Throughout the Sicilian sequence, the audience has indeed enjoyed an Olympian distance upon Leontes' jealousy, secure in its awareness of the actual state of events. The audience, in other words, stands in the position of superior awareness that Bertrand Evans considers one of the characteristic dramatic principles of Shakespearean drama;[11] and although its awareness is far from complete, the audience's understanding of temporal outlines is more closely aligned to that of Time than to that of the action's participants. Once the truth is revealed, though, subsequent actions become open-ended: although the oracle's pronouncement suggests further resolution, this final clause is cast as a riddle and contains no details about how the resolution might be achieved. Uncertainty, therefore, replaces inevitability; the outcome of events becomes less determinate, less subject to rigorously constrained consequence. Ironic awareness is replaced by uncertainty, and the audience, like Perdita, is left in the wilderness—a wilderness, in this case, of the stage and its unpredictability.

Second, the coherent narrative of the first part is replaced by a remarkable sequence of incidents, each of which is characterized by striking immediacy, and all of which stand in sharp juxtaposition to each other. Immediacy is achieved partly through a dazzling array of "theatrical" effects: effects of sound, movement, and spectacle that display the stage at its most physical. Such effects are strikingly absent from the Sicilian sequence of the play's first half: although the earlier sequence is characterized, as Daniel Seltzer points out, by numerous examples of "intimate stage business" between characters,[12] there is nothing to compare with the storm effects (suggested by the text), the famous bear, the sound of hunting horns, or the archaic staginess of Time's entrance. The immediacy of the sequence's incidents is heightened by their almost Brechtian juxtaposition: the mixture of tones and effects gives each a kind of discontinuous autonomy on stage, and this sudden, unprepared-for variety, following the vastly more streamlined narrative of the first half, forces abrupt, disorienting shifts in audience response.

Matchett observes that this sequence wrenches us "from our response to the plot and the action to a wider perspective. . . . Challenging our awareness, it opens us to fresh experience."[13] He discusses this shift in terms of the art/nature opposition, but his observations apply still more valuably to the basic level of audience attention that this sequence engages. On this level, the sense of "fresh experience" is a result of elements that draw attention away from broader temporal outlines and heighten the autonomy of individual stage moments, much as the storm scenes do to the dramatic world of *King Lear*. Such "fresh experience" in Shakespearean (as in all) drama is that experience uniquely available in the theater: of a stage present existing in its own right, intruding itself into the very "tales" that dramatists make it tell. When Time stands forward to signal the leap of years, in other words, he addresses an audience that is already undergoing its own experiential leap, from prescience and irony to uncertainty and surprise, in the face of a stage turned strange and new.

As with the graceful present of the play's first scene, this scenic presence is diverted and distanced. The couplets of Time's soliloquy telescope the seacoast sequence into the past and return the audience to the play's main narrative line. But this line, with its rigid chain of consequence, has been weakened by the appearance of incidents and stage elements outside its projected outcomes, and the theatrical moment in all its presence and autonomy looms large in time's subsequent developments. Indeed, the stage is now set for the sheep-shearing scene, one of the longest scenes of heightened stage presence in all of Shakespeare. This scene is introduced three times—by Time, by Polixenes and Camillo, and by Autolycus—and each introduction contributes a nonnarrative "timelessness" to its action. The first two are usually viewed as connective scenes, linking past and present, and indeed (as we have seen) each does include references to the play's first half. Oddly, though, these references are less conjunctive than disjunctive: Time's reference to Leontes, after all, is offered to take "leave" of him (IV.i.17), and Polixenes finally urges Camillo to "lay aside / the thoughts of Sicilia" (IV.ii.51–52). Both scenes look ahead to Florizel and Perdita, and both do so, in part, by distancing the play's first half. As a result, the sheep-shearing scene bears few reminders of the Sicilian past, and even the Bohemian past is rendered less consequential to the festival present: Shakespeare omits the marriage plans that Greene's Egistus made for his son Dorastus and has Polixenes visit the Shepherd's cottage as much from curiosity as from suspicion.

The third introduction to the sheep-shearing scene also introduces one of its main participants. Despite the number of critical attempts to integrate Autolycus into the play's thematic structure,[14] this stage rogue continues to baffle the play's readers (while delighting its spectators). He is introduced later (IV.iii) than probably any other pivotal Shakespearean character, yet he plays no part in the play's concluding scene. He becomes almost a *genius* of the pastoral festivities, yet he was once a member of Florizel's retinue, a detail introduced so casually (between stanzas of a song) that it risks being missed. But if we put aside attempts to incorporate Autolycus into the play's thematic framework and concentrate, instead, on his stage presence, his dramatic function within the play (and within the sheep-shearing scene in particular) becomes clearer. In a play that counterpoints modes of time and presence, Autolycus represents life (and drama) at their most theatrically immediately.

Speaking to the Clown in a self-dramatizing third-person, Autolycus characterizes himself as a figure of Protean identity:

> I know this man well; he hath been since an ape-bearer, then a process-server, a bailiff, then he compass'd a motion of the Prodigal Son, and married a tinker's wife within a mile where my land and living lies; and, having flown over many knavish professions, he settled only in rogue. Some call him Autolycus. (IV.iii.94–100)

On stage, he displays a similar fluidity of roles, moving between them with an improvisational randomness that suggests his opportunism and delight in mischief. Like the mischief figures of morality drama, he plays upon the moment, and the impulsiveness of his actions makes them strikingly self-contained. His major contribution to the main plot (discovering the Old Shepherd's secret and deciding to act on it) originates largely out of whim: "Though I am not naturally honest, I am so sometimes by chance" (IV.iv.712–13). Moreover, like Nowadays, New-Guise, and Nought, his incessant acting and tumbling prose are charged with a vibrant self-assertiveness that draws attention away from more serious matters and toward himself. His wonder at the rustics' response to his ballads—"No hearing, no feeling, but my sir's song, and admiring the nothing of it" (IV.iv.612–13)—captures much of the distracting effect of his stage presence as a whole. Like the wares he hawks, Autolycus himself is largely an "unconsider'd trifle" (IV.iii.26), "inconsequential" in the strictest sense, a carefully placed dramaturgical tangent to his world's fixed sequence.

His appearance before and during the sheep-shearing scene, then, contributes to its self-contained immediacy: along with the Shepherd's dance that precedes him and the "Saltiers" who succeed him, his presence during the scene—with his "ribbons of all colors i' th' rainbow" (ll. 204–5), songs and ballads, and other antics—constitute some of the play's most frenetic stage activity. Even before Autolycus' entrance as ballad-monger, this scene has drawn characters and audience alike into an experience of atemporality. Among the characters, the past is suspended almost by consent: as we have seen, Polixenes and Camillo suspend memories of Sicilia, and Perdita and Florizel "strangle" thoughts of his superior rank. Time and its effects (as well as its threat) remain present during the scene, especially in the disguised visitors, but the emphasis is on the moment, and even age is brought within its domain. Matching Florizel's "timeless" admiration, Camillo tells Perdita: "I should leave grazing, were I of your flock, / And only live by gazing" (ll. 109–10). Polixenes, too, participates in the festival atmosphere to an extent not generally acknowledged in discussions of the scene; his famous debate with Perdita concerning the "streak'd gillyvors," for all its potential allusion to Perdita's station and its implications, is largely playful, a quality more evident in the theater than in the text, and one that tends to undercut threat. Moreover, when later in the scene the Clown remarks that "My father and the gentlemen are in sad talk" (l. 310), Polixenes is "refreshed" enough by the entertainment to request the Saltiers. It would be a mistake to claim that Polixenes "forgets" his mission, even temporarily, but it would also be a mistake to neglect the extent to which even he surrenders to his disguise and submits to the scene and its diversions. Both visitors could, with truth, join Perdita in her confession: "Methinks I play as I have seen them do / In Whitsun pastorals. Sure this robe of mine / Does change my disposition" (ll. 133–35).

The audience, too, is offered a "fresh experience" of the stage present, one that tends to subsume awareness of time and its consequences. Francis Berry claims that the audience, remembering the play's first half, "frames" the sheep-shearing scene and modifies its response to the lovers in light of their parents' experience.[15] But pictorial metaphors such as this are misleading, since the theater is a temporal as well as a spatial medium: earlier moments are rapidly distanced in performance, and memory often requires explicit reminders if it is to "frame" the stage present with what has already occurred. Such reminders are few, and the audience's awareness of threat is subordinated, in large part, to the scene's compelling immediacy, an immediacy heightened by the innocent love of Perdita and Florizel, by Autolycus' antics, and by a gracefulness of gesture finding its natural culmination in dance. The

audience never completely abandons its apprehensive detachment
from the lovers, but we must not underestimate how much the
stage draws all who watch into its easiness.

With the exit of the dancing Saltiers, however, and Polixenes'
interruption of the festivities, the audience is abruptly returned to
an awareness of consequence and the claims that time exerts on
the present. If Leontes' earlier attack of jealousy is painful because
of the idyllic picture we have been given of his childhood friendship with Polixenes, the latter's remark to Camillo—"'Tis time to
part them" (l. 344)—is even more chilling, because we have been
given an extended stage version of such carefreeness. Like Prospero's truncation of *The Tempest*'s wedding masque, Polixenes'
subsequent explosion completes the disillusionment for the audience and for Perdita and Florizel, returning the former to its
awareness of consequence as it returns the latter to the realities of
their disparate stations. Perdita tells Florizel:

> Beseech you
> Of your own state take care. This dream of mine
> Being now awake, I'll queen it no inch farther,
> But milk my ewes, and weep.
>
> (ll. 447–50)

Just as Time makes "stale" the "glistering" present, so Polixenes'
rage makes the festival timelessness seem itself a dream.

When Camillo persuades the lovers to sail to Sicilia, the audience returns one last time to the play's broader narrative outline,
resuming a more privileged distance concerning events. Freed
from the tragic irony of the first part, the audience now enjoys the
perspective of comic irony. With the secret of Perdita's birthright
secure, the audience watches the characters, each of whom lacks
at least one piece of information, move toward a reconciliation
with romance inevitability. All converge on Sicilia: Florizel with
Perdita, Polixenes with Camillo, Autolycus with the rustics and
their secret. Audience attention centers on the logic of events,
which unfolds with a neatness both providential and artistic; time,
"that makes and unfolds errors," begins to right the situation, and
the audience is allowed the omniscience to appreciate its workings. Anticipation runs high, looking forward to a reconciliation
that will redeem the present from the apparent irrevocability of

the past, awaiting the wonder on the part of the characters when the apparently miraculous is disclosed.

It is a measure of the dramaturgical complexity of *The Winter's Tale* that these expectations are at once fulfilled, unfulfilled, and more than fulfilled. On one hand, the Gentlemen who report the reunion between Leontes and Perdita underscore the miracle of the encounter, calling it "so like an old tale, that the verity of it is in strong suspicion" (V.ii.28–29). On the other hand, despite Neville Coghill's attempt to defend the effectiveness of these messenger speeches,[16] if there is any clear *scène à faire* in the play, the disclosure of Perdita's identity is it—since, in fulfilling the oracle's prophecy, it gives Leontes an heir, Florizel a wife, and Perdita a royal family. The reunion effects a reconciliation between age and youth, past and present, Sicilia and Bohemia. Such a scene the audience expects to see; ironically, the messenger scene is disappointing precisely because *The Winter's Tale* is not a tale but a play, and a play's most powerful moments are its stage moments. The very quality of the reunion that "lames report to follow it, and undoes description to do it" (ll. 57–58) is that quality of immediacy the stage provides. We want the scene to be represented as dramatic present, not deflected into a narrative past.[17]

The usual justification for the messenger scene is that the reunion is described to lend focus to the final scene, but this explanation underestimates both the disappointment of the former and the theatrical coup of the latter. For the audience, there is no play beyond this reunion; at least this is what the earlier scenes have indicated. The oracle's only prophecy concerns the lost child, as does Time's anticipation of the play's second half:

> What of her ensues
> I list not prophesy; but let Time's news
> Be known when 'tis brought forth. A shepherd's daughter
> And what to her adheres, which follows after,
> Is th' argument of Time.
>
> (IV.i.25–29)

In terms of the audience's expectations since the shipwreck, Perdita's return represents the projected end of the narrative movement, and the audience has anticipated it as final. To extend the play beyond this promised conclusion is to press stage action, once again, beyond the apparent confines of plot.

We have been studying *The Winter's Tale* in terms of two interrelating perceptions: that of time, evidenced through its effects of change and consequence, and that of the moment, experienced as something seemingly beyond these effects. We have explored, too, how the play represents a complex dramaturgical manipulation of temporality as it is experienced within performance: drawing attention away from narrative outlines into the stage present, distancing the present by the perceived intrusion of time and its effects. In the play's own vocabulary, occasioned by Perdita's gift of "rosemary and rue" to the disguised king and counsellor, we have been exploring the interacting rhythms of something like "grace and remembrance" (IV.iv.74–76) and the ways in which Shakespeare builds these rhythms into the play's dramaturgy and stagecraft. The statue scene, justly praised as one of the culminations of Shakespeare's art, represents the play's crowning interpenetration of these two realms of temporal experience.

As in *The Tempest,* the final reunion of this play is orchestrated by a master of ceremonies in command of the secrets behind external events. When Paulina reappears with Leontes at the beginning of the fifth act, however, she does so, not as a provider of second chances, but as a spokesperson for memory at its most fixed, keeping fresh the remembrance of an apparently irretrievable past and feeding its hold on the present with almost unpleasant insistence. Cleomines appeals to Leontes to "Do as the heavens have done, forget your evil, / With them, forgive yourself" (V.i.5–6), and Dion urges him to consider his heirless kingdom; but Paulina, who "hast the memory of Hermione . . . in honor" (ll. 50–51), pressures his conscience with the claims of the past:[18]

> Were I the ghost that walk'd, I'ld bid you mark
> Her eye, and tell me for what dull part in't
> You chose her; then I'ld shriek, that even your ears
> Should rift to hear me, and the words that follow'd
> Should be "Remember mine."
>
> (ll. 63–67)

To the servant's praise of Perdita's beauty, Paulina laments:

> O Hermione,
> As every present time doth boast itself
> Above a better gone, so must thy grave
> Give way to what's seen now!
>
> (ll. 95–98)

Her lines deny the possibility that loss can ever be replaced, or that the present can in any way heal the past. At the same time, unknown to Leontes and to the audience, these lines are half-truths, since the play's conclusion will dramatize a transcendence of memory and a better "present" that will fill time's grave. In their paradoxical truths and untruths, Paulina's lines anticipate the transformation of time that structures the statue scene itself: a transformation from the realm of memory, associated with life-lessness and sepulchral coldness, to the more vibrant present of "what's seen now."

This transformation, when it occurs, is seamless in its move-ment from one temporal vision to the other. Leontes' initial re-sponse to the statue's unveiling is an acute "remembrance," di-rected toward a past so cunningly recreated in stone that its image is resurrected, with equal vividness, in memory: "O, thus she stood, / Even with such life of majesty (warm life, / As now it coldly stands), when first I woo'd her!" (V.iii.34–36). The statue, in other words, confronts Leontes with the past and with his re-sponsibility for its loss, while paradoxically bringing it so vividly into the present that this loss seems to vanish. As he continues to gaze, the harsh line between past and present blurs, shading the memorial presence of the statue into the living presence of Her-mione. In a word that reverberates throughout the scene, time's apparent irrevocability is "mocked" by a reappearance that seem-ingly occurs outside time's laws, and memory is both dissolved and brought to life in the face of the present's revelation. With this dramatic stroke, Shakespeare moves beyond Aristotle, whose third form of *anagnorisis* bears striking resemblance to the statue scene: "The third kind of recognition is through memory: we see one thing and recall another, as a character in the *Cyprians* of Dicaeogenes saw the picture and wept, or the recognition scene in the lay of Alcinous, where Odysseus listens to the bard and weeps at his memories, and this leads to the recognition" (*Poetics*, XVI).[19] As Aristotle's examples make clear, art serves a function much like memory, giving form to the flux of experience, and in Aristotle's moments of recognition it points to the life from which it has been abstracted. Recognition in *The Winter's Tale*, by contrast, moves beyond memory into the miraculous: it occurs when what is seen actually becomes what is recalled, through a transformation that merges past and present, image and life, narrative and a moment beyond its predictions.

Paulina commands the statue to "Strike all that look upon with marvel" (l. 100), and the final accomplishment of Shakespeare's stagecraft in *The Winter's Tale* lies in the audience's inclusion in the striking marvel of this scene. The stage reconciliation that the audience was denied in V.iii takes place, but the disclosure that makes it possible, Hermione's survival, comes as a revelation for the audience as well as for the characters. The earlier image of Hermione falling to the stage floor, Paulina's confirmation of her death, Leontes' plans to bury her, and Antigonus' ghost-like dream apparition (recalling "visitors from the dead" elsewhere in Shakespeare), all establish the Queen's death as a dramatic reality for the audience, breaking sharply with Shakespeare's usual practice (in plays such as *Twelfth Night* and *Pericles*) of making his audience confidants to all secrets and partners to all contrivance. Much more in the manner of Beaumont and Fletcher, Shakespeare withholds a narrative detail, the revelation of which transforms both the outcome of the play and the significance of what has preceded it. That the play hinges on such a deception is, by now, a commonplace in criticism of *The Winter's Tale*. But, like many Shakespearean commonplaces, its full implications for audience response remain imperfectly understood, even though dramaturgical decisions invariably adjust the audience's relationship with the developing stage action. Most obviously, the audience is forced into a collective experience that mirrors that of the stage characters, chiefly Leontes, whose discovery constitutes the scene's principle focus. Like Leontes, the audience is initially forced into its own moment of remembrance. It matters little at what point the audience realizes that Hermione is alive; when the statue shows signs of life, the audience scans its memories, recalling the play's earlier scenes, trying to find the connections that could justify a development so beyond expectation. Hermione explains to Perdita that she remained in hiding to await the fulfillment of the oracle's prophecy, but this detail, like all others in the closing scene, is subsumed in the moment itself, luminous in its freedom from anticipation. In place of the ironic superiority over characters usually enjoyed during such dramatic reconciliations, Shakespeare creates a theatrical experience for which, as we noted earlier, the critical lexicon lacks descriptive terminology, an experience that constitutes the opposite of irony, for in this instant, as the statue becomes that which it has commemorated, the present is vastly more than we thought: fuller and richer, freed from irony's frameworks.

By setting the statue scene outside the audience's comprehension of plot and time, and by making the stage action, literally, beyond the anticipation that has sought to contain it, Shakespeare allows the stage itself, one last time, to assume a heightened autonomy. As in the sheep-shearing scene, attention is directed toward individual objects, movements, and gestures, carefully orchestrated by dramatic speech highlighting the particular.[20] Polixenes' "The very life seems warm upon her lip" and Leontes' "The fixure of her eye has motion in't" (ll. 66–67) recall, in their specificity, Autolycus' ribbons, the "flow'rs of winter," and (most tellingly) Florizel's admiration of Perdita's movements:

> When you do dance, I wish you
> A wave o' th' sea, that you might ever do
> Nothing but that; move still, still so,
> And own no other function.

> (IV.iv.140–43)

Ewbank writes of this scene: "Speeches are short, the diction plain, the language almost bare of imagery: as if Shakespeare is anxious not to distract attention from the significance of action and movement. . . . An unusual number of speeches are devoted just to underlining the emotions and postures of people on stage, as in Paulina's words to Leontes: 'I like your silence, it the more shows off / Your wonder' [ll. 21–22]."[21] This shift of emphasis away from language and toward gesture is heightened by the audience's own attention on the actress playing Hermione, as it watches for signs of breathing and movement, trying to detect the gesture that will reveal whether or not Hermione lives. The final discovery of *The Winter's Tale,* then, lies in a surrender to the moment; and for the audience, this involves a surrender to the stage moment, in which the most riveting activity is pure gesture outlined, almost pictorially, within the stillness of performance, and to which the most appropriate response is rapt attention and "wonder." With the accompanying music, movement and gesture acquire balletic expressiveness.

It is easy to see why the play's conclusion has tempted critics toward Christian interpretations of the play, especially in light of Paulina's reference to redemption from death and her pronouncement that "It is requir'd / You do awake your faith" (ll. 94–95), and in light of the word *grace,* which recurs throughout the play like a musical motif.[22] Though strictly Christian frameworks are hard to attach to the play as a whole, the final scene is indeed charged with an almost religious sense of grace as something freely given, beyond desert. Hermione's reappearance provides characters and audience with a development beyond the apparent consequence of events as the play has suggested them, with "the experience of restoration after total loss."[23] In this sense, the scene is beyond time, or at least beyond time as it has constituted a reality in the minds of characters and audience. If time participates in the play's denouement, it is less the stock figure of the play's middle than a force of mystery, always outside comprehension's hold, revealing itself in the miracles of the present. For the audience, grace is born in the "wink of an eye" (V.ii.110), when the stage action severs itself from rigorous connection with the "dramatic time" that has ruled for much of the play.

In the midst of its transformations, however, such grace is never completely free of remembrance. The first four acts have presented grace in terms of freshness, innocence, and gracefulness of gesture and bearing: Hermione has been called "a gracious innocent soul" (II.iii.29), and Perdita was described by Time as "now grown in grace / Equal with wond'ring" (IV.i.24–25). This grace, like the youth of Polixenes and Leontes, is timeless because it has not yet been subjected to the laws of change and consequence. The "grace" of the final scene, however, is richer because more dearly bought, and the passage of time from which it emerges leaves traces to spark remembrance. For one thing, the scene contains reminders of irreversible change. Hermione has grown old: "Hermione was not so much wrinkled, nothing / So aged as this seems" (ll. 28–29). And while Perdita has found a mother, she has also acquired a history, which, like Prospero's narration to Miranda in Act I of *The Tempest,* marks her emergence into a world that contains, among other things, time and its changes. Also apparent are reminders of consequences not redeemed by the present. Paulina recalls the dead Antigonus with moving regret, and Leontes' decree that she should marry Camillo does not fully dispel this awareness of "wither'd" loss (l. 133). Similarly, the scene lacks Mamillius, who actually was buried. Although he is never explicitly mentioned in the final scene, he has been mourned as recently as V.i, and his absence leaves the reunited family vaguely incomplete. While Florizel serves as a replacement for Mamillius, he also stands as a reminder of his loss.

The play's conclusion, in other words, resolves the plot with its image of a world ransomed from time, but it nevertheless remains marked by the memory of what time has destroyed. The paradox of temporal experience resolves itself into a duality of perception, a double vision in which time and actuality infuse and qualify each other, a balance of faculties appropriate to a world of coexistent loss and gain. The play has shown that time's effects are inescapable, since action, for all the world's miracles, does have consequences. One cannot escape the reality of change in a sublunary world ruled by mutability's "staling" hand. Festivity must end: Perdita and Florizel enter the cycle of the generations, and Autolycus, after his appearance in the penultimate scene, simply vanishes. Nonetheless, through Shakespeare's manipulation of the stage and its narrative possibilities, the audience feels the rigor of temporality open, again and again, into a stage presence always slightly beyond time's changes and consequences. Sicilia gives way to the wilderness of Bohemia; Polixenes, despite his age and station, succumbs in part both to the festival's liveliness and Perdita's charm. Most of all, in the play's final stroke, the audience discovers that, when it tries to predict time's outlines and outcomes, it risks amazement—that the present can mock not only consequence, but comprehension as well.

CHAPTER FIVE

Ben Jonson, *Volpone,*
and the Assault
of Incident

It is hard to approach Ben Jonson's plays without sensing the uneasiness evident in almost four centuries of response to his dramatic canon. This second greatest of all English dramatists has suffered in both the theater and the critical arena for some of the very sources of his brilliance: his intelligence and technical skill, his fondness for dramaturgical innovation, and a particularizing sensibility and sternness of purpose at once Juvenalian and deeply native. T. S. Eliot's assessment remains illuminating: "The reputation of Jonson has been of the most deadly kind that can be compelled upon the memory of a great poet. To be universally accepted; to be damned by the praise that quenches all desire to read the book; to be afflicted by the imputation of the virtues which excite the least pleasure; and to be read only by historians and antiquaries—this is the most perfect conspiracy of approval." [1] Such regard, with its implicit removal of Jonsonian drama from the theater to the shelves of dramatic history, hides a deep bewilderment with the premises of his dramatic art, an art that exploits theatrical potentials not allowed for within conventional notions of dramatic form and theatrical effect. This bewilderment is understandable, for Jonson's plays are dramaturgically innovative even within the parameters established by his Elizabethan and Jacobean contemporaries, to the point where they reflect not only accidents of historical development, but radical conceptions of form and effect.

At the heart of this dramaturgy is its almost inhuman difficulty on all levels: intellectual, linguistic, intonational, visual, kinetic. On the level of narrative, where the audience works to structure stage activity into coherent patterns of dramatic action, Jonson's plays reveal a dramaturgical impulse to liberate the stage's anarchic potential and to explode patterns of comprehension through a barrage of theatrical material, which tests the audience's cognitive limits as it tests the capacities of the stage itself. From the Boschian stage confusions of *The Alchemist* to the vast acreage and equally sprawling action of *Bartholomew Fair,* Jonson's is a drama of overwhelm, a drama that reveals the stage's ability to accost and assault, to stretch and defeat, to rub "salt" (in Jonson's words) in comprehension's "cheeks."[2] If *Everyman* shows the subjection of stage to narrative and idea, Jonsonian drama highlights the stage's intrinsic disruptiveness, its everpotential freedom from conceptual patterns. The collision of this disruptiveness with Jonson's theoretical insistence on formal pattern and moral contemplation renders his drama, and its underlying dramaturgy, one of the most richly problematic within the English dramatic canon.

Few dramatists have suffered more than Jonson from the comprehension bias in dramatic tastes, rivaled (as he was) through most of his career by the dramatist who reflected and helped establish these tastes. For all its gaps, confusions, moments of presence loosened from the hold of narrative, Shakespearean drama maintains a ruling clarity, and its narrative lines effect structuring continuity. Narrative sequences may be forgotten in the course of a Shakespearean play, but they are generally reintroduced in a return to pattern that subsumes uncertainty and highlights, by contrast, those few narrative elements that remain outside its control. Theseus reenters to close the confusions of identity in *A Midsummer Night's Dream* and to preside over the play's quartet of romance pairings, while Hal's escapades at the Boar's Head Tavern are punctuated by reminders of the rebellion that he will eventually combat, and of the even broader historical line of kingship against which the rebellion is taking place and within which he will assume his place as Henry V. A Shakespearean play, in other words, has at least one narrative line, usually more, to which pressured comprehension has eventual recourse, even if this line is as sinister as Iago's seduction or as remote as the Venetian senate to which Lodovico alludes at the end of *Othello*.

In Jonson's plays, by contrast, chance and accident rule, and events are dominated by characters adept at playing opportunity's dice: Autolycus assumes the throne of Bohemia, and Mischeff and his rogues swamp Mercy's providential exhortations. Narrative collapses within stage activity as characters normally given stability (in Shakespearean drama, for instance) become subject to the entropy and changeability that characterize Jonson's dramatic world. *Volpone*'s four Avocatori are gulled by the courtroom performance Mosca introduces, and more than one critic has been disturbed by the degree to which the fourth Avocatori partakes of the play's bare opportunism by planning to wed his daughter to the newly wealthy parasite. Even Lovewit, whose return is forecast in *The Alchemist*'s opening lines, dispels chicanery, not by setting into motion a process of judgment beyond the corruption that has held the stage, but by entering the play's action and proving its most skillful opportunist. By contrast, those characters who most firmly uphold patterns of justice and law are often the most readily victimized: Surly's honesty is overwhelmed by the manipulations of Face and Subtle; Adam Overdo, entering Bartholomew Fair to expose its enormities, ends up in the stocks; and Celia and Bonario, for all their pleas to Providence, are vindicated not by their virtue, but by the self-canceling maneuvers of others. Indeed, whatever its moral implications, the victimization of characters such as these is, to some extent, dramatically justified within Jonson's dramatic universe, since their constancy easily becomes a version of the Jonsonian humor, or *idée fixe*, which renders characters unable to adapt to a world of deceptive appearances and Protean shifts. To a degree that has considerable implications for narrative stability, the Shakespearean figure of order, secure in the possession of integrating social values, becomes the Jonsonian fool—a paradoxical transformation that we have observed before, when Mercy appears momentarily ridiculous in the face of Mischeff's taunts.

With long-range action the property of folly—always liable, as the "projections" of the gulls in *The Alchemist,* to disappear "in fumo" with the intrusion of the unexpected—the Jonsonian comic plot moves without the Shakespearean central plot strands that might impel events, and guide anticipation, along clearly structured lines. Instead of such lines, around which incidents could coalesce, Jonson provides isolated activities: a father setting out to follow his son; several groups going to a fair, unaware of what they might find. Even the predatory intrigues of *Volpone* and *The Alchemist* develop without anticipating their own conclusion; to an extent even beyond that of normal intrigue drama, they move by adjustment and improvisation, balancing precariously upon the accidents and opportunities of chance, continually redirecting movement instead of developing toward clearly formulated ends. What Mosca refers to as "our trade," and Doll "the commune work," are activities that exist more for the sake of the virtuosity they display than for the material gains they bring in their wake. The exception is *Epicoene,* in many ways unusual among Jonson's major comedies. From the first act, in which its main characters conceive the plot to reinstate Dauphine in his inheritance, it moves with un-Jonsonian linearity, most of its activities standing in direct relationship to this goal. Yet even this play, with its almost Restoration-comedy central intrigue, approaches Jonson's more typical unpredictability in the final two acts, when the gentlemen exercise their wit on the ladies and buffoons for wit's own sake.

The pressure toward randomness and discontinuity is reflected, as well, in the peculiarly Jonsonian absence (until the *The New Inn* [1629] and the incomplete *Sad Shepherd* [c. 1635–36]) of a stable romance plot, the unifying spine of most comedy. Romances anticipated near the beginning of plays generally fail to materialize (Brisk and Saviolina, Winwife and Dame Purecraft, Audrey and Squire Tub), while the relationships that survive develop near the end (Edward and Bridget, Lovewit and Dame Pliant, Quarlous and Dame Purecraft, Winwife and Grace). Almost afterthoughts, they have little weight in the conclusion compared to the cadences provided by Shakespearean pairings; the seemingly inevitable union of Celia and Bonario, which offers unifying resolution to the close of *Volpone,* is denied, like the failed unions at the end of Chekhov, with a noncomic sense of opportunity lost. Jonson's man-woman relationships become simply additional elements in the workings of contingency, their cohesiveness generally less strong than the divisive, solipsistic impulses that govern them in Jonson's dramatic society: vanity, jealousy, sterile wit, promiscuity. In Jonson's hands, this traditional source of nar-

rative cohesion becomes yet another testimony to isolation and
fragmentation.

Jonsonian narrative, then, moves in un-Shakespearean directions in un-Shakespearean ways, abandoning linearity for abruptness and apparent randomness. As Jonas A. Barish writes, "Few
dramatists of his stature depend so little on suspense, on tying
episode to episode and evolving one incident out of another. In
Shakespeare, each scene germinates out of causes planted in previous scenes, and becomes in turn the germ of future scenes. In
Jonson, scene after scene has only its own existence to contem-
plate. In Shakespeare, people have missions, they go on errands,
they seek each other out. In Jonson, they meet by accident; they
just happen to turn up."[3] In the absence of traditional narrative
technique, activity spins free, and the stage assaults its spectators
with incidents that overwhelm their resources for receiving and
ordering them. When Ananias enters the stage in IV.vii of *The
Alchemist,* for instance, a stage that has already been thrown into
confusion by the invasion of Surly, he announces his arrival by
proclaiming: "Casting of dollars is concluded lawful" (l. 43). In a
plot summary, with its outline and liaison, the significance of this
moment in the overall narrative is fairly clear: Ananias has suc-
ceeded in obtaining the blessing of the brethren for Subtle's chicanery. On Jonson's stage, though, memory buckles, pressed beyond its cognitive limitations: Ananias has remained offstage for
nine and a half scenes (since III.ii), and with each Jonsonian scene
representing at least one new entrance, the audience has seen (in
this interval) Dapper, Drugger, Kastril, Mammon, Dame Pliant,
Surly (in two roles), Doll (in three roles), and Face and Subtle (in
a number of roles). Ananias himself is involved in only one of
many intrigues in this brilliantly complicated play, a plot strand
variously tied in with the others (the brethren, for one thing, are
supplying the metal that will be sold to Mammon), and he is a
secondary figure in this intrigue, subordinated to the more important, and more flamboyant, Tribulation Wholesome. His mission
to the brethren, his narrative link with the earlier scene, is cloaked
in the indirection of passive voice ("Is concluded lawful"), further
isolating the present moment from its antecedents. The abruptness
of Ananias' entrance, onto a stage already crowded with other
activities (each asserting its own claim to attention) is quintessen-

tially Jonsonian, and for a brief instant we may not even know who he is, let alone why he is there. This is true, in varying degrees, for the six other characters who hold the stage at this moment, since the narrative connections between them are too complex to comprehend fully and clearly in this assault of the stage and its bodies. One does not need the psychologist's calculations to recognize the ruthless demands this dramaturgy places on audience memory, or the failures it inevitably precipitates. Our appreciation of Jonson's plotting skill, and his intricate narrative links, develop when moments like this are over, in the more abstract calm of recollection. To call *The Alchemist* one of "the most perfect plots even planned," Coleridge must have seen (or more likely read) it several times.[4]

Whether Jonson's narrative dramaturgy results from his "humors" conception of dramatic character, or the boundaries of character are a function of Jonson's entropic view of action and incident, the temporality of this discontinuous dramatic world places severe cognitive demands on characters and audience alike. For the characters, survival in Jonson's world depends on perception and flexibility, on the ability to understand and engineer activity in a world continually verging on anarchy. On the part of the audience, Jonson's plays demand similar sharpness; with the complexity of their self-contained and shifting incidents, they force the audience into a distinctly pressured cognitive activity. As *The Alchemist* demonstrates with such boldness, this mental improvisation forces comprehension to, and beyond, its boundaries, as characters and audience work to assimilate incidents always edging beyond control. It establishes, too, the distinctively Jonsonian tension between cognitive and moral patterns and the particular world of behavior and action that these patterns are designed to order.

With its close connection between character action and audience effect, *Volpone* offers much to the study of Jonson's narrative dramaturgy. Indeed, through its thematic deployment of the word *plot,* the play seems to invite such a focus. Mosca reassures Voltore that he has "a plot for you, sir" (III.ix.21); Sir Politic credits England with "my dearest plots" (II.i.8); Peregrine vows and executes "a counterplot" (IV.iii.24); Volpone exults "We must

pursue as well as plot" (V.iii.107); and the first Avocatori brands
Mosca "the chiefest minister, if not plotter, / In all these lewd im-
postures" (V.xii.108–9). As a glance at the word's development
indicates, *plot* was a resonant word in the early sixteenth century,
a mixture of meanings traditional and new, its literary and nonliterary applications still metaphorically interdependent. As a
noun, its literary applications developed, in the mid-sixteenth century, out of its earlier designation as a "ground plan," the area on
which a building is situated and constructed. Casting a literary
work's narrative structure as a kind of foundation, such a usage
employs an explicitly spatial metaphor, establishing within English terminology the conceptually atemporal notion of plot that
infuses the earlier *Poetics*.[5] That Jonson himself was drawn toward this topographic conception of narrative, with its incidents
fixed within a kind of architectural abstraction, is evident from his
section on "fable" and "action" in *Discoveries:*

> If a man would build a house, he would first appoint a place to
> build it in, which he would define within certain bounds; so in the
> constitution of a poem, the action is aimed at by the poet, which
> answers place in a building, and that action hath [its] largeness,
> compass, and proportion. But as a court or king's palace requires
> other dimensions than a private house, so the epic asks a magnitude
> from other poems, since what is place in the one is action in the
> other; the difference is in space. So that by this definition we con-
> clude the fable to be the imitation of one perfect and entire action,
> as one perfect and entire place is required to a building. (VIII: 645)

From the point of view of theatrical performance, it is this notion
of narrative form that underlies the use of *plats* by Elizabethan
companies, scene outlines serving as synopses of dramatic action.

But if Jonson's classical temperament drew him toward the
formal abstraction of a narrative whole, with its "largeness, compass, and proportion" conceived in geometric completion, his theatrical instincts drew him toward more recent meanings that had
accrued to the word *plot*. By the end of the sixteenth century, *plot*
had established its connection with action and intention, and
in its newer uses as "purpose," "scheme," and "project" it designated a present no longer secure in its groundplans, but one de-
stabilized by the promise (and threat) of change. Influenced, most

likely, by *complot,* the word also acquired its familiar meaning of "conspiracy" and its associations with contrivance and illicit purpose, as when Shakespeare's Richard boasts (in 1592): "Plots have I laid, inductions dangerous" (*Richard III,* I.i.32). The word's political overtones of conspiracy and intrigue, and the accompanying disruptions of order that they imply (and which Sir Pol finds so tantalizing), gained particular currency after the "Gunpowder Plot" of November 1605—a fact of significance to *Volpone*'s dramaturgy, since the play (supposedly written in five weeks) was first performed that winter. With these usages, and its concurrent appearance as a verb, *plot* entered the realm of time and its contingencies, locating pattern within the scheming mind and developing against a world of eventuality made available to personal ordering. This emergence of the actional from the spatial is reflected, in the word's literary designations, by the concurrent emergence of the notion of artistic plotting, of the author's activity as shaper of literary material.[6]

Jonson's drama reveals his particular obsession with the word *plot's* conflicting meanings, literary as well as political. As these meanings suggest, *Volpone* stands at a historical meeting ground of rival conceptions of narrative form: a conception that stressed conceptual mastery of dramatic form, its temporal outlines flattened to almost spatial contours; and a conception that stressed the generation of form within the arena of action, against the deflections always threatened by a temporal world peopled with others. In the tension between its spatial and temporal significations, between its twin conceptions of design and sequence, *plot* suggests the conflicting pulls of Jonsonian stage narration—the Fletcherian onstage symmetry of the four pairs of characters in III.iv of *Every Man out of His Humor,* on one hand, and the frenzied entrances and exits of *The Alchemist*'s climactic scenes, on the other—and the dialectic that characterizes narrative activity within his plays and within his audience. Characters and audience share the burden of plotting a play like *Volpone:* they must impose their own conceptual orderings on the play's incidents, and this activity involves each in the collision of fixed comprehension of situations with the relative, the particular, and the unexpected.

Volpone's main characters, all plotters in this predatory world, scheme fiercely to control events within the limits enforced by their conceptions of those events and by the interested actions of characters around them, each determined to enact a drama with himself or herself as protagonist. In this mutual struggle of plot and counterplot, these characters can be ranked according to the accuracy and extent of their perception and the success of their attempts to control. At the top work Volpone and Mosca, the prime manipulators, who enact an elaborate death-bed routine to induce a secondary group of characters to compete for the play's equivalent of the philosopher's stone, Volpone's will. Below them, the suitors engage in a similar desire to manipulate events, and Volpone and Mosca play upon this, controlling them by flattering their desire to direct the outcome of Volpone's "death." Volpone and Mosca, in other words, control events by exploiting the same urge in others, a tightening of action that distinguishes *Volpone* from the earlier comedies. In *Every Man in His Humor,* Brainworm gulls Stephen into buying a cheap sword from him, but in so doing he plays upon simple vanity; he employs little of the insinuation that Mosca displays in his language to Voltore:

> And, gentle sir,
> When you do come to swim in golden lard,
> Up to the arms in honey, that your chin
> Is borne up stiff with fatness of the flood,
> Think on your vassal.
>
> (I.iii.69–73)

Like the other predators who flock to Volpone's chambers, Voltore joins the interlocking chain of manipulation, surrendering actual control for the imaged control seemingly within his grasp. Volpone and Mosca are obvious dramatists, but we must recognize, through Jonson's matrix of ironies, that their play is peopled with other dramatists, each intent upon casting events to his or her own end.

Mosca's success in controlling the plot, like that of Face and Subtle in Jonson's later play or that of Iago and Milton's Satan, lies in his ability to manipulate the story, or the *account* of the play's events. Controlling the story constitutes the primary source of power in *Volpone,* a play of coercion remarkably free of the exercise of physical force, and this control assumes two forms. As the vision of "golden lard" attests, control of the projected story is central to the play's manipulations; and at this, Mosca is a master performer. His manipulation succeeds because of his ability to phrase desire, and because of the subtlety with which he invites its realization. The promise "Only you" reverberates throughout Mosca's insinuations, locating each character at the center of a personal narrative (the common Renaissance spelling—"Onely you"—preserved in Jonson's Folio text, underscores the singularity of Mosca's promise). Since the desire for such centrality is the driving force behind their delusions, the suitors embrace Mosca's temptation, "lard" his promises with projections of their own, and jealously defend their privileged status against all threats, including the ever-looming, and inevitable, threat of the truth. Even Volpone is incredulous at the self-contained projections of their hopes:

> That yet to me 's the strangest; how th'ast borne it!
> That these, being so divided 'mongst themselves,
> Should not scent somewhat, or in me or thee,
> Or doubt their own side.
> *Mosca.*   True, they will not see't.
> Too much light blinds 'em, I think. Each of 'em
> Is so possessed and stuffed with his own hopes
> That anything unto the contrary,
> Never so true, or never so apparent,
> Never so palpable, they will resist it.
>
> (V.ii.18–27)

Mosca keeps each of the suitors "divided" from the others, lost in his own story, merely by reminding him of it, and its promised fulfillment; as he remarks to Volpone, "You know this hope / Is such a bait it covers any hook" (I.v.134–35). All Mosca needs in order to manipulate this certainty is his voice, painting the barrenness of the present with a future that exists in language alone but nonetheless asserts, for the gulls, a compelling reality. So dazzling is the imaginary within this world, so tangible its promise, that the play's emblematic image might very well be one of its final ones, when the suitors try to indicate Voltore's demon—"In shape of a blue toad, with a bat's wings!" (V.xii.31)—by pointing at air.

Story control also involves controlling the account of what has already happened, and this poses more difficulties for the "lim-

ber" Mosca. At first, such control involves simple assurances of
Volpone's favor. But as incidents start to splinter off with Jonson's
typical centrifugality, Mosca's multiple assurances must struggle
to keep pace. After the first major intrusion of the unexpected—
the fiasco with Bonario in the closet—Mosca must refashion a
story for each of the suitors, reaffirming his single commitment to
each and providing them with modified courses to follow. Such
control necessitates an almost algebraic awareness of constants
and variables, and of the relational matrix within which story elements are increasingly compounded. The self-imprisonment of
characters in the Humors plays is here reinforced by the fact that
every figure on stage has an individual version of what will happen
and what has already happened in the play. Story, in other words,
has become the intrigue version of the *idée fixe,* and Mosca's in-
genuity is strained to the utmost by the need to keep such stories
separate yet consistent. As in *The Alchemist,* the effort to maintain
mutually distinct stories accounts for the precarious equilibrium
of group encounters in *Volpone.* Corbaccio and Voltore eye each
other suspiciously as one enters and the other exits, but actually
crossing the stage are discrepant understandings of events, each
anxious to make the moves that will pull the play in its direction.
When individual stories work in concert with one another, one has
the brilliant contrivance of the trial scene, a masterpiece of fictional orchestration by which "so rare a music" is struck "out of
discords" (V.ii.18). The three suitors, Lady Would-be, and the
puppeteer Mosca—each with an individual story, agreed only in
the need to condemn Celia and Bonario—manage to shout down
the couple and substitute their improvised stories for the truth.
"These be strange turns!" exclaims one Avocatore (IV.v.59); "I do
begin to doubt th' imposture here," confesses another (l. 141). But
the "strange turns" are, in reality, a complex configuration of im-
postures, partially conscious to those who participate in them and
fully apparent only to the director, Mosca, who watches their
triumph over actuality. Perhaps nowhere else in the play is the
power established by controlling the story more obvious, or more
damaging for those unable, or unwilling, to play narrative's game.
Celia and Bonario cannot contend: innocent though they are, they
remain woefully inadequate storytellers.[7]
    The security of such narrative structures collapses, for the

suitors, in Mosca's *coup de richesse* and in the exposure with
which Volpone ends the game of imposture and the play itself.
With these two blows, the victims must confront the external
world to which "light" has blinded them, discover, like Stoppard's
Rosencrantz and Guildenstern three centuries later, that they represent secondary characters in the drama to which their hopes had
laid claim, and face the harsh facts that their exposure lays bare:
"This, his own knave; this, avarice's fool; / This, a chimera of
wittol, fool, and knave" (V.xii.90–91). For the suitors, story rup-
tures against the truth, a truth that denies them the centrality and
control they had sought. Yet as this final scene makes clear, the
puppeteers themselves—Volpone and Mosca—have likewise
proved themselves subject to the terminating disruption of events
beyond their control. In *Volpone*'s central irony, they too eventually succumb to the play's assault of incident.

Volpone and Mosca have distinguished themselves from
those they have gulled, and acquired mobility within their dramatic world, by their flexibility and their improvisational skills in
the face of circumstance. But if circumstance presents opportunity—Celia, for instance—it also presents accident, and Volpone
and Mosca must repeatedly reform and redirect their improvisa-
tions in order to incorporate the unexpected. The suitors, though
reliable in the single-mindedness of their self-interest, represent, at
the same time, much of the threat of accident, and the unpredictability that their self-interest involves disrupts stage action like the
repeatedly unexpected "One knocks." The honest Bonario, whose
gullibility is nonetheless balanced by the clear-sightedness of
suspicion, represents further unpredictability: his remark about
Mosca—"I do doubt this fellow" (III.vii.16)—suggests the threat
that he poses to Mosca's manipulations, constituting, as it does,
the first aside not spoken by Volpone or Mosca. Ingenious as the
two cozeners are, their abilities to predict behavior are pressed to
the limit by the independence evident in both folly and goodness.
Accident (and the likelihood of further accident) increase, and Volpone and Mosca hurriedly shift to maintain control as, again and
again, new events propel their plots and "quick fiction[s]"
(III.v.25) toward the precipice of ruin. Volpone is abruptly beaten
away from Celia's window; Mosca, plotting anew, induces Corvino to offer Celia for Volpone's recovery; Corvino, overeager, ar-

rives before he is expected; Bonario is thrust into the closet. With each intrusion of the unexpected, Mosca and Volpone are themselves momentarily subjected to Mosca's judgment on Corbaccio's illusion of youth: "And with these thoughts so battens, as if fate / Would be as easily cheated on as he, / And all turns air!" (I.iv.157–59). Jonson's stage direction at this point makes the precariousness (and its irony) clear: "*Another knocks.*"

The play's closing act, with its disastrous final strokes of the unexpected, exposes the limits of Mosca's and Volpone's ability to transmute accident into fortuitousness and to endow flux with an almost artistic shape. Mosca senses this boundary when he cautions Volpone after the courtroom scene: "We must here be fixed; / Here we must rest. This is our masterpiece; / We cannot think to go beyond this" (V.ii.12–14). The suggestion, though, is short-lived, rejected by a Volpone eager to escape a sudden onslaught of melancholia and a Mosca strangely willing to risk disaster, and the decision to victimize the suitors one last time signals their fatal overextension.[8] For one thing, they miscalculate the backlash of disillusionment; Voltore, recovering from the speechlessness that afflicts the suitors and characterizes other Jonsonian characters abruptly brought "out of their humors," reveals all to the Venetian court in an unprecedented move of self-disclosure. Even this, though, is brought within precarious hope of control, until Voltore's recantation is rendered irrelevant by the ultimate unpredictability: Volpone and Mosca themselves. By this point, the alliance that has served as foundation to the play's carnival of gulling has cracked, a fissure given visual embodiment by the two characters' physical separation as Volpone wanders away to witness the reactions to his "death," Mosca to gull Volpone. Neither foresees the other's bid to assume center stage, to become supreme orchestrator of the play's actions, and neither anticipates becoming a pawn within the other's master game. Their overextension reveals them to be limited in the inescapably Jonsonian way, locked within the confines of their self-gratifying comprehension, constrained—like the suitors by their greed and Celia and Bonario by their paradoxical goodness—by their ultimate inability to predict and control. Gabriele Bernhard Jackson captures the ironies of centrality and tangentiality that this exposure illuminates: "The manipulator, though gifted with more consciousness of his surroundings than the people he manipulates, is still rigid in acting out his conviction that he defines the universe, that only the creations of his intellect are really real, and that events are arrangeable for his exclusive benefit. In the end his line of force, too, crosses another, and the collision overthrows him; he discovers that the action to which he is central is itself tangential to another which he did not comprehend."[9] As Truewit remarks in *Epicoene*, "That falls out often . . . that he that thinks himself the master wit is the master fool" (III.vi.48–49). Volpone and Mosca each reveals himself to be the protagonist of his own personal narrative, and plots that heretofore worked in concert now work to subsume one another.

For all its moral inversions, the dramatic world of *Volpone* is driven by a powerful logic, through which the very impulse to control leads, with an inevitability akin to physical law, to its own defeat. As control seeks to extend its domain, and as it encounters the unpredictabilities that such an extension invites, it generates a counterimpulse toward fixity to which it is dialectically bound. What Alexander Leggatt terms Volpone's "suicide"[10] is, paradoxically, Volpone's final gesture of control, an ultimate gesture of self-assertion when the story of his death and fortune are wrestled from his control. He regains control, not by escalating deception, but by exposing the truth in its static bareness, even if this results in his own imprisonment. He chooses, in the end, a simpler story—"This is called mortifying of a fox" (V.xii.125)—and though this story leads to the fixity and immobility that Volpone fears so intensely, it is his own, as author and protagonist. *Volpone*, then, traces the shape of control in a world where such control must always face contingency's deflections: extending itself through a widening field of circumstance, it reaches its boundaries, collapses inward upon itself in a spasm of self-negation, and fixes itself in a final, rigid stasis, like Volpone "cramped with irons" (V.xii.123). Essentially the same movement as *The Revenger's Tragedy*, this self-canceling logic helps explain why *Volpone*, more than any other Jonsonian comedy, approaches in action and tone the Jacobean tragedy of blood. The conclusion of *The Alchemist*—Face's timely capitulation and Subtle's return to the stalls of Pie-corner—is far less severe.

The "plottings" of *Volpone*, in other words, collapse into a closing configuration as immobile as any ground plan. But though this reduction of activity into stasis occurs through impulses embodied within the activity of control itself, it is hard to escape the sense of moral arbitrariness that characterizes the play's conclusion, hard not to credit Jonson's claim (in the Epistle Dedicatory) that he could have varied the ending. Volpone's ruses have ended, but this represents nothing more than the failure of a mechanism burdened to the breaking point. There is little external resolution and no fundamental change in the principle of entropy that has shaped the play's activities and created the field within which fools and cozeners spring to life. That such a principle survives the moral judgment that seems to signal its end—"Let all that see these vices thus rewarded, / Take heart, and love to study 'em" (V.xii.149–50)—is made obvious by Volpone's temporary escape both from the arms of the Venetian law and from the dramatic illusion to which he has been confined, in the Epilogue that solicits approval for his plots and counterplots. Action may whirl itself into stasis, but stasis is not the same as stability: moral order stands precariously against the play's vertiginous spinning.

Jonson's defense of the play's conclusion against "the strict rigor of comic law" reflects the inseparability of actional content and dramatic form, and the uncertain ability of judicial and aesthetic law to curb the impulses toward anarchy within each. To address questions of plot and incident within the realm of dramatic action, then, is inevitably to raise questions of dramatic form, and to consider the often discordant interaction in Jonsonian drama between pattern (in its structuring capacity) and the moment (in its improvisational randomness). And to explore formal questions in Jonson's plays is, to an extent unrivaled throughout dramatic history, to face his audience: contemporary, present; actual, theorized; addressed in his prefatory material and harangued from his stage; dramatized through the performance-watching that takes place incessantly in his plays. "Jonson . . . [used] the stage to formulate propositions about his spectators, and the response of those spectators was as much a part of the theatrical event as the stage action." [11] A rhetorician of the theater always attuned to response, Jonson's dramaturgical instincts were directed beyond the stage, and the interaction that mattered most to him was between his play and audience.

We have detailed some of the differences from Shakespeare that render Jonson's narrative technique radically more demanding on comprehension, and we have considered a manifestation of its entropic conception of incident within the crowded intrigue narrative of *The Alchemist. Volpone,* at first sight, appears significantly less exacting than a play like *The Alchemist,* its action subject to more deliberate narrative control. For one thing, this action is markedly simpler, streamlined to a greater extent than the later play's dramatic intricacy. Unlike *The Alchemist's* characters, those in *Volpone* (though more numerous) remain in generally stable groups of no more than four: Volpone and Mosca, until the final act at least, form a recognizable group, as do Peregrine and Sir Politic, the three suitors, Celia and Bonario, the Avocatori, and even Nano, Castrone, and Androgyno. Lady Would-be, who moves between the suitors and the Peregrine/Politic plot, is one of the few characters (other than Volpone and Mosca) who engages in major action in two groups. Accordingly, even the play's most densely active scenes—the courtroom sequences—are more clearly marked out in comprehensible narrative groupings (accusers, victims, judges) than *The Alchemist's* brilliantly proliferating gulling scenes. In keeping with this relative conservatism, *Volpone* has two central manipulators compared to *The Alchemist's* three.

For another thing, *Volpone* provides a greater wealth of narrative source material than *The Alchemist*—material which, because it offers contextualizing outlines and a texture of fictionality, has often been thought to provide determining shape to the play's narrative and moral development. Foremost among these, of course, is the framework of the beast fable, classical in origin and medieval in development, which gives the play and its primary characters their names and furnishes Jonson with *Volpone's* central situation. The literary tradition of Reynard the Fox and the moral traditions of Aesop infuse the play's opening scenes, as when Volpone contemplates his suitors: "Vulture, kite, / Raven, and gorcrow, all my birds of prey, / That think me turning carcass, now they come" (I.ii.88–90). On a slightly lesser scale, the play evokes characters and situations from morality narrative (Volpone calls Mosca "My good angel" [III.iv.116]) and from the *commedia dell'arte* (decrying Volpone's mountebank performance, Corvino shouts: "Signior Flaminio, will you down, sir? down? / What, is my wife your Franciscina, sir?" [II.iii.3–4]).[12] *Volpone*, moreover, contains a suggestively narrative symbol in the transmigration sequence mentioned in the Pythagorean entertainment (I.ii. 1–62) and reinforced by the history, which Volpone recounts, of Scoto's "poulder" (II.ii.225–45).[13] Narrative patterns abound in *Volpone*, encouraging perceptions of narrative and moral order throughout, and above, the play's moment-by-moment unfolding.

Closer study of *Volpone*, though, reveals that its aids to comprehension are subject to the radical undermining of Jonsonian dramaturgy as a whole, and that overarching patterns are fragmented through the particularity of individual characters and individual moments. The very challenges that we have discussed in terms of the play's characters—the improvisational nature of its central activity, the solipsistic autonomy of its characters' projects, the instability that makes itself felt from the play's earliest moments in the pivotal alliance of Volpone and Mosca, and the escalation of plot as contingency asserts itself—constitute challenges to the audience as well: they subvert the effects of Jonson's narrative devices and, by forcing attention onto the momentary and the provisional, undermine confidence in organizing frameworks. In Jonson's actual handling of its motifs, for instance, the beast fable lacks the tight hold over action so often assumed in interpretations of the plays. Jackson asserts that "the names of the characters are no comparison, but a complete identification. . . . Voltore *is* a vulture, Volpone *is* a fox; they cannot escape the meanings of their names even if they try." [14] But Jonson's use of dramatic names was, throughout his dramatic career, complex and varied, and even the most narratively explicit of these names exist in uneasy relationship with the revelation of Jonson's characters on stage.[15] In *Volpone*, complete and consistent beast-fable identification is elusive: Volpone's reference to "Vulture, kite, / Raven, and gorecrow, all my birds of prey" contains a bird that does not appear in any character's name (kite) and applies four birds to three suitors, unless we include the more marginal Lady Would-be, who is associated (through Sir Pol, her husband, and through her own verbal credentials) with a different kind of bird. Volpone's animal identification, too, is loosely handled during the play; in the final scene, he is linked with both fox and wolf.

Even more significant for the audience's theatrical experience of *Volpone* and its attempts to structure dramatic action, references explicitly linking the play with beast-fable narrative appear inconsistently, clustered at the play's beginning and at its conclusion. Noting the absence of animal imagery from the play's middle acts, Edward B. Partridge speculates that "Jonson may have thought that, once he started the comparisons working, he ought not to stress them, lest the emphasis be taken away from the human point of view." [16] In the theater, though, where characters are played by actors and where memory is limited in the scope and availability of its conceptual information, metaphorical identification must be underscored for characters to be seen as anything but human. From a theatrical perspective, the play's animal associations recede from its middle action, at which point even the metaphorically Italianate names appear infrequently and Mosca (for example) refers to Voltore simply as "your advocate" (V.ii.43). As for the beast-fable components of the Would-be subplot, it is worth noting that Sir Pol is onstage for twenty-five lines before he is named, and almost one hundred lines of dense dialogue before he is called "Sir Pol"; that he is imprisoned as a turtle, not a parrot; and that his "hawk-like" predator Peregrine is named only in Jonson's *dramatis personae.*

This is not to deny that the beast fable exerts organizing influence in *Volpone,* or that, like the play's other narrative allusions, it serves to set characters and events within sharp narrative and moral relief. These observations are meant to suggest that the outlining provided by allusions to the beast fable form only half of the dialectic governing Jonson's dramaturgy, that such patterns are necessarily incomplete, and that, unlike the organizing patterns that retain external stability in Shakespearean narrative, Jonsonian pattern is warped within the dramatic action it seeks to contain. It is significant, for instance, that the majority of beast-fable references occur within Volpone's lines (as, in fact, do most of the play's other references to external narrative material), a fact that suggests the intimate connection between such references and Volpone's own sensibility. This sensibility, as we have seen, is an improvisatory one, projecting little beyond the most immediate events, treating clusters of these events as episodes, each a small masterpiece to be savored in its self-contained artistic shape. His beast-fable references are accordingly directed at distinct "scenes"—the arrival of the birds of prey, the mortifying of a fox—fragmenting the overall dramatic narrative into the situational one-acts in which he revels. Volpone projects himself through narrative—one of his fantasies with Celia, after all, is to "act Ovid's tales" (III.vii.221)—but the impulsive, short-range nature of these projections collapses outline into the moment, mitigating against secure audience application of the beast fable (or any of his narrative allusions) to the narrative as a whole.

As one of the consummate actors in a world animated by performance, Volpone's sensibility is also brilliantly histrionic, and his actions further reduce the broader applicability of narrative devices through their focus on his individual stage presence and on the moment of his theatrical performance. Self-display charges Volpone's narrative references, as when he describes himself to Mosca as "a fox / Stretched on the earth, with fine delusive sleights / Mocking a gaping crow" (I.ii.94–96) and calls for his furs to embellish the role. As in *Mankind* and the Autloycus scenes of *The Winter's Tale*, theatricality undermines broader comprehension by focusing attention on the self-referentiality of performer and performance. In Jonson's play, it also subverts the ruling influence of any single narrative device, since as Volpone draws upon the play's store of narrative fragments and motifs, he shifts his narrative performance, Proteus-like, in response to shifting dramatic opportunity or the threat of sudden disaster. When he hears of Celia's beauty, he abandons his beast-fable role for that of the well-storied Scoto; later, when Lady Would-be unexpectedly arrives in his chamber, he casts her verbal barrage as a Vice's torment by calling for his "good angel" to rescue him.

Volpone's histrionic temperament, like that of Mosca, constitutes only the most obvious manifestation of the play's broader current of theatricality, its fascination with the moment's brilliant self-assertiveness. For the world of *Volpone*, like that of Jonsonian drama as a whole, is a world of sights and sounds, of individual gesture and mannerisms, of the ornate and the grotesque, relished up close and stared at from afar. This fictional particularity, evoked within the play's dramatic world, is heightened by Jonson's stage, dense in its props and its clusters of characters, baroque in its visual complexity. Idea recedes into the background, in part, through the sensory stimulation that comes so thick on Jonson's stage. Both evocations of the transmigration motif, for example—considered by at least one critic to stand as the play's organizing metaphor[17]—are explicitly staged, plays-within-the-play that stand theatrically self-contained. The Pythagorean sequence is performed by Volpone's three grotesques, the narrative alternating between the visually striking Nano and Androgyno in clumsy tetrameters. Mosca concludes the performance by singing a song, a musical intrusion into the sequence further heightened if Volpone joins in. The transmigratory history of Scoto's "poulder" is located, similarly, within the play's most elaborately staged performance: Volpone's mountebank scene. His stage encircled by the disguised Mosca and Nano, Volpone overruns the scene's conceptual relationship with the play's narrative as a whole through an oration thick with the jargon of charlatanry, achieving a histrionic magnetism reinforced by the two songs that punctuate the oration and by the distinctly Jonsonian commentators in the wing (Peregrine and Sir Pol), who focus attention on the performance and on themselves as audience through the one's snide perception and the other's gullible misperception.[18] Transmigration lies at the heart of the play's moral and conceptual realm, but its performance impact on audience perception, like much else in this realm, risks vanishing "in fumo" as a result of the play's theatrical density.

Language itself, so central to narrative and other conceptual formulations, is charged with the theatrical self-display that characterizes *Volpone*'s world as a whole. Although Barish considers *Volpone* "a momentary shift of Jonson's attention away from specifically linguistic caricature,"[19] both the play's prose and its verse are characterized by a typical Jonsonian emphasis on verbal performance, on language's noninformational functions, and on the imagistic and phonetic features of words, displayed, like the other surfaces of Jonson's dramatic world, for their own sake. Semantic links collapse within *Volpone*'s verbal pastiche, against the tight clusters of imagery and sound that animate the play's language; conceptual detachment buckles against the glut of sensory speech. Corvino, for example, disparages the mountebank to Celia:

> All his ingredients
> Are a sheep's gall, a roasted bitch's marrow,

> Some few sod earwigs, pounded caterpillars,
> A little capon's grease, and fasting spittle;
> I know 'em to a dram.
>   (II.vi.17–21)

With its compacted syntax, spliced rhythms, and puncturing dissonances ("bitch's marrow," "fasting spittle"), this violent cluster
of images reverberates beyond sense into pure sound, like the frenetic jabbering of *Mankind*'s mischief figures. Jonson may have
exhorted his audience to be "wise, / Much rather by your ears than
by your eyes" (Prologue to *The Staple of News*, ll. 5–6), but Volpone's stream of words from the mountebank platform, the un-
guent catalogue of pleasures with which he seeks to soften Celia's
conscience, and the mesmerizing repetition of Mosca's exhortation to Corvino—"Think, think, think, think, think, think, think,
sir" (II.vi.59)—suggest how fully Jonson's dramatic language actually participates in his stage's assault of incident. Volpone himself must endure this assault when he finds himself at the mercy of
Lady Would-be's verbal intrusion in Act III, and the imagery with
which he articulates his own distress applies with equal force to
the audience's theatrical perception of *Volpone* as a whole: "Another flood of words! a very torrent!" (III.iv.64); "The bells in
time of pestilence ne'er made / Like noise, or were in that perpet-
ual motion!" (III.v.5–6); "such a hail of words / She has let fall"
(ll. 10–11). Far from aiding composure and comprehension, Jonson's "poetry of the surface" (to borrow Eliot's phrase)[20] is shaped
more by the energies of the stage than by the demands of understanding.

In short, by overwhelming the narrative controls that offer
shape to its events, *Volpone* implicates its audience in the moral
and perceptual difficulties that characterize its dramatic world. Its
multiplicity of incident, dramaturgically freed of anticipations and
liaisons, gives the play's development in performance a complication always burdened with the imminent and the unknown, and
consequently effects an enormous strain on the audience's efforts
to organize incident into narrative. *Volpone*'s audience, like its
characters, must struggle to plot the play's barrage of activity, a
barrage that topples comprehension with a single stage knock and
forces it to recover. This rhythm of comprehension, confusion,

and recovery constitutes the narrative pulse of *Volpone*'s most characteristically Jonsonian moments—those moments of confusion and surprise when assurance collapses in an anarchy of possibility. It characterizes, too, the narrative experience of the play as a whole. *Volpone* develops from the relatively simple narrative of the beginning, with its beast fable underpinning, through the increasing complications of the play's middle, where events intrude with growing unpredictability and ever-widening consequence. After the brief stasis at the start of Act V, the action plunges even deeper into the unknown, as intriguer finally stalks intriguer and events hang precariously in the balance. In the end, the play reverts to stark narrative simplicity, and comprehension reasserts itself against the dance of eventuality, when Volpone halts the plot, bringing the narrative and its incidents once again into our control and his. But, as we have seen, even this moment of narrative stability is undermined by Jonson's dramatic art, in the theatricality that the magnifico displays as he steps forward to command applause. At every moment, even those most tightly bound by narrative pattern, *Volpone*'s assault of incident involves an equally pervasive (and equally subversive) assault of the stage.

If we consider the voices that emerge from his prologues and prefaces, his onstage representatives, and his poetry and prose, it is hard to escape the conclusion that Jonson strongly resisted the radical implications of his own dramaturgy. Like all who study his drama, we are left, in the end, with the paradox of Ben Jonson, a dramatist profoundly ambivalent toward his own theatrical instincts. A moralist suspicious of theatricality, he nevertheless peopled his greatest plays with actors like Volpone, Mosca, Face, and Subtle. An advocate of moral abstraction who crafted the Would-be subplot with the thematic parallels to the main plot so carefully noted by Barish,[21] he nevertheless filled his stage with a frenetic brilliance more distracting than any spectacle of Inigo Jones. Finally, a theorist who considered narrative as conceptually stable as Penshurst's foundations, he nevertheless composed plays of rapid particular incidents, in which broad narrative frameworks are drawn into episodes, warped by actions and interactions, and fragmented by the limited projections and self-absorptions of the characters who seek to shape them. Jonson's symbol of moral and social stability may have been the circle, but his drama dealt with the relativity of theatrical circumferences, obscuring the circle's formal abstraction in the sensory immediacy of performance.[22] Jonsonian drama is brilliant, and problematic, in large part because his moral and theatrical instincts remained so fiercely at odds.

Jonson's audience found (and still finds) itself at the center of the Jonsonian paradox. On the one hand, this most demanding of dramatists clearly expected his audience to meet his demands, and he lost no opportunity to remind his audience that attention, comprehension, and proper judgment lay within their power. In the Choruses to *The Magnetic Lady*, devoted (like much of Jonson's onstage commentary) to discussion of proper audience response, Probee explicitly outlines the audience's responsibility for full and accurate narrative comprehension: "Our parts that are the spectators, or should hear a comedy, are to await the process and events of things, as the poet presents them, not as we would corruptly fashion them. . . . Follow the right thread, or find it" (Chorus after Act IV, ll. 10–20). Proper judgment depends on proper comprehension of the narrative "thread," and narrative comprehension in turn depends on a clear, intent mind. Jonson refused to do for his audience what he felt to be its proper work: defending the entrance of masque figures without introductory explanation of their allegorical significance, he wrote in the *Masque of Queens*: "For to have made themselves their own decipherers, and each to have told, upon their entrance, what they were, and whether they would, had been a most piteous hearing, and utterly unworthy any quality of a poem, wherein a writer should always trust somewhat to the capacity of the spectator, especially at these spectacles; where men, besides inquiring eyes, are understood to bring quick ears, and not those sluggish ones of porters and mechanics that must be bor'd through, at every act, with narrations" (ll. 95–110).

Jonson, then, held to his ideal of "judicious spectators" (Induction to *The Magnetic Lady*, l. 124), epitomized in the Dedicatory Epistle to *Volpone* by the "most learned Arbitresses," who were characterized, along with their ability to judge correctly, by their cognitive "capacity" and by their willingness to exercise it. Yet it is precisely in terms of these faculties that Jonson's audience most consistently failed him. His prefaces and prologues berate his audience for their limitations: their preference for spectacle over matter, their constant liability to miscomprehension and misinterpretation. *Volpone* warns against "invading interpreters" who "utter their own virulent malice under other men's simplest meanings" (Dedicatory Epistle, ll. 65–67), and the Induction to *Bartholomew Fair,* though addressed to "the understanding gentlemen o' the ground here" (ll. 49–50), nevertheless contains "articles of agreement" between playwright and audience designed to ensure correct behavior and judgment on the part of the latter. When Jonson dramatizes spectators onstage, he often portrays them cut in the same mold of self-absorption as the other characters within his dramatic world: Sir Politic before Volpone's mountebank performance, Bartholomew Cokes at Littlewit's puppet show, Probee and Damplay, the Gossips in *The Staple of News,* and the theater audience described in *The Devil Is an Ass* and represented, onstage, by Fitzdottrel. Among Jonson's few competent spectators, some (Mitis in *Every Man out of His Humor* and the Boy in *The Magnetic Lady*) are made—almost defensively—"acquaintances" of the author, sharing his privileged omniscience concerning narrative and moral designs.[23]

In terms of even the most fundamental levels of comprehension, Jonson's audience failed to meet the cognitive standards that the playwright set for them, and he berated them for abdicating their responsibilities as thinking men. In all fairness, they could not have done otherwise, since Jonson's theatrical demands consistently surpass both his moral demands and the powers of audience comprehension. Inevitably, perhaps, Jonson's recourse was to the printed page, where comprehension finds the controlling authorial voice that Jonson was at such pains to establish within his plays, as well as the reading leisure necessary to meet Jonson's intellectual demands. Here, in the defenses and explanations, the elaborate character descriptions, and the plot summaries cast as prose "arguments," acrostics, and marginalia, one sees Jonson's uneasiness with the complexities of his drama, and his efforts to present stable literary outlines to counteract the threats to comprehension within his dramatic action. Champion of the streamlining "unities," Jonson the dramatist himself did what he condemned in playwrights who violated them: "that but shows how well the authors can travail in their vocation and outrun the apprehension of their auditory" (*Every Man out of His Humor,* Introduction, ll. 284–86). Cognition, after all, is itself a kind of "humor," structurally limited in what it can grasp; its understandings are easily "outrun" by a world that resists its orderings. To the extent that Jonson resented the cognitive limits that his drama repeatedly transgressed, there is truth as well as pathos in the judgment passed on his audience in "Ode to Himself," appended to *The New Inn:* "They were not made for thee, less thou for them" (l. 10).

But Jonson's personal failure was the theater's gain, since his plays constitute, en masse, an innovative dramaturgy that explores multiplicity, fragmentation, and the boundaries of his audience's comprehension of the theater and the world. Jonson's narrative technique, his confrontation of pattern with theatrical profusion, addresses his spectators as it does his characters: facing them with a world always one step more complex than the conceptual frameworks constructed to match it, confronting the self with a theatrical moment irreducibly and brilliantly other. That the moment so often prevails in its vivid particularity suggests that Jonson's instincts lay in the terrains beyond comprehension that he so consistently mapped out. In his explorations of these boundaries, even Jonson's failures constitute powerful illumination of the theater's own boundaries, its narrative possibilities and impossibilities, and the vigorous theatrical effects available in the negotiating ground between audience and stage. His drama is difficult, but its difficulty is an investigative one, rough and exhilarating, relentless in what it exposes about the activity of play-watching. No dramatist before Jonson exploited more fully the demands of the stage on audience response, or explored with more brilliance a dramaturgy of overwhelm; until our own century, few followed him. We can learn much about Jonson by studying the theater, and much about the theater by watching Jonson press it to, and beyond, its limits.

CHAPTER SIX

Shaw's Comedy of Disillusionment: *Major Barbara* and *Heartbreak House*

A number of years ago, the *New Yorker* printed a remarkable cartoon, at once ludicrous and poignant. It consisted of a snowman, assembled with more eagerness than skill, stick arms propped awkwardly in its side. Leaning slightly forward and to one side, it stared into the middle distance with an expression mixing alarm with unfathomable despair. As the cartoon's caption explained it: "The snowman realizes what he is."

Frozen both physically and spiritually in its icebound *anagnorisis,* the snowman enacts a gaze that lies at the heart of Western drama. For while drama clearly lies within what Langer calls "the mode of Destiny"[1]—springing along its vectors of project and action, "always great with things to come"—it is no less characterized by those moments when forward movement halts, when the dramatic character must confront the self in the stillness and silence that characterize the theater as a narrative medium. Typically, such pauses are moments of discovery: a guiding misperception collapses in the face of a more actual state of affairs, and the character must reconstruct perceptions of the self and others in light of these new realizations. Othello, driven by an increasingly blinding delusion, is brought to the point where delusion buckles, in the realization of how he has been manipulated, what he has done, and how deeply it has cost him. Othello realizes what he is, and despite its rhetorical and poetic self-aggrandizement, his concluding speech reflects this insight: "I pray you, in your letters, / When you shall these unlucky deeds relate, / Speak of me as I am" (*Othello,* V.ii.340–42).

Although our Aristotelian heritage has stressed the centrality of such reversals and recognitions in tragic drama, it is arguable that comedy constitutes the more fertile ground for disillusionment as a dramatic subject. Comedy, after all, combines a notion of character organized much more tightly around singlemindedness with a principle of multiplication that generates increasingly intricate lines of action and brings characters into increasingly inevitable collision. We have explored these two tendencies in the comedies of Ben Jonson, where radically delineated characters—each dominated by a ruling preoccupation, or "humor"—are propelled along lines of action continually subject to deflection and interruption. The logic of Jonsonian comedy leads to the exposure of these preoccupations, and individual characters suffer the sudden disillusionment of discovering that events are sharply different from what they had supposed. Quintessentially Jonsonian, and typically comic, is the moment in III.ix of *Volpone* when Mosca, momentarily surprised by the suspicious Corvino ("You are his, only? And mine, also, are you not?"), responds with blank, incomprehending monosyllables ("Who? I sir?") (ll. 19–20); or the crowning moment in Act V, when the three suitors (and, to a lesser extent, even Volpone and Mosca) stand gape-mouthed, "out of their humors," exposed to the Venetian Avocatori and to themselves.

No dramatist came closer to Jonson's fascination with delusion and disillusionment than George Bernard Shaw, whose major plays, though tamer in their management of incident than Jonsonian comedy, are nonetheless dramatic matrices of mistaken perception, animated by pulses of revelation. In this design, Shaw was helped (as he so often was) by his nineteenth-century dramatic background, particularly the legacy of the well-made play that he often decried and just as readily exploited. This legacy provided Shaw with a dramaturgy founded on discrepant and incomplete awareness among characters, and a dramatic logic founded on misperception and subsequent discovery. The comedy of Scribe and Sardou sends a number of characters into motion, each lacking some important piece of the scheme of events, and multiplies the intricacy of error until it is resolved in a clarifying denouement. Disillusionment, the exposure of inaccurate understanding by the sudden light of actuality, is a sine qua non of the well-made play, the determining element in its characterization and the cornerstone of its suspense and *éclaircissement*.

If *disillusionment* seems too strong a word for the moments of exposure in Scribean drama, this is because the consequence of illusions, and their loss, are in the end very slight. Error, in the world of the well-made play, constitutes an aberration, and its correction makes possible reconciliation and personal and social union. In the denouement of Scribe's intrigue comedy *The Glass of Water* (1840), for example, Queen Anne discovers that her ensign Masham, with whom she has been in love, is himself in love with a shopgirl, a disappointment with potentially disruptive consequences for characters and play alike. Confronted with this jolting realization, though, she blesses their betrothal and turns her ever-roving eye on the handsome guardsman outside, subordinating feeling to the proper development of incident.[2] Such characters may be temporarily ruled by *idées fixes,* but their illusions are flimsy things that may be abandoned or modified for the sake of the well-made play resolution. With Shaw's characters, on the other hand, illusion and error occupy the realm of the self where they are most uncompromising: the realm of conviction. "There is only one way of dramatizing an idea," Shaw wrote; "and that is by putting on the stage a human being possessed by that idea."[3] Ideology animates Shaw's characters, locates them within Shaw's ethical universe, and generates the structures through which they organize and express intentionality. Even such determinedly anti-ideological characters as Lady Britomart are inhabited by ideas: not abstract notions but complex and specific wholes, including codes of relationship, ethical distinctions, and private fictions that fuse conceptions of past and future to a notion of personal role often akin to a calling. With their inbuilt conceptions of history—personal, social, universal—such "ideas" are specifically narrative structures, contextualizing time as well as action within firmly designated frameworks (indeed, one of the keys to Shaw's psychosociology is the inseparability of the ideological and the cognitive). The bulwarks of self-perception in Shaw's dramatic world, these complexes are as fiercely held as the "life-lies" of *The Wild Duck* or the "pipe-dreams" of *The Iceman Cometh*.

Such personal constructs provide autonomy from certain aspects of life while facilitating participation in others, and their rupture implicates Shaw's characters with devastating suddenness in moral systems and networks of events and relationships against which they had previously found moral identity. This crisis is generally precipitated by revelations of neglected fact that expose illusion by unearthing deeper levels of the truth. Barbara, for instance, begins her play possessed by an evangelical divine scheme, a teleological vision cast against the complacency of the upper class and the brutality of the lower: "Theyre all just the same sort of sinner: and theres the same salvation ready for them all" (p. 90).[4] This conviction collapses into disillusionment when Barbara discovers that her salvation framework, tragically conventional at the heart of its unconventionality, is incomplete, for it neglects the economic structure of society, the mechanisms of which derive the Salvation Army's financial backing from Bodger and Undershaft—sources that also fuel the social conditions the Army seeks to redress. It neglects, too, human intransigence in this society: when Barbara learns that Snobby Price, newly repentant, has pocketed the coins left on the drum, she discovers "faith" at the service of greed. As so often in Shavian drama, reality punctures the idealism that disguises it, and Barbara implicitly shares Vivi Warren's admission (to Crofts) when she learns in Act III of *Mrs. Warren's Profession* that her income has derived from economic and sexual exploitation: "I believe I am just as bad as you" (I: 331). Convictions shattered, Barbara watches the Salvation Army march away in a parody of her missionary zeal.

For this kind of moral capitulation, *disillusionment* is probably too tame a word: recognition like this shares the self-negating impact of Jonsonian exposure. Vivie's confession—"I feel among the damned already" (I: 332)—is no rhetorical trope; it reveals a metaphysical depth to her moral loss. In *Widowers' Houses*, Trench displays an almost Sartrean vertigo when confronted with the tainted sources of his money. Shaw's stage direction is explicit: "*Trench does not at once reply. He stares at Sartorius, and then hangs his head and gazes stupidly at the floor, morally beggared, with his clasped knuckles between his knees, a living picture of disillusion*" (I: 94). Barbara's disillusionment is only slightly less visceral: "I stood on the rock I thought eternal: and without a word of warning it reeled and crumbled under me. I was safe with an infinite wisdom watching me, an army marching to Salvation with me; and in a moment, at a stroke of your pen in a cheque book, I stood alone; and the heavens were empty. That was the first shock of the earthquake: I am waiting for the second" (p. 170). If the dramatic technique of Scribe and the other well-made play dramatists focused on the clarifications and resolutions of the truth learned, Shaw often chose to dwell on the repercussions of illusions lost, and on the personal impoverishment that such a rupture leaves in its wake. When Shaw turned his eye to the reality unearthed by disillusionment, as we shall see, it was often problematic: volatile, unstable, eluding both confident formulation and cognitive grasp.

Shaw's interest in disillusionment and its consequences has a further dimension, one that ties his "drama of ideas" even more closely to the stage for which he wrote. When Shaw defined comedy as "the fine art of disillusion,"[5] he meant to suggest that comedy's function was to disrupt complacency and illusion as they existed both in the world of his characters and in the auditorium of the spectator. Ibsen's greatness, Shaw maintained, lay primarily in his dramatic assault on his audience, his "terrible art of sharpshooting at the audience, trapping them, fencing with them, aiming always at the sorest spot in their consciences." Among the vehicles through which Ibsen attacked the prejudices and outworn ideas of society at large, Shaw specifically praised his narrative technique, the management of sequential action by which Ibsen attacked audience perception within the theater. "The new school," Shaw wrote, "will trick the spectator into forming a meanly false judgment, and then convict him of it in the next act, often to his grievous mortification."[6] Suggesting as much about Shaw himself as it does about his Norwegian predecessor, this line reveals an interest in dramatic temporality and the sequential operations of theatrical cognition, as well as an almost judicial fascination with dramaturgical attack. That Shaw's own drama hinges on surprise and inversion comes as no surprise, nor that the audience is subjected to their impact. But Shaw's manipulation of audience response was more powerful, and more fundamental, than the simple inversions of popular convention with which he is generally, and rightly, credited.[7] Shaw subjects his audience to rhythms of comprehension and its undermining significantly analogous to movements of understanding and "disillusionment" within the dramatic world. True, audience comprehension is never held with the conviction of character illusion, nor is its surrender as devastating, for the aesthetic nature of dramatic representation guarantees that our construction of a play's temporal meanings never has the personal consequences with which we invest our private roles, fictions, and judgments. But to the extent that narrative comprehension does involve the generation and structuring of meaning, then its undermining is a kind of "disillusionment," one that returns the spectator—like Othello, Corvino, and Barbara—to a world that lies outside structures of meaning, even if this world is the safe one of the stage. Moments of explicitly narrative disruption are legion in Shaw, and we must not use our retrospective familiarity with outcomes to downplay their theatrical impact: Cleopatra's remark that the object of Caesar's rhapsodic tribute "isnt the great Sphinx" (II: 185) comes as a jolt to the audience as well as to Caesar, forcing a sudden disruption in response, amused bewilderment, just as the report of Ferrovius blindly slaying the Roman gladiators in the final act of *Androcles and the Lion,* unprepared for, plunges audience expectation into momentarily turmoil.

Before we consider the implications of this subversion for the cognitive rhythm of individual plays, though, we must consider the other dimension of Shaw's dramaturgy, a hypernarrativity that gives his drama its distictively Shavian dialectic and serves as backdrop and occasion for his disruptive strategies. Compared to the drama of Ibsen, Strindberg, and Chekhov, Shaw's plays are remarkable for their proliferation of narrative techniques and their pronounced, often literary storiness. A dramatist of ideas who believed that "dramatic invention is the first effort of man to become intellectually conscious," Shaw worked determinedly to make the stage subservient to conceptual frameworks, to provide it with *Everyman*'s power of illustration, and to heighten the intellectual component of playwatching.[8] Shavian drama reveals prolific use of those devices with which dramatists have conventionally sought to highlight narrative context and connection: clear delineation of dramatic segments, use of known stories, *raisonneurs* and other figures of narrative authority, devices of outline and liaison. Indeed, the Shavian canon as a whole serves as a showcase for many of these devices and techniques: *Caesar and Cleopatra, The Man of Destiny, Pygmalion,* and *Androcles and the Lion* join numerous other Shaw plays in proposing history and legend as signifying contexts for onstage action; *Saint Joan* reveals a deliberate manipulation of setting and scene division to arrange the worlds of court, camp, and countryside in ideological counterpoint; and many of his plays feature the central intellectual presence of the Shavian *raisonneur,* who orders and articulates the ranging social, economic, and ethical points of view, and whose seeming grasp of events approaches clairvoyance. Through such devices, we see Shaw the dogmatist, working to impose order on the flux of performance just as, in his prose, he sought to impose order on history, behavior, and thought.

On the surface, *Major Barbara* represents the culmination of this impulse in Shavian dramaturgy, for Shaw constructed the play with an abundance of controls to streamline its narrative development and to highlight the intellectual level that this development underscores. Shaw's three acts, for instance, break the setting into three locations and time spans stylized with an emblematic force reminiscent of morality drama or, to choose a literary text Shaw greatly admired, of *Pilgrim's Progress*:

> UNDERSHAFT . . . Where is your shelter?
>
> BARBARA In West Ham. At the sign of the cross. Ask anybody in Canning Town. Where are your works?
>
> UNDERSHAFT In Perivale St Andrews. At the sign of the sword. Ask anybody in Europe. (p. 91)

As the play unfolds, the contending ethical standpoints represented by these settings are displayed to the audience with illustrative directness. Narrative and moral explicitness is especially pronounced in the second act, which Shaw called "a play in itself," [9] and which features discrepant points of view set in overtly ironic relationship to each other: salvationism, Undershaftianism, and the violence and chicanery of West Ham itself. Character interactions draw out the contrasts: Jenny Hill with Snobby Price, Barbara with Bill Walker, Barbara with Undershaft, Undershaft with Mrs. Baines. The theatrical effect of such explicitness and contrasts is an intense clarification of events and issues that reaches its ironic climax at the act's conclusion in the almost pictorial arrangement of points of view: Mrs. Baines receiving Undershaft's signed check ("The longer I live the more proof I see that there is an Infinite Goodness that turns everything to the work of salvation sooner or later" [p. 134]), Bill Walker looking on triumphantly, Barbara standing alone in her despair, and Cusins ecstatically drawing out the ironies: "The millennium will be inaugurated by the unselfishness of Undershaft and Bodger. Oh be joyful!" (p. 134). Even by the standards of his other plays, seldom is Shaw's ironic counterpoint—between discrepant understandings of events, and between these understandings and the stage action itself—so explicit, and seldom is the audience allowed such insight concerning irony's shape.

Guided, then, by this mutually illuminating opposition of points of view, by the clear demarcation of setting and action, and directed into the final act by the central soul-struggle between Barbara and Undershaft, the audience of *Major Barbara* is permitted a high degree of comprehension concerning the temporal and ideological development of what they see on stage. In light of these features, one might be tempted to agree with Francis Fergusson that *Major Barbara* is a "thesis," [10] shaped by its broad conceptual development—from Wilton Crescent to West Ham to Perivale St. Andrews—and by Barbara's conversion to reality within this scheme. But even this radically streamlined play reveals the undermining that characterizes all but the most dogmatic of Shaw's plays. As *Major Barbara* moves into its final act, it becomes clear that the play's narrative and ideological development is undermined in significant ways, and that the theater audience finds its Olympian comprehension of events and positions significantly disturbed. After a brief respite in Wilton Crescent at the start of Act III, the scene shifts to Undershaft's domain. Up until this point, Undershaft has served as a kind of arch-*raissoneur*, guiding the audience's narrative and intellectual perspective through his apparently irrefutable insight into the events and ethical stances of the play's world: "You shall see. All religious organizations exist by selling themselves to the rich" (p. 121). With its almost divine right historical succession, his ideology seems the inevitable replacement for Barbara's shattered salvationism. When Undershaft's world becomes the dramatic setting, however, his omniscience becomes problematic for an audience that has been led to accept it. Earlier in the play, Undershaft's narrative authority was displayed in situations where he stood outside, or to one side, of events, calling attention to the truth beneath worlds and societies other than his own. The gunpowder shed, on the other hand, so potentially explosive that single matches must be dropped into a fire bucket, reveals that Undershaft's prophetic insight does not necessarily involve control. Paradoxically, the massive power of the foundry serves to expose Undershaft's individual powerlessness, and he admits this: "It does not belong to me. I belong to it" (p. 162). As he later warns Cusins: "From the moment when you become Andrew Undershaft, you will never do as you please again. Dont come here lusting for power, young man" (p. 169). Like the Mephistopheles to whom he is compared (p. 124), the price of Undershaft's personal forcefulness is subordination and subservience.

This powerlessness has distinct implications for the play's conclusion and how it is traced and anticipated in the theater. Where we might expect events to shape themselves toward a resolution, onstage or projected, the future fades into uncertainty, for Undershaft's moral insight (and the narrative authority that it has supported) are now shown to lack an end that might guide the formidable power which he has amassed. When asked by Cusins: "And what drives the place?" he replies "[*enigmatically*] A will of which I am a part" (p. 169). Such a statement may intend a kind of Providential assurance, but—in the range of voices occupying the stage in this final act—it cannot escape the darker echoes of Cusins' initial response to the foundry and the city in the distance: "Not a ray of hope" (p. 158). Undershaft offers his armaments to all buyers, and Cusins's accusation that the foundry is "driven by the most rascally part of society, the money hunters, the pleasure hunters, the military promotion hunters; and he is their slave" (p. 169) is never satisfactorily answered. The overwhelming theatrical impact of the physical setting, its cannon trained on the background town, reflects the dangerous amorality of Undershaft's philosophy and the threat implicit in its open-endedness. As Robert F. Whitman points out: "The failing of Undershaft's religion . . . is that all his money and gunpowder have no purpose, no goal, except to create themselves and perpetuate themselves. And it carries in itself the seeds of its own destruction." [11] With a dramatic

gesture midway between Ibsen and Pirandello, Shaw renders problematic the play's apparent ethical—and narrative—center: the realist credo against which vision has already crumbled. And he
does so through an appeal to the stage itself, now loosened from
argument's clear outlines.

True, Barbara reasserts the claims of salvation in the play's
closing moments, proclaiming a new mission through the synthesis of evangelical vision with Undershaftian realism: "through the
raising of hell to heaven and of man to God, through the unveiling
of an eternal light in the Valley of The Shadow" (p. 184). Osten-
sibly, vision has restored its teleological harness on the power of
the present. But the synthesis of Shaw's dialectical marriage remains problematic for an audience that has witnessed the collapse
of salvationism and, by implication, of all frameworks that seek
to project beyond the present. Shaw provides no evidence that illusion has not been replaced by further illusion, no suggestion
about how any visionary framework might survive the earthquake's second shock when it arrives. As Barbara stands on the
battlements, dummies sprawled in straw at her feet, the future remains ominous and obscure. By this point, disillusionment has
crossed the boundaries between play and audience: in one of the
central ironies of *Major Barbara*, Barbara's "return to the colors"
takes place against deepening audience apprehension.

But even this feature of the conclusion resists easy formulation, for the play's final-act disillusionment is also a liberation, and
a theatrical one at that. As the conceptual clarity of the previous
acts gives way to uncertainty and ambivalence, the stage itself
stands out with increasing autonomy, free of subjugating theses
and narrative lines. One of the most physically imposing of Shaw's
sets, its lines are bold and angular, drawing the eye off balance.
Cluttered with props and actors, pervaded by an atmosphere of
awe, this stage becomes a source of energy in itself, the theatrical
equivalent of Undershaft's munitions, a contagious space which
the audience cannot help but share. In this regard, the conclusion
constitutes an appropriate climax for the play as a whole. Shaw
may have claimed that *Major Barbara* was about poverty, but it
deals much more fundamentally, as does all of Shavian drama,
with power in all of its forms: Blood and Fire, Money and Gunpowder. Power courses through the play's confrontations: Lady

Britomart with Stephen, Barbara with Bill Walker, and Undershaft with Barbara, as he looks hypnotically in her eyes and says: "Tell him, my love, what power really means" (p. 170). Drums roll, horns play, people march in ecstatic procession, a stage setting looms huge with explosive power. Such power is death, but it is also life, and in both capacities it lies in uneasy relationship to cognitive frameworks that seek to control or deny it. In moments when these frameworks weaken, it exists as a charged and unmediated presence, both for the characters who grapple with it and for the theater audience that witnesses its triumph. It is through such underminings and liberations that we encounter the Shaw most consistently neglected by admirers and detractors alike: the theater artist who reveled in performance and all its potential anarchies, who welcomed the continual pressure that theatrical performance exerts against structures of audience comprehension, and who embraced the inescapable relativity through which the stage undermines exclusively "authoritative" standpoints.

Major Barbara, then, reveals the tension at the heart of Shavian dramaturgy. Both dogmatist and theater artist, Shaw combined a commitment to the coherence of events and ideas with a persistent disillusioning impulse designed to undercut the structures of comprehension that support this coherence. In the confrontation of these two impulses, alternately deliberate and ambivalent, we can recognize the source of both the power and the difficulty of Shavian drama, since his finest plays derive their characteristic energies less from the clear comprehension of certain "ideas" than from the energy with which they confront comprehension itself. Writing anonymously about *Major Barbara* in 1915, Shaw made a remark that applies to his dramaturgy as a whole: "It made demands on the audience but the demands were conceded. The audience left the theater exhausted, but felt the better for it and came again." [12]

When the second shock finally came, in the Great War that exploded the complacency of Georgian England, its destructiveness exceeded Undershaft's most optimistic calculations and Shaw's greatest nightmares. In the midst of his own disillusionment over the triumph of militaristic nationalism and the apparent failure of his evolutionary program, Shaw wrote a play that many, impressed by its darkness bordering on nihilism, have considered an exception—albeit a brilliant one—among his plays. Yet the dark fantasia of *Heartbreak House* merely represents an intensification of the disillusioning impulse present in Shavian drama as a whole and evident even in the more tightly shaped world of *Major Barbara,* an impulse pressed to its logical ends both in the realm of action and on the level of audience response. The play's darkness, one might say, is as much technical as philosophical, and its roots lie deep within Shaw's dramatic and theatrical art.

Disillusionment—christened *heartbreak* by the play's characters[13]—disrupts the world of *Heartbreak House* much more ruthlessly than it does the world of *Major Barbara.* For one thing, it is much more widespread. Disillusionment in the earlier play is, after all, largely restricted to Barbara. According to Cusins, Undershaft "completed the wreck of my moral basis, the rout of my convictions, the purchase of my soul" (p. 142), but the disillusionment that he describes occurs offstage and contains little of the dramatic force of Barbara's centerstage crisis. Nor do we react with tremendous concern to the moral wreck of a character whose "moral basis" has remained so enigmatic; a "sort of collector of religions" (p. 115), one of a long line of Shavian ironists, Cusins shows more relish for the discrepancies between points of view than for any position of his own. For the rest, characters are marked by the extent to which they sidestep disillusionment: Lady Britomart rests firm in her self-possessed propriety; Stephen in his morality of "character"; and Mrs. Baines in her rapturous single-mindedness. Bill Walker, brought to the brink of disillusionment, escapes back into the London underworld and its primitive ethic. In *Major Barbara,* it seems, heartbreak is the prerogative of the morally elite.

Disillusionmemt is spread much more democratically among the characters of *Heartbreak House,* where the exposure of truth beneath illusion recurs with polyphonic frequency. Those characters who undergo it the least (Hesione, Shotover, Nurse Guiness) have, one suspects, few illusions remaining. Nor is heartbreak limited to the Pauline single strokes of the earlier play: Ellie undergoes a trio of major disillusionments: discovering that Marcus Darnley is actually Hesione's husband, that Mangan was the agent of her father's ruin, and that the Captain's mysticism is spiked with rum.

The unfortunate Mangan, bedeviled throughout this play, must suffer even more. Underlying these larger crises is a steady pulse of smaller disillusionments, a background of heartbreak that reverberates like the offstage bombs in Act III and that none of the characters manage to escape.

Furthermore, disillusionment in *Heartbreak House* occurs at a personal level unusual even for Shavian drama, far more akin to the emotional battlefields of Edward Albee and Harold Pinter. The central interactions of *Major Barbara,* by contrast, attack illusion at the ideological level, drawing ammunition from the external social and economic realms, and while this level is powerful in its spiritual repercussions it is generally free of more narrowly private concerns. In the portrayal of Barbara's pivotal disillusionment, attention is actually deflected from its personal dimensions: Cusins asks: "What is a broken heart more or less here?" (p. 135), and Undershaft later chides: "Come, come, my daughter! dont make too much of your little tinpot tragedy" (p. 170).[14] In Shotover's house, on the other hand, characters are exposed at their most vulnerable: Ellie's romantic imagination and her adoration of her father, Mangan's age and livelihood, Ariadne's emotional frigidity, Randall's infatuation. Shaw underscores the personal devastation of this manipulation: Mangan compares the experience of hearing Ellie and Hesione talk about him to a man hitting a woman in the breast (pp. 127–28), Randall *"chokes"* (p. 154), and Mangan himself *"breaks into a low snivelling"* (p. 171). Even Mazzini Dunn, the most poised of the house's visitors, acknowledges disillusionment's edge: "I have learnt a good deal about myself from you, Mrs Hushabye; and I'm afraid I shall not be the happier for your plain speaking" (p. 119).

Hector tells Randall: "In this house we know all the poses: our game is to find out the man under the pose" (p. 151). The word *game* is significant, for it suggests the extent to which the activity of heartbreak in this play is pursued as an end in its own right. Disillusionment in the Shotover house lacks the contextualizing purposiveness of Barbara's conversion ideology and Undershaft's almost religious arch-realism; instead, personal details are hurled, and poses stripped, as part of a deeper maneuvering for control—control apparently sought, like that at a card table, for the game of it. The tactics of move and countermove, as well as the jockeying for dominance, provide the logic behind the following interaction between Ellie and Hesione:

> MRS HUSHABYE [*rising superbly*] Ellie: you are a wicked sordid little beast. And to think that I actually condescended to fascinate that creature there to save you from him! Well, let me tell you this: if you make this disgusting match, you will never see Hector again if I can help it.
>
> ELLIE [*unmoved*] I nailed Mangan by telling him that if he did not marry me he should never be able to see you again [*she lifts herself on her wrists and seats herself on the end of the table.*]
>
> MRS HUSHABYE [*recoiling*] Oh!
>
> ELLIE. So you see I am not unprepared for your playing that trump against me. Well, you just try it: thats all. I should have made a man of Marcus, not a household pet.
>
> MRS HUSHABYE [*flaming*] You dare!
>
> ELLIE [*looking almost dangerous*] Set him thinking about me if you dare.
>
> MRS HUSHABYE. Well, of all the impudent little fiends I ever met! Hector says there is a certain point at which the only answer you can give a man who breaks all the rules is to knock him down. What would you say if I were to box your ears?
>
> ELLIE [*calmly*] I should pull your hair.
>
> MRS HUSHABYE [*mischievously*] That wouldnt hurt me. Perhaps it comes off at night.
>
> ELLIE [*so taken aback that she drops off the table and runs to her*] Oh, you dont mean to say, Hesione, that your beautiful black hair is false?
>
> MRS HUSHABYE [*patting it*] Dont tell Hector. He believes in it.
>
> ELLIE [*groaning*] Oh! Even the hair that ensnared him false! Everything false!
>
> MRS HUSHABYE. Pull it and try. Other women can ensnare men in their hair; but I can swing a baby on mine. Aha! you can't do that Goldylocks.
>
> ELLIE [*heartbroken*] No. You have stolen my babies. (pp. 125–26)

Mangan wails, "In this house a man's mind might as well be a football" (p. 130), and his image reflects the competitiveness and violence that often underlie the play's manipulations and unmaskings. In its less predatory moments, as in Hector's romantic impersonations, the game of disillusionment is played out of mere whim.

As *Heartbreak House* moves toward its final act, roles and self-identifying fictions are steadily stripped away, and truth emerges from the wreckage of illusion. Before considering Act III, however, and the problematic nature of this truth, we must recognize how fully the audience, too, has been an object of the play's relentless attack. Gone is the streamlined clarity of the first two and a half acts of *Major Barbara,* and in its place is a more disturbing triumph of multiplicity and indeterminacy.

Chief among Shaw's dramaturgical decisions in *Heartbreak House* is the deliberate omission of a character (like Barbara or Undershaft) whose story or point of view might focalize the action. Ellie begins the play as its likely protagonist, and her story does achieve prominence during certain sequences, but the competing pressures of other characters and rival concerns cause her story to merge with the rest in a general melange of incident and motif. Similarly, Shotover contributes a far less dominating perspective on events than his counterpart in *Major Barbara,* whose insights and mastery remain firm until the qualifications of the final act. Unlike Undershaft, Shotover spends much of the play offstage, and his grasp of events never emerges with the munition-maker's assertive straightforwardness. His remarks, though blunt, are enigmatic and evasive, leaving characters and audience alike in uncertainty. Ariadne warns Ellie: "My father is a very clever man; but he always forgot things; and now that he is old, of course he is worse. And I must warn you that it is sometimes very hard to feel quite sure that he really forgets" (p. 69). Mystic vision is suggested by Shotover's pursuit of "the seventh level of concentration," but his omniscience is suspect even before its dependence on rum is exposed at the end of Act II. Sharing the play's broader tone of mystery and ambiguity, Shotover provides little guidance concerning the play's narrative outline or moral center.

Nor do time and place demarcate action into comprehensible units. All of the activities of *Heartbreak House* take place in a single evening and are bound to the house that gives Shaw's fantasia its name. One of the most striking of Shavian sets, its almost sentient presence is underscored by the characters themselves, who allude to it over thirty times during the play.[15] Yet this setting, lacking the Hegelian explicitness of the three settings of *Major Barbara,* neither clarifies our understanding of the action nor guides its directions. Attempts to set Heartbreak House in thematic opposition to Horseback Hall, and to fit the play's characters into the emblematic framework of Shaw's Preface, risk neglecting the play itself, where Heartbreak House is named only in the final act and Horseback Hall is never mentioned. Until then, the set serves largely as a location, like the city parks of Restoration comedy or the claustrophobic rooms of Harold Pinter, where characters often do little more than arrive. It is constructed to resemble *"the after part of an old-fashioned high-pooped ship with a stern gallery"* (p. 59), but it is a ship adrift, both for the characters who ride aboard it and the audience that seeks to comprehend its course.

As always in the theater, an absence of guiding narrative devices throws attention onto the moment-by-moment unfolding of the stage action. Here, we can note the demands that *Heartbreak House* places on audience comprehension, demands that effect a considerable amount of cognitive pressure.[16] *Heartbreak House,* for one thing, has only ten characters compared to the fifteen of *Major Barbara,* but the latter are arranged in clear groupings, generally appear only in specific settings and during certain acts (with the exception of Undershaft, Barbara, and Cusins, who traverse all three of the play's moral realms), and are no doubt given further demarcation by costume. Entrances and exits are infrequent, and are often anticipated when they occur: with the exception of the final scene, for instance, each of Undershaft's entrances is announced: by Morrison at Wilton Crescent and by Snobby Price at the Salvation Army yard. The characters in *Heartbreak House,* on the other hand, appear individually, quickly lose any strong sense of grouping, change costume, and enter and exit with disjunctive randomness.[17] This confusion is deepened by a bewildering multiplicity of relationships, extending and receding in complexity: Hector, infatuated with Ariadne (also pursued by Randall), is husband to Hesione (Ariadne's sister), as well as the object of Ellie's infatuation, and so on. Discussing Billy Dunn, the pirate, Charles A. Berst observes that he is given "a confusion of relationships which Strindberg would glory in."[18] The implications of this complexity for comprehension in the theater are inescapable: confronted with such randomness of stage activity and intricacy of relationship, the audience is frequently pressed to a level of perplexity well beyond what it can comfortably comprehend—a condition of confusion and forgetfulness humorously played upon in Hesione's attempt to introduce Mazzini:

> MRS HUSHABYE [*introducing*] Mr Mazzini Dunn, Lady Ut—oh, I forgot: youve met. [*Indicating Ellie*] Miss Dunn.
>
> MAZZINI [*walking across the room to take Ellie's hand, and beaming at his own naughty irony*] I have met Miss Dunn also. She is my daughter. [*He draws her arm through his caressingly.*]
>
> MRS HUSHABYE. Of course: how stupid! Mr Utterword, my sister's-er-
>
> RANDALL [*shaking hands agreeably*] Her brother-in-law, Mr Dunn. How do you do?
>
> MRS HUSHABYE. This is my husband.
>
> HECTOR. We have met, dear. Dont introduce us any more. (pp. 93–94)

Ironic superiority over Hesione during this exchange is slight, for with the unfettered complexity of *Heartbreak House*'s network of relationships, an audience would have to be truly Olympian to comprehend more than she.

The play subverts its audience's structures of comprehension even more directly through intrusions of the unexpected. Nurse Guiness warns Ellie in the opening scene—"This house is full of surprises for them that dont know our ways" (p. 62)—and her warning could serve as well to the play's audience. In the environment of the theater, the series of revelations in *Heartbreak House* affects the audience as it does the characters, abruptly compelling the spectator to reconstruct his or her understanding of a scene or a plot connection when confronted with a new detail. Ellie's romantic reminiscences of Marcus Darnley may occasion increasing skepticism as she naively recounts the outrageous details of his past, but the audience is little prepared for Hesione's sudden, almost whimsical disclosure when Hector enters: "What a lark! He is my husband" (p. 83). The play is full of such moments when the audience, too, is surprised—even instances when the audience is clearly misled. From what Ariadne has revealed about herself, for instance, the audience joins Hesione in believing Randall to be

Lord Hastings when he first arrives (a misperception Randall plays upon); like Hesione, the audience is subsequently jolted when he answers her accusation—"I dont believe you are Hastings Utterword"—by agreeing: "I am not" (p. 91). Likewise, the audience is given no indication that Mangan is awake during the long second-act conversation between Ellie and Hesione, and must accordingly reformulate its memory of the scene to incorporate this disclosure.[19] *Heartbreak House,* in short, intensifies the pressures on comprehension exercised so teasingly in the well-made play and thereby involves its audience more fully in its characters' misperceptions and abrupt disillusionments.

As facts are disclosed, and as characters are shown alternately in control and out of control of events, the gap between individual fictions and the events they seek to explain widens, and narrative outlines become mountingly obscure. The bedrock of reality that grounds disillusionment in *Major Barbara* (and in most drama before the modern period) has begun to surrender its narrative outlines to the ambiguities of dream. Mangan was Mazzini Dunn's benefactor; Mangan was responsible for Dunn's ruin; Dunn operated all along with an awareness of Mangan's incompetence. Such revelations, finally, do not supersede each other as more accurate accounts of a past grown solid; instead, they stand beside one another as markers of a past always edging beyond comprehension's reach. *Heartbreak House* is a fantasia of discrepancy in which the audience becomes increasingly suspicious of what it sees and what it is told, where character fictions and audience formulations both give way in what Ellie calls "this silly house, this strangely happy house, this agonizing house, this house without foundations" (p. 171). In Barbara's earlier words, "There must be some truth or other behind all this frightful irony" (p. 156).

Francis Fergusson claims that the dramatic interest of *Heartbreak House* is focused on "the fateless fate and the bodiless farce of the emancipated mind itself."[20] In the theater for which Shaw wrote the play, though, the opposite is true, and this intensifies as the play develops. For as disillusionment piles on disillusionment and outlines blur, both characters and audience come to rest, not in any "bodiless farce," but in the moment with all its concreteness and immediacy. This surrender to the present is most pronounced, of course, in the terrace scene, when two acts of disillusionment have run their course. By this point in the play, individual fictions have been detonated so frequently that characters occupy the stage strangely detached from past and future. Character configurations reinforce this sense of a present stripped of its context, in which time before and time after feel as remote from the present as Shotover's Zanzibar. In contrast to the union of Barbara and Cusins, which represents an extension forward of the Undershaft lineage, pairings cloaked in futility open Act III of *Heartbreak House:* Hesione escorting Mangan, and Randall mournfully playing his flute for Ariadne. Rejecting Mangan, Ellie announces her betrothal to Shotover—"Life with a blessing! that is what I want" (p. 169)—but the stage picture of a young girl with an old man who has just referred to himself as "half dead" denies her the promise, however qualified, of Barbara's visionary projections. More faithful to the final act's eerie aimlessness and inertia, with plans and memories both torn away, is Hector's pronouncement: "We have been too long here. We do not live in this house: we haunt it" (p. 171).

Against this foreground of collapsed illusion, the house—as well as the rest of the outdoor setting—stands out with growing autonomy. For as the mind succumbs to the difficulties of *Heartbreak House,* attention rests in the eyes and the other senses. At this point, the setting grows in overt significance, acquiring, for the first time, its symbolic correspondence with an England drifting perilously close to the rocks: "And this ship that we are all in? This soul's prison we call England?" (p. 177). Individual illusions give way, as they did in *Major Barbara,* to a setting charged with explosive power—here, the dynamite stockpiles at home and the enemy bombs from abroad. Yet this setting is more deeply ominous than Undershaft's munitions factory, for its symbolic significance and underlying destructive potential are highlighted at precisely the point when any vision capable of guiding them has vanished for good in the eddies of disillusionment. By the end of *Heartbreak House,* it has become clear, there are no colors left to return to.

"How is all this going to end?" asks Hector in the middle of the act (p. 174), and we can see the play's conclusion as a polyphonic sequence of answers to that question. The stated possibilities range from Mazzini's assertion of an overruling Providence to

Shotover's warning of a ship smashing against the rocks, from Ariadne's assurance that Hastings is in charge to Ellie's simple affirmation that "life must come to a point sometime" (p. 174). Earlier in the act, Hector prophesies with apocalyptic resonance when he warns: "I tell you, one of two things must happen. Either out of that darkness some new creation will come to supplant us as we have supplanted the animals, or the heavens will fall in thunder and destroy us" (p. 159). *Heartbreak House,* in short, approaches its conclusion with the same possibilities held in uneasy balance at the end of *Major Barbara:* redemption or destruction. Of course, in the darker world of this play, the current of reality that emerges from disillusionment seems to sweep inexorably toward annihilation. Mangan's disclosure of his government position bears out Cusins' fear that "The most rascally part of society" holds the harnesses of the world's power, and the clients of Undershaft's munitions factory arrive overhead to drop their bombs. Mired in ineffectuality, none of the characters resist the forces of destruction; instead, when the aircraft arrive, two run to the dynamite pit, while the rest flood the house with light, making it a beacon— in their suicidal ecstasy—for the aerial attack. The movement of events and tones in these final moments seems to confirm Shotover's warning: "The next one will get us. [*He rises.*] Stand by, all hands, for judgement" (p. 178).

The next one, though, does not get them, and although both Mangan and the burglar are killed in the gravel pit, the aerial attack passes with the house left standing, ablaze with light. "Yes, safe," Hector laments. "And how damnably dull the world has become again suddenly!" (p. 181). It is the play's final disillusionment, its final frustration of outline and resolution, that neither redemption nor destruction occurs. Although the threat of the bombers' return maintains the atmosphere of danger, expectations of judgment and apocalyptic closure, like most of the other predictions offered by the play's characters, pass as themselves likely illusions. The conclusion of *Heartbreak House,* then, presents a possibility even bleaker, perhaps, than cataclysm: the possibility that, as Mazzini earlier suggested: "Life doesnt end: it goes on" (p. 174). The stage, in turn, embodies more (and less) than the immanent energy of *Major Barbara's* conclusion; presided over by Randall's wistful flute, it becomes a manifestation of stasis and inertia in the face of a powerlessness grown routine. Such, one may speculate, is surely the most disillusioning "Nightmare of a Fabian"[21]: that even the purgations of destructive change are unlikely. "The tragedy of modern life," Shaw commented in 1912, "is that nothing happens, and that the resultant dulness does not kill."[22] If the first two acts anticipate Pinter's fierce conversation struggles, the play's conclusion, with its setting cut loose from past and future, looks ahead to inert theater worlds of Samuel Beckett.

In the midst of Barbara's devastation, Undershaft remarks to her: "You have learnt something. That always feels at first as if you had lost something." This paradox lies at the heart of Shaw's comedy of disillusionment, and we can appreciate the peculiar ambivalence that charges his plays by underscoring the tension between its two halves. On one side is the deepening sense of reality that comes about for Shaw's characters when they are stripped of limiting fictions about the world; as Shotover chides Mangan: "Think of this garden in which you are not a dog barking to keep the truth out!" (p. 167). Shaw himself wrote in his Preface to *Major Barbara:* "If a man cannot look evil in the face without illusion, he will never know what it really is, or combat it effectively" (pp. 61–62). Evident, too, are the deeper purposes frequently available to these characters as they discover a more fundamental movement in life—the variously formulated versions of the Shavian Life Force, such as Undershaft's "will of which I am a part"— as well as the jubilant energy released when Shaw's characters grasp their freedom from limited roles and private comprehensions. In this respect, the Dionysian allusions in *Major Barbara* constitute a revealing metaphor for the inner liberations of Shavian drama as a whole. As Nietzsche wrote in *The Birth of Tragedy:* "Schopenhauer has described for us the tremendous awe which seizes man when he suddenly begins to doubt the cognitive modes of experience, in other words, when in a given instance the law of causation seems to suspend itself. If we add to this awe the glorious transport which arises in man, even from the very depths of nature, at the shattering of the *principium individuationis,* then we are in a position to apprehend the essence of the Dionysiac rapture, whose closest analogy is furnished by physical intoxication."[23] Cusins marches in rapture; Barbara stands exultant on the battleworks; Hesione says of the bombings: "It's like an orchestra: it's like Beethoven"; "By thunder, Hesione," Ellie exults: "it is Beethoven" (p. 178).

On the other side are those moments of stunned silence and vertigo before jubilation, when the *principium individuationis* has just collapsed and characters stand frozen, confronted by the self in its personal poverty. It is because Shaw understood so well the strength of private fictions and the consequences of their abandonment that he once claimed that *Major Barbara* could easily have been a tragedy.[24] Even in their most liberating intoxication, Shaw's characters are marked by the pain of loss; some (like Vivie Warren and Mangan) never move beyond it. Moreover, as *Major Barbara* suggests, the tremors of disillusionment tend to undermine the visions and purposes that succeed it, to challenge the security of any self-guiding projection beyond the moment. Reality may mean the death of illusion, but it also signals the end of dreams. It threatens to leave Shaw's characters in limbo, unable or unwilling to set up new frameworks of vision to guide their power and longings into action, surrounded by the shells of former belief. Such is a frightening prospect within the Shavian universe, for its currents are often dangerous ones, and hell (Juan tells us) is the home of the drifters. The barrenness and futility of the final act of *Heartbreak House* are the inevitable outcome of a principle deeply embedded in Shaw's dramatic vision, a comic principle turned darker that confronts all conviction with disruption, all forward movement with stasis. It is no doubt in response to this immanent loss of purpose in Shavian drama that we encounter the massive prefaces and stage directions, filled with Shaw's own insistent purposes, attempting to preclude through exhortation the inertia inherent in his plays.[25]

As we have suggested, Shaw involves his audience in a similar movement between conceptual frameworks and their undermining, binding his comedy of disillusionment to the stage and its effects. Drawing upon performance's ability to frustrate as well as facilitate comprehension, Shaw's dramatic technique shifts attention between cognitive structures and physical immediacy, deflecting it from objects to the lively play of mind and from mental constructions back to the stage itself. This interplay at the heart of Shavian drama is a source of its undeniable theatricality. Despite the sacrosanctity of thought in this "drama of ideas," many of Shaw's most riveting moments are those when the mind is set against a physical background that isolates it—Don Juan speaking in the void, Caesar before the Sphinx, Barbara against the munitions works—or when ideas are actually subsumed by the stage, as they are at the close of *Heartbreak House*. Recalling a performance of the play, which he had seen years earlier, Stark Young wrote: "Evidently the impression from the Theatre Guild production of *Heartbreak House* that had remained so strongly in my mind as the years went by came from the terrace scene and the company talking there in the moonless blue night. It was a long time ago and I had forgotten nearly all they said, but not that haunting tone composed of the scene, the voices, the vibration of characters, the impending blind ruin."[26] "I had forgotten nearly all they said": it is rather surprising testimony to Shaw's theatrical instincts that this playwright of "discussion"—who once claimed that his drama was "all talk"[27]—had such powerful recourse to the stage and its wordless presence.

CHAPTER SEVEN

Not I and Footfalls:
Beckett and the Edges
of Narrative

To close this study with the contemporary theater is, somewhat paradoxically, to find ourselves where we started and, Janus-
like, to gaze backward in the very act of looking ahead. For the
diversity and innovation of contemporary drama, as well as the
theoretical self-consciousness the dramatists of today share with
their age, have occasioned fundamental reexaminations of dramatic art, radical insights into its possibilities and limitations, and
(as a consequence of these insights) a wealth of models by which
the drama of its predecessors can be understood and valued. Innovation in the present illuminates achievement in the past, highlighting dramatic effects that have eluded attention and, in a sense,
"discovering" more intricate features of previous dramatic exper-
iments. Ionesco's investigation of linguistic breakdown retrospectively foregrounds the threat of such breakdown throughout earlier drama, providing dramaturgical perspective (for instance) on
the proto-absurdist game of "vapors" in *Bartholomew Fair*. Similarly, the gazebos of sexual disguise so prominent in Genet and
Orton suggest the dislocations of gender identity on the stage of
Shakespeare and Middleton, with its boys playing women and
"women" cross-dressed as men. Bond rewrites *King Lear*, like
Soyinka *The Beggar's Opera*, but specific adaptations are only one
way in which the plays of the past fifty years, through their dramatic and dramaturgical explorations, "rewrite" earlier drama for
our understanding.

Perhaps chief among the twentieth century's "discoveries" is
the theater itself. While critics continue, for the most part, to work

with literary models of dramatic form, the dramatists of our century have displayed a keen awareness of their medium, exploring with unprecedented interest the boundaries that characterize it and the responses it engages. From the slip-time of Vaclav Havel through the "choreopoems" of Ntozake Shange, contemporary drama foregrounds performance as the center of dramatic and theatrical art, allowing the physical environment of dramatic action its weight and movement, giving theoretical justification for what has been, throughout dramatic history, largely a matter of unspoken practice. In so doing, it has highlighted the complex relationship between narrative and performance, exploring through strategies of cognitive disruption the ambiguous interfaces between dramatic space and performance space, between the domain of fiction and the more fundamental domain of the stage. Led by Pirandello's "plays of the theater within the theater," dramatists such as Genet, Weiss, Stoppard, and Williams have dramatized the lines of theatrical illusion, confronted the problematic distinctions among levels of theatrical reality, and (in plays such as *The Balcony, Marat/Sade, Rosencrantz and Guildenstern Are Dead,* and *The Two-Character Play*) extended this ontological confusion to the audience's experience of the dramatic object in performance, throwing attention metatheatrically upon the complexities of illusion and actuality in the theatrical moment. Following Brecht's dramatic precedents, Arden, Dürrenmatt, Müller, and Churchill have explored similar interfaces through a dramaturgy of alienation, counterpointing narrative representation with the presentational realities of performance and sharpening the edges of story with the stage's self-sufficiency. From its earliest *causes célèbres* in Paris, Berlin, and Zurich to its more sophisticated development in the work of Rozewicz and Handke, Grotowski and Foreman, the avant-garde has shattered the foundations of narrative logic, substituting disruption, opacity, and fragmentation. Finally, even naturalism has sought its performance roots in the subversion of conventional dramaturgy: extending the discontinuity and indeterminacy that pervade or threaten early Strindberg, later Ibsen, and all of Chekhov, the theater of Pinter, Shepard, Mamet, and Fornes is characterized by gaps and surprises, disparity and confusion, encroachments of the fabulous and the mythic, and the infringements of a subjectivity that denies the assurances of narrative outline. Despite differences of style and ideology, these dramaturgical currents reveal a similar strategy: to subvert patterns of temporality as they do all ordering structures, and to unearth and explore the theatrical regions at narrative's edge.

Of all the explorations within contemporary drama of the stage/narrative duality, none is more powerful than that of Samuel Beckett. As a dramatist, Beckett effects an unprecedented disclosure of the theatrical moment, allowing it a substance and a place within his action unrivaled in the dramatic canon, foregrounding the mutual displacements of narrative and performance through rigorous dramaturgical strategies. His three longer plays—*Waiting for Godot* (1953), *Endgame* (1957), and *Happy Days* (1961)[1]—suggest the innovations of Beckett's dramatic technique. Attacking at its roots the conventional transformation of performance into narrative, Beckett exploits a dramaturgy of reduction and discontinuity, and a theatrical heightening of the present's inertness. With the stage a sphere of tedium and stasis and future action as remote as the arrival of a Godot who will never come, plot flattens into the present and action into activities that express little more than a need to fill the emptiness of time and space. *Godot* opens with the words "Nothing to be done" (p. 7a), for the ancestral dramatic world of projects and overarching action has reduced itself to a country road, a shelter, and a mound where characters are divorced from the ability to act, save in the barest of routines. Buried to her waist, then neck, in the stage's center mound, Winnie is the most constrained of these early Beckettian characters, but her physical immobility reflects a broader powerlessness to move that constrains them all, even at their most mobile. "Time has stopped" (p. 24b), and action recurs with the repetitive patterning of Vladimir's song ("A dog came in the kitchen / And stole a crust of bread," pp. 37a–b), modified only by the perceptible diminishments of decay. When events happen, they are quickly forgotten by the characters who undergo them, especially across the indeterminate breaks between acts. And when the past is referred to at all, as in Vladimir's recollection of the Macon country (p. 39b) and Winnie's earlier "happy days," it appears strangely incongruent with the starkness of the present, its vividness alive only as a kind of linguistic echo, surrounding the stage moment itself with the blankness of temporal uncertainty. Words like *still, once, already,* and *was* reverberate through these plays as reminders of a past that (perhaps) once was, but the only changes that happen are for the worse, and the temporal realm that owns the stage is that of the present, empty of the developments and reversals from which plot is built. "Yes," Winnie notes, "something seems to have occurred, something has seemed to occur, and nothing has occurred, nothing at all" (*Happy Days,* p. 39).

This flattening of plot throws emphasis not only onto a dramatic present severe in its stasis, but also onto the actual contours of performance. Much as the curve of a single brush stroke foregrounds the painter's canvas, the relative absence of narrative detail renders Beckett's minimalist stage worlds more assertive in presence, thrusting them upon the audience's attention in their bareness. Individual props—carrot, turnip, handkerchief, three-legged toy dog, panama hat, toothbrush, parasol, gun—grow to fill the vacant space surrounding them, through an inert immediacy that focuses the audience's senses as well as the characters' on object and space. The absence of a structuring plot likewise throws attention onto physical activity: pulling off a boot, falling down, wheeling a chair around the perimeter of a room, peering through a magnifying glass, craning one's neck to see behind a mound. Imitating the visual gags of slapstick and pantomime, as well as more classically histrionic routines and poses, the characters in these three plays participate in an unprecedented gestural language, often addressing the audience less through the words they use than through the postures and motions they are forced to undergo, acting with the pattern of circus clowns and freezing gesture into physical image: Vladimir and Estragon stand like marionettes, "*motionless, arms dangling, heads sunk, sagging at the knees*" (p. 13b); the heads of Nagg and Nell "*strain towards each other, fail to meet, fall apart again*" (p. 14); and Winnie stares ahead, "*eyes front*" (p. 64). It is revealing of Beckett's dramatic craft as a whole, and his striking reliance on the gestural, that the London premier of *Endgame* featured, as afterpiece, the mime *Act without Words I*.

Beckett's dramatic art, then, draws attention away from the vicarious sphere of fictional narrative and onto the *mise-en-scène* itself. Even language, which normally transcends the theatrical moment in order to establish a narrative dimension, remains bound to the movements and objects of performance. Stripped to its syntactic minimum, language itself becomes gesture, the material of crosstalk routines, the occasion for rhetorical performance. As Lucky discharges his stream of words (". . . quaquaquaqua . . . ," p. 28b), as Estragon barks "Crritic!" (p. 48b), and as Winnie struggles throughout Act I to read and pronounce "genuine pure hog's setae," words revert to sound—the grunts, growls, and whines to which language's phonemes can finally be reduced. Beckett's stage is a harshly denotative one, where sights and sounds subvert all efforts to escape them and where all collapses, magnetically, within the pauses and silences that lie at the heart of Beckett's theater. In these silences, narrative devolves into the stage's presence, direct and inescapable, a presence that frames and isolates gestures of meaning.[2]

In short, Beckett's is a radical dramaturgy, concerning itself with the foundations—or "roots" (*radix*)—of theatrical art itself. The foregrounding of performance introduced in Beckett's full-length plays, and the subversions of conventional narrative through which this is accomplished, are sharpened even more powerfully within his shorter dramatic pieces, the "ends and odds" that have occupied Beckett's dramatic interest from the pivotal *Krapp's Last Tape* (1958) through *Play* (1963), *Come and Go* (1966), and the powerful late plays of the '70s and early '80s.[3] Focused and enriched by Beckett's parallel work within radio, film, and television, these plays reveal—in their radical distillation—a deepening awareness of the theatrical medium and of the nonnarrative power this medium can be made to exert upon its audience. Indeed, the plays since *Happy Days* represent a culmination of those moments of presence which we have isolated throughout this study—the grinning face of a Cambridgeshire stage devil, Shakespeare's moving statue, Lady Would-be's torrent of words, the haunting inertness of *Heartbreak House*'s terrace scene—extending such moments from the rhythmic pulses rippling through the longer plays, gaps of solitude and failure, into the very forefront of dramatic performance.

In keeping with Beckett's artistic minimalism, and his dramatic credo "that less is more,"[4] these plays represent further condensations of dramatic elements and a more ruthless paring away of theatrical inessentials. All pretense of conventional plot is abandoned, as the stage is made to display the barest of activities performed by the most reduced of characters: three heads speaking from urns; an illuminated face listening, opening and closing its eyes, smiling a toothless grin; a woman rocking; two men sitting at a table, one reading, the other listening. Framed by stillness, movement in these plays loses its strict connection with fictional development and serves, increasingly, as a component of stage imagery, both kinesthetic and visual. Beckett's detailed stage directions for these plays, and his growing role as director, reflect the deepening precision of his performance requirements, as he seeks to shape position, height, depth, angular relationship, sound, movement, and light with a mathematical precision that moves beyond blocking into choreography.[5] The spare stage directions of *Godot* (*"A country road. A tree. Evening."*) have become the precise specifications of lighting and voice for *Play*, the instructions concerning costume, movement, and light in *Rockaby* (1981)— "Incongruous frivolous head-dress set askew with extravagant trimmings to catch light when rocking" (p. 22)—and the stage diagrams for *Come and Go* and *What Where* (1983). The location and strength of spotlights, the volume of music, the timing of silence—traditionally subsidiary elements become determined and foregrounded to the point where they become agents within the theatrical action, constituting a performance "text" that rivals the more conventional linguistic one.

This concern with quintessences and with the plasticity of the *mise-en-scène*, locates Beckett within a theatrical tradition often overshadowed by the movements of modern drama outlined earlier: a tradition, extending backward through the verse drama of William Butler Yeats into the plays of Maeterlinck and the symbolists, which accords primacy to the theatrical image in its multisensory complexity and to poetic effects and resonances beyond the conceptual (Yeats' "reverie," for instance).[6] With innovative boldness, Beckett surpasses the earlier dramatists of this tradition in his reduction of action into activity, narrative into gesture, seemingly abandoning a poetics of narrative for a distilled poetics of space. But despite his elevation of the theatrical, Beckett's late plays stop short of pure performance poetry, and of more traditionally nondramatic forms like dance; indeed, they situate themselves squarely within a tradition of narrativity. They do so (in part) through the heightened narrative activity on the part of their characters, an activity that provides a surprising amount of story material to counterpoint the reduced narrative of the present. Here, too, Beckett's miniatures represent extensions of the earlier plays. Not only do Vladimir, Estragon, Hamm, and Winnie have continual recourse to the "past" of memory, they supplement the images bequeathed by this past with a conscious fictionalizing within the present. Hamm's story of the crawling man (recounted with an appropriately "narrative tone") and Winnie's tale of Milly represent central actions of *Endgame* and *Happy Days*, and they suggest the general importance that narrative activity holds for Beckett's characters, serving both as fictional refuge from the present's bleakness and as surrogate reality within which the anxieties of that present can be given indirect articulation.[7] "No, one can do nothing," Winnie states blankly (p. 39), her words weighed by the bracketing pauses, but her fortunes over two acts suggest otherwise: she can counterpoint the present's bareness with the outlines of narrative and fill the silences of being with the sound of words. In a more optimistic moment, Winnie consoles herself with the recourse that all of Beckett's characters share: "There is my story of course, when all else fails" (p. 54). Her story shares the protective function of such narrative activity throughout Beckett's plays; in the words of *That Time* (1976), "just one of those things you kept making up to keep the void out just another of those old tales to keep the void from pouring in on top of you the shroud" (p. 230).

As Beckett's dramatic action becomes increasingly constrained in the late plays, and as the remaining vestiges of plot are dispensed with, the stage becomes more insistently filled with storytelling voices, recounting events existing in the half-space between memory and fiction. Echoing the narrative performances of the earlier plays, the characters of Beckett's late drama often produce their own monologues, propelling the play through compulsive speech-acts as mechanical in their production as the linguistic babble of Lucky's speech: the endlessly recurrent fragments delivered by the urn-bound characters of *Play* and spliced together by the spotlight's merciless beam; the single speech, a tapestry woven with recurrent incident, in *A Piece of Monologue* (1979); or the "sad tale a last time told" (p. 287) by the Reader in *Ohio Impromptu* (1981). But just as frequently in these plays, the stage produces its own voices, given objectified existence from the stage figures who listen. Still in the mode of earlier Beckett, Krapp plays back the recorded statements of his previous selves, making possible a complex superimposition of voices and subjects within a broadly naturalistic context; by the production of *That Time,* though, the voices of an earlier self reverberate toward the Listener (and toward that other listener, the audience) from the darkness that surrounds them both. Liberated from the remaining constraints of naturalism, and encouraged (no doubt) by Beckett's intervening work with the dismbodied speech of radio, the late plays bring directly to the stage the voices that exist, in *Godot,* only within description:

> VLADIMIR: What do they say?
> ESTRAGON: They talk about their lives.
> VLADIMIR: To have lived is not enough for them.
> ESTRAGON: They have to talk about it.
> VLADIMIR: To be dead is not enough for them.
> ESTRAGON: It is not sufficient. (p. 40b)

The paradoxes of Beckett's art intensify within his later work, for the more inert the moment of performance, the more insistent the compulsion to counterpoint it with a stream of broken fiction. As Beckett foregrounds the stage, in other words, and its freedom from narrational voice, the stage increasingly echoes with voices of its own. The theater has seen no dramatist more fascinated by its material inertness, and yet none more drawn toward its vocal opportunities. The result, crystallized within his shorter dramatic pieces, is a profound juncture of narrative and presence, where each becomes luminous with the other's reflection and where the interface between comprehension and direct experience is revealed with unprecedented richness.[8] To enter the individual stage worlds of Beckett's late plays is to plumb the depths of narrative activity on the part of dramatic character and theater audience alike, and to inhabit those theatrical margins where cognitive boundaries verge on the unknown.

*   *   *

It is a measure of how far Beckett has traveled from the elements and categories of conventional drama that one often finds it hard to refer to the stark figures who people his late drama as "characters" at all. In few plays is this more evident than in the brilliant and disturbing *Not I* (1972), where character is reduced to a mouth, lit up within the darkness eight feet above stage level, and a hooded figure, motionless except for four raisings and lowerings of the arms—"a gesture" (Beckett tells us) "of helpless compassion" (p. 14). The play consists of Mouth's monologue: a series of phrases—some recurring, none longer than eight words—narrating fragments of incident and experience belonging to a protagonist known only as "She." One of the fixed points of this fractured narration is an incident in a meadow, when She underwent an unexplained trauma and found herself "in the dark," her ears filled with buzzing:

> . . . coming up to seventy . . . wandering in a field . . . looking aimlessly for cowslips . . . to make a ball . . . a few steps then stop . . . stare into space . . . then on . . . a few more . . . stop and stare again . . . so on . . . drifting around . . . when suddenly . . . gradually . . . all went out . . . all that early April morning light . . . and she found herself in the [. . .] found herself in the dark . . . and if not exactly . . . insentient . . . insentient . . . for she could still hear the buzzing . . . so-called . . . in the ears . . . and a ray of light came and went . . . came and went . . . such as the moon might cast . . . drifting . . . in and out of cloud . . . but so dulled . . . feeling . . . feeling so dulled . . . she did not know . . . what position she was in . . . imagine! . . . what position she was in! [. . .] whether standing . . . or sitting . . . or kneeling . . . or lying . . . . (p. 15)

At four points within the monologue, Mouth struggles to assert its independence from the narration—"what? . . . who? . . . no! . . . she!"—pausing briefly before continuing the stream of words. The play ends, as it opened, with ten seconds of Mouth's monologue spoken unintelligibly behind the curtain, acoustically connected with the onstage lines.

Like *Play, Not I* literalizes the dismemberment implicit throughout Beckett's work (one thinks of the directions in *Happy Days,* phrased to dissociate body parts from a central self: "head down," "eyes close," "hand reappears," "smile off").[9] But *Not I* extends its principle of disjunction beyond the physical dismemberment of the earlier play. As its title suggests, *Not I* dramatizes the dissociation of self from discourse, of the narrating subject from the subject of narration. In *Play,* the first-person "I" serves to attach the stories to the figures who narrate them, asserting the linkage common to personal history ("I said to him, Give her up. I swore by all I held most sacred," p. 148), and establishing a linguistic continuity between the past of story and the present of narration. Mouth's "vehement refusal to relinquish third person" (p. 14), on the other hand, drives a wedge between the speaking voice and what it recounts, severing the narrative stream from necessary connection with the present moment and its tortured speaker. Autobiography enters a problematically fictional realm, for without the secure point of a remembering "I" and its attendent subjectivity, memory shifts into the less personalized realm of story. Without this continuity between self and discourse, in other words, and the first person that guarantees it, the backward extension of the self in time effected through memory splits into the disparate worlds of story fragment and "mouth on fire" (p. 19).

But such dissociation is seldom complete with this playwright, whose favorite word is *perhaps.* The very vehemence of Mouth's refusal to surrender suggests a more fundamental, and more anxious, refusal to accept, and a powerful unspoken acknowledgement of the narrative's personal claim on its narrator. This sense of connection is underscored in the monologue itself, by the recurrent doubling of Mouth's onstage condition within the narrative fragments: references to the sudden darkness and the stream of words, to "whole body like gone . . . just the mouth" (p. 19) and "sudden urge to . . . tell" (p. 22), and to a life that even in mobility was characterized by self-enveloping loneliness. It is this continuity which Mouth rejects, for acceptance of *I* would force the self-confrontation (and self-disclosure) feared by all Beckett's characters—by the protagonist of *Film,* for instance, who carefully maneuvers throughout his cinematic world in order to protect his eye/I.[10] First-person acknowledgment of the fractured life pieced together by its monologue would implicate Mouth in a dual subjectivity and force ownership both of the fictional life that was never lived and of the absence embodied in this "godforsaken hole" (p. 14). Mouth, then, plays the Beckettian game with narrative, wearying of its incessant demands ("and the whole brain begging . . . something begging in the brain . . . begging the mouth to stop . . . pause a moment . . . if only for a moment," p. 20), compulsively editing its details, but equally dependent upon its broken contours, which blanket the present with the pretense of fiction. Auditor's "gesture of helpless compassion" occurs in each of the momentary pauses, but Mouth's monologue spills out, undiminished, an endless evasion of silence.

Like all the figures in Beckett's late plays, Mouth shares a narrative bondage with the playwright's prose characters, who are compelled to narrate, in part, by the printed text's self-contained linguistic world. But although a number of Beckett's prose pieces have been adapted for theater, the stage remains a separate world, different in its opportunities for linguistic exploration. Like the other late plays, *Not I* transfers vocal narrative activity into the theatrical medium and, in so doing, draws the audience into the world of narrative creation and relinquishment, forcing a conflict of the cognitive and the experiential that is uniquely the theater's province. In its attempts to naturalize this play's searing imagery, to transform its strangeness into comprehensibility, the audience participates in narrative's broader efforts to structure performance and in the failure of these efforts on Beckett's stage.

For the audience, too, is implicated in the disjunctions that characterize Mouth's narrative activity. Within the monologue that contains the play's story clues, narrative is disjoined from itself, fragmentary and incomplete. One can locate individual episodes in Mouth's monologue, accorded relative stability by their recurrence within the vocal stream: among them, the moment of birth; a courtroom scene; an incident of compulsive talking inside a supermarket; a time in "Croker's Acres"; and the traumatic moment in an unnamed field. Among these moments glimmer other moments, recounted images and feelings, fleeting indices of past time. But unlike Wordsworth's "spots of time" or the vivid products of Proust's involuntary memory, these details of memory/narrative provide no unity; fragments of a life, they are little more than isolated snapshots, sharing a minimum of continuity, and the gaps between them have at least as much impact as the reduced images they provide. Mouth's linguistic snapshots are poorly developed, suggesting pivotal experiences ("just as the odd time . . . in her life . . . when clearly intended to be having pleasure . . . she was in fact . . . having none . . . not the slightest," p. 16) but leaving the precise contours of these experiences, and their connection with other experiences, obscured within the monologue's splintered temporality. Unlike Prospero's narration to Miranda in *The Tempest*'s first act, which provides a past to contextualize the present, its details harmonizing within the audience's efforts to integrate them, the narrative fragments of *Not I* resist both clarification and integration, forcing audience comprehension into tentativeness and uncertainty. Was She raped in the field? The victim of a stroke? As Bam's Voice remarks to conclude *What Where*—a play whose title sums up the narrative problem in a play like *Not I*—"Make sense who may" (p. 316).

The uncertainty resulting from Mouth's narrative, and its structural disjunctions, is heightened by this speaker's insistent disowning. For the refusal to admit the first person into the narrative sphere has consequences, not only for Mouth's self-confrontation, but for the audience's own engagement with the theatrical present. By asserting a link between speaker and utterance, "I" constitutes a linchpin within the stage/narrative continuum, representing a point of contact between the linguistic projections of story and the physical immediacy of the stage. Its banishment from Mouth's speech accordingly severs a crucial connection between the dramatic and theatrical planes, releasing each into a strange and jarring autonomy. The doubling of details within story and stage image suggest teasing continuities, but the connections are inexact: the theatrical "beam" of light is not "flickering on and off" (p. 20), nor, at eight feet above stage level, could Mouth be recognizably "standing . . . or sitting . . . or kneeling . . . or lying." An imperfect match, Mouth's narrative both meets and deflects the visual dimensions of the theatrical present, maintaining a state of tension with a present boldly independent of subordinating outlines. Thus objectified, narrative stands on its own as a stage element alongside all others.

This disjunction between story and stage, between the narrative world of She and the more immediate world of Mouth and Auditor, liberates the latter in its visceral immediacy. Those elements within Mouth's monologue that do correlate with the stage serve, not surprisingly, to underscore its physical presence: its darkness, the volume and pace of its sounds, the movement of its speaking lips, its inquisitorial beam of light. The narrative stream, in other words, indirectly foregrounds those components of performance most physically autonomous from narrative, least available to comprehension's abstractions. Though Beckett's minimally descriptive names (Mouth, Auditor) are available only within the stage directions, the word *mouth* appears six times in the play's monologue, along with references to the tongue, lips, jaws, and cheeks, and to the physical process of speaking. Such references bear significance within the narrative sphere, as experiences of a She intensely aware of her vocal activity, but they refer more immediately to the actual, non-narrative presence of a mouth onstage, visually independent of the monologue's words. Beckett has taken pains to establish this independence, of Mouth and of the stage as a whole, locating both Mouth and Auditor unnaturally high above the stage floor, sculpting the stage area with darkness and a starkly narrow range of colors (grey, white, red), rendering the play's spare movement rigid and mechanical. The presence of Auditor, witness to Mouth's tortured monologue and one of a long line of Beckettian listeners,[11] contributes to the stage present's narrative impenetrability. Mouth's monologue contains repeated references to the act of listening, but these revolve largely around "her" own perception of the "stream of words." External figures who listen within these narrative fragments do so with suspicion, abhorrence, or neglect, not "helpless compassion." There is, in other words, no narrative link to explicate the presence of this strangely hooded figure, and although critics have offered various explanations concerning this figure's relationship to the Mouth and its monologue (audience surrogate, prompter/censor, confessor), the play itself leaves this relationship unspecified. Even the concept of *relationship* is suspect, given this strange stage configuration: in the theater, it is not necessarily clear that Auditor *listens*, much less that this listening is compassionate, and although Auditor faces Mouth, responding gesturally to the monologue's overt points of evasion, Beckett has given no indication that Mouth, for its part, necessarily faces Auditor (the monologue itself avoids the second person as scrupulously as it does the first: this play could, with justification, also be titled *Not You*). Mouth speaks into an ambiguous space of uncertain address, seemingly unaware of Auditor's existence, and with the differences of lighting ("*faintly lit*" white skin versus "*fully faintly lit*" black djellaba) the two figures appear to inhabit distinct dimensions, vaguely "alone together" (*Ohio Impromptu*, p. 286). For all the interaction between them, Mouth might as well be a screen image or holographic projection.

Mouth's voice itself partakes of the stage's immediacy, battering the imaginative world of narrative through the sheer force of its own delivery. Even the most alert of the play's spectators has attested to the immense difficulty involved in comprehending Mouth's monologue, with its already fragmentary phrases blurred by the speed with which they are spoken ("and now this stream . . . not catching the half of it . . . not the quarter . . . no idea . . . what she was saying . . . imagine!" p. 18). In a revealing instruction, Beckett told Jessica Tandy, the actress who played the demanding role of Mouth in the play's premiere, "I am not unduly concerned with intelligibility. I hope the piece may work on the nerves of the audience, not its intellect." [12] As elsewhere in Beckett, the result of such calculated barrage is a continual reversion of sense to sound, as a word will do if repeated past the point of meaning, and of the imaginative realm of narrative into the physical properties of vocal utterance. The play begins and ends with incomprehensibility, as the voice drones behind the curtain, but incomprehensibility represents a continual pressure during the play's onstage performance, for Mouth's monologue etches grooves onto the audience's nerves less through what it signifies than through how it sounds. Subjected to this performance, the audience is forced to lock itself in attention, "straining to hear . . . the odd word . . . make some sense of it" (p. 21)—but such efforts are bound to fail, for Mouth's verbal stream presents a cognitive overrun, rendering speech itself a subversion of narrativity.

The audience's experience of *Not I* involves a fading in and out of narrative, for the details of a story/past are dwarfed by the enveloping darkness and crushed by the force of Mouth's vocal performance. As Enoch Brater observes of *That Time* (which Beckett considered a "brother to *Not I*"), "Our attempts to order the bits and pieces, to place them in a hierarchy, a chronology, and a progression, lead nowhere but back to the images themselves." [13]

It is here, in the imagery of the stage, that *Not I* works on its audience's nerves, as narrative and presence alternate with the uncanny continuity of an optical illusion. The play assaults the senses, animates its spectator as it does its anatomically diminished protagonist, and assures a residual experience more direct than the vicarious satisfaction of story or the abstract resolution of "meaning." Peter Brook, we recall, has argued that a powerful theatrical event "scorches on to the memory an outline, a taste, a trace, a smell—a picture." Beckett's theatrical minimalism has, as its goal, the creation of such traces, and it achieves this effect in *Not I* through the joint offering and subversion of narrative context. When the play is over, it leaves its powerfully reduced and fragmented world as its scorching "silhouette": story images freed of outline, a piercing stage image, and the play's penetrating voice, which drones on within the audience's mind, in a kind of auditory "afterimage" or echo, long after it has ceased in the theater: "all the time the buzzing [. . .] dull roar in the skull" (p. 16).

Not I foregrounds the static image, etched into three-dimensional stage space with pictorial immobility, and the rapid pulsing of a stage voice that fills the surrounding darkness with its mechanical urgency. *Footfalls* (1976) introduces and shapes a slightly different set of theatrical variables: patterned movement, tonal vibration, and a set of stage polarities (movement/stillness, light/dark, sound/silence) between which the play gently modulates. If *Not I* constitutes a sensory and cognitive assault, *Footfalls* encourages relinquishment, a surrender to the shadings and the emptiness that exert such pull in Beckett's late drama. Through its modulations of vocal performance, the play explores the status of stage voice, the narrative demarcations it variously suggest, and the performance environment to which it finally yields.

Like *Not I*, *Footfalls* represents a theatrical condensation, its stage world reduced to the barest of elements. Its central figure is a woman named "May"—"*dishevelled grey hair, worn grey wrap hiding feet, trailing*" (p. 42)—who traverses the stage along a central strip in careful, measured paces (nine steps both directions), turning at each end and occasionally halting to face the audience. The lighting, dim throughout, fades upward toward the darkness surrounding this acting area: "*strongest at floor level, less on body, least on head.*" In remarks on the play to its first German actress, Beckett has stressed the centrality of this moving image—"the walking up and down"—to the play's conception, claiming, in fact, that "the text, the words were only built up around this picture." [14] One of Beckett's closest dramatic approximation to the structure of a chamber piece—he himself has refered to the play as "chamber music"—*Footfalls* is divided into four movements, the first three framed by a single chime note reverberating through the theater darkness, the final movement a brief image (fifteen seconds) of the empty stage, faintly lit, "*no trace of May*" (p. 49). [15]

Words may have constituted later additions to the play's visual text, but they are nonetheless central to its narrative and theatrical impact. Like *Not I*, *Footfalls* undermines the linguistic foundation of conventional drama, through which words link performance and narrative, identifying speaker and establishing the conceptual world of dramatic fiction. *Not I* achieves this subversion through its severance of discourse from speaker and through its fierce pressing of language into the drone of stage sound. *Footfalls* mounts its attack from within the convention of dramatic speech, relocating language in an ambiguous half-world where its status as utterance (and the status of its utterances) become, like the play's eerie central figure, mountingly indeterminate. The play's four movements play distinct variations upon the relationship of voice to stage, problematizing the play's linguistic and narrative groundwork, releasing both into a shadowy swirl of possible meaning and endowing the environment of performance with a complex, richly ambiguous autonomy. In the first movement, curtain and light come up on a conversation between the pacing woman and an offstage voice. Each identifies the other: the woman calls the offstage voice "Mother," and it responds "Yes, May" (pp. 42–43). Punctuated by a striking number of pauses (thirty within two pages of text), their spare dialogue echoes the modified naturalism of Beckett's earliest drama: May is Clov to a Hamm now invalided offstage, and their interchange recalls *Endgame*'s repetitive, symbiotic dependecy:

> M: Would you like me to inject you . . . again?
> V: Yes, but it is too soon.
>
> *Pause.*
>
> M: Would you like me to change your position . . . again?
> V: Yes, but it is too soon. (p. 43)

Narrative relationship makes itself available to comprehension here with an ease unusual in Beckett's late work: mother (age "eighty-nine, ninety") and daughter ("forties"), the latter pacing with an urgency that the former can detect even in her sleep, externalizing through these steps an inner preoccupation: "Will you never have done . . . revolving it all? [. . .] In your poor mind. (*Pause.*) It all. (*Pause.*) It all" (p. 44). Through such detail, and despite occasional dissonances (the onstage figure looks closer in age to the old Woman in *Rockaby* than to a woman in her forties), the present acquires a relatively secure narrative context, its strangeness largely naturalized by the dialogue and the dramatic situation it describes.

After the dissolve into darkness, and the faint chime's echo, movement two begins with May standing still, face front, with the offstage voice now all that is heard. Though Beckett, directing the play in performance, has specified the theatrical duration of this (and subsequent) breaks, the duration in terms of dramatic time is left indeterminate, producing the temporal disjunction evident between acts of *Godot* and *Happy Days*. In keeping with this disjunction, the relationship between figure and voices has also shifted. The offstage voice now describes the woman's position, and her movements when she resumes her steps ("See how still she stands, how stark, with her face to the wall. [. . .] But let us watch her move, in silence," p. 45). It recalls May's childhood pacing, establishing such potentially expository material through narrative and through narrated dialogue: "The mother: The motion alone is not enough? May: No, Mother, the motion alone is not enough, I must hear the feet, however faint they fall" (pp. 45–46). But though this voice is recognizable as the offstage voice ("Mother") of the earlier movement, and though it shares the point of view of the mother within its narrative, the voice now surrounds the stage, attaining a disembodied omniscience it seemed to lack in the earlier dialogue. Moreover, while (like Mouth) it never identifies itself as "I" within its narrative, it employs the first person, at the monologue's opening, to identify itself with the walking figure: "I walk here now. (*Pause.*) Rather I come and stand." But despite such suggestions that the voice is now a kind of verbal pacing within the stage figure's "poor mind," even this identification is left tantalizingly insecure: Beckett removed explicit indications that this was the case from the dramatic text in revision; left the voice a separate one, to be performed by another actress; and specified in production that the actress playing May was to accompany parts of "the mother's text" by twice moving her lips, a gesture that both owns and disowns the actual speech.[16] Through these carefully conflicting suggestions, Beckett has left the voice in the indeterminate region that has increasingly come to constitute his dramatic territory: a space that is at once subjective and objective, internal and external, recalling the hauntingly externalized inner voice of the television play *Eh Joe* (1966) and anticipating the vocal indeterminacy of *Rockaby* and the television play *but the clouds* (1977).[17]

Movement three presents a third and final stage configuration of figure and voice. Standing still, save for brief spans of pacing, May assumes the narrative tone of Hamm and Winnie, Henry in the radio play *Embers* (1959) and the Reader in *Ohio Impromptu* (1981), recounting the "Sequel" of a fictionalized story of a girl named "Amy" and her mother, "Mrs. Winter." In a voice now clearly her own, May becomes a taleteller, recounting incidents from the life of her protagonist with the formulaic constructions of literary narrative: "But many also were the nights when" (p. 46) and "Old Mrs. Winter, whom the reader will remember" (p. 47). Yet, as with all of Beckett's narrators, the story she tells bears connections with herself, connections which emerge through May's reactions to her tale (her voice breaks at one point in her narrative) and through thinly disguised similarities with the play's earlier details. As a number of critics have pointed out, *Amy* represents an anagram for *May*, just as the fictional *Millie* is made to echo *Winnie* in *Happy Days*. May's story displays more direct connection with its narrator, and the events we have already been told, than the often more covert tales of Beckett's other protagonists, and its details (in conjunction with the others) nearly add up to that rare thing in Beckett, a life.

But, as Beckett notes, what this figure displays on stage is something much less than a life: "A life, which didn't begin as a life, but which was just there, as a thing."[18] The play's three movements, each highlighting a narrative mode and a relationship between voice and figure that Beckett has exploited elsewhere, work upon each other in a way that undermines all three, calling into

question the epistemological basis of the clarity that each seemingly provides. The dialogue between Amy and Mrs Winter that
the shadowy figure recounts as part of her narrative sequel echoes
(and problematizes) the dialogic form in the monologue of movement two as well as the actual dialogue of movement one; the
offstage voice's identification with May in movement two makes
us wonder about its counting of her steps in movement one; and
the phrases that echo or recur in two or more movements ("Yes,
May"/"Yes, Mother," "It all"/"It all") establish haunting scenic
equivalences. As a result, each movement is infused with narrative
modes not its own, and the play as a whole becomes a wintry
fantasia in which subject and object, mother and daughter, past
and story merge through complex, partial superimpositions. Is the
mother there? Was she ever there? Where can the line be drawn
between truth and fantasy? "Where is she, it may be asked" (p.
45). In the swirl of uncertainty that surrounds this narrative material, attention rests on the figure onstage, increasingly reduced
to a pair of feet in the diminishing stage light, alternately moving
and standing still. And as the light dims, this figure in her tattered
clothes seems a kind of ghost, her voice increasingly independent
of her darkened face, a precarious presence amidst the echo of
voices, vanishing to a memory in the fourth movement's emptiness. In this final emptiness, even May's existence is called into
doubt, as she enters the nowhere realm into which the offstage
voice has already vanished. Through its shifts and vanishings, and
its echoic repetitions, *Footfalls* provides an eerie stage equivalent
to the words of *A Piece of Monologue:* "Nothing stirring. Faintly
stirring. Thirty thousand nights of ghosts beyond. Beyond that
black beyond. Ghost light. Ghost nights. Ghost rooms. Ghost
graves. Ghost . . . he all but said ghost loved ones" (p. 269). Beckett himself described May's "faint tangle of pale grey tatters" (p.
47) as "the costume of a ghost." [19]

The play's final movement is, in many ways, its most resonant. Barely visible, the stage stands empty of figure and voice, the
only "events" the movement of light and the pulsing vibration of
a chime note dying out. With its final image of emptiness, and its
closing silence, the last movement represents a powerful and unusual end for Beckett, since nothingness in his plays usually constitutes a point both feared and desired, but one which indicates

within the asymptotic movement of decay, a zero-point never to be reached. The irreversible narrowing that characterizes Beckettian drama—Pozzo's blindness, Winnie's reduced mobility, the diminishment of bodies to heads upon urns, the lessening of Auditor's gesture—approaches stasis, but however large this condition looms it remains elusive, momentarily touched in the pauses and silences but finally unattainable. If Beckett's slender dramatic action is an arrow, it is Zeno's, moving by halves, doomed never to pierce the emptiness toward which it is weakly directed. In its own diminishments—light, movement, two voices to one—*Footfalls* represents one of the few of Beckett's plays to reach this still point, and to attain the absence that elsewhere seems so immanent yet so remote. "*Chime even a little fainter still. Pause for echoes. Fade up to even a little less still on strip. No trace of May. Hold fifteen seconds. Fade out. Curtain.*" (p. 49). In this stunning visual conclusion, and the stillness that envelopes the play's final chime, *Footfalls* achieves a point of closure at which the activities of narrative and action, so richly problematic throughout the preceding movements, cease. It is the moment that Hamm longs for, and that—unaware of Clov's motionless presence—he thinks he has reached at the end of *Endgame*: "Moments for nothing, now as always, time was never and time is over, reckoning closed and story ended" (p. 83). The rest, says Hamlet, is silence.

But this silence, though empty of all the sounds and movements that have filled it to this point, is anything but an *absence,* as the word is commonly understood. The object of a room full of eyes, the faintly lit stage floor asserts depth and presence, and the closing light illuminates a stage presence all the more powerful for the diminishing world we have seen it contain. The revolvings of figure and voice yield to the performance field that has supported them, a space that constitutes their theatrical ground of being and that asserts (in this final image) the essence of *mise-en-scène.* By boldly closing with an image of the stage, Beckett brings to the forefront that immediacy that is the ground of all drama, liberating the presence that we have pursued through all the plays we have studied. In this way, *Footfalls* offers a different conception of the stage than *Not I.* In the earlier play, the stage represents the site of a twin alienation. On one hand, it threatens the annihilating silence of self-exposure, when being is faced with its nullity and stares into the void; within the play's monologue, this silence is imaged as incapacity and stasis, and the rest it offers (presided over by the mysteriously shrouded Auditor?) is a rest like death, "sweet silent as the grave" (p. 18). At the same time, the stage effects a continual deflection of this silence through a barrage of unintelligibility, the steady drone of the impenetrable that nonetheless teases with its fragments of sense. The play hurries around silence, rolls over it, but the silence it offers is most evident in the urgency with which it is evaded.

Footfalls reveals the other dimension of the Beckettian stage, the presence that counterpoints its anxiety of absence. The play's closing movement may represent the silence of death, but this silence is curiously full, textured with the afterimages and aftersounds of the preceding action, its faintly lit space carved out of the theater's darkness. The word *again,* which appears five times in the opening movement, is replaced by the word *still,* which recurs five times throughout the rest of the play (in addition to four times in Beckett's stage directions). The words are close in meaning, but the shift is nonethless pronounced, for the mechanical repetitiveness of the former (a less urgent version of the *on* that drives *Not I*) gives way to the latter's sense of motionlessness and persistence. Telescoped by this shift in words is the emergence of an almost palpable emptiness, less the destruction of being (perhaps) than its source, powerful in the stage's halflight.

> Will you never have done . . . revolving it all? (*Pause.*) It?
> (*Pause.*) It all. (*Pause.*) In your poor mind. (*Pause.*)
> It all. (*Pause.*) It all.
>
> *Pause. Fade out on strip. All in darkness.*
>
> *Pause.* (p. 48)

The words *It all* echo the haunted revolving which has joined the voices and details of the first three movements, but they also suggest a transcendence of this repetition in a muted acceptance. Fading beyond the borders of light and sound, these words point to a nothing strangely like everything, an ontological and theatrical *tabula rasa,* the "dark whole" of *A Piece of Monologue* (p. 268) or "that MINE" of nothing in *but the clouds* (p. 261).

Footfalls is a play of shadings: of light into darkness, of movement into immobility, of a musical note into the silence where its vibrations cease. As in Japanese landscape painting, such shadings contribute a striking presence to the regions they penetrate and to the blank spaces they contain. At the center of Beckett's dramaturgical shadings is the shading of narrative into the "empty space" from which it arises and to which, with every closing curtain, it inevitably returns. Beckett's roots are the theater's roots, and in the dramatic distillation of a play like *Footfalls*, we find a crystalline image of theatrical duality. If Beckett dramatizes the limitations of narrative, its evasions and its failed transformations, he does so to uncover its source, in a medium so actual that it impedes, in the end, all attempts to transform it into the "other realm" of dramatic illusion. If Beckett dramatizes the human mind projecting itself through narrative, and forces his audience to share this activity, he also dramatizes its surrender, illuminating the stage as a space where narrative activity must, and can, finally cease. In so doing, he allows the theater its paired voices in the fullness of their delicate interplay: the voice of its fictions, and the equally reverberating voice of its silence.

Afterword: Masha Reading

Of the six figures who crowd the stage in the opening minutes of Chekhov's *The Three Sisters,* perhaps the most remarkable is Masha, the character who says the least. Dressed in black, "her hat on her lap," Masha engages in that surprisingly rare stage activity, "reading a book." Characters in drama allude to books, even perceive the world through books, but—with occasional exceptions such as Faustus, Hedvig, Ellie Dunn, and the Reader of Beckett's *Ohio Impromptu*—they seldom attempt to read these books onstage. The living room of James Tyrone's summer house contains two bookcases, and its volumes "have the look of having been read and reread," [1] but the reading of these books occurs off-stage before the dramatic action as it is crafted for performance and outside the setting we are given to watch. In the multiactioned world of theatrical performance, it would seem, there are few activities deemed less stageworthy.

A moment's thought suggests why, since the activity of reading is flatly nonhistrionic: motionless, time-consuming, solitary, and usually silent in its interior projections. Through Masha, then, Chekhov establishes a counterpoint in keeping with the larger ironies of *The Three Sisters:* contrasting the scene's ensemble structure with a point of absent self-enclosure embodied in one of the most self-involved of all activities, the act of reading. But Chekhov also creates a more explicitly formal counterpoint, one that reverberates across the border between performance and play. For Masha reading is witnessed by an audience watching, and the space that opens up between the two is a generic gap between print and performance, containing the dissonance of these disparate realms. Her private participation in the world of Pushkin—glimpsed only through the mesmerizing line she recites ("'A green oak by a curved seashore, upon that oak a golden chain . . . upon that oak a golden chain,'" p. 240)—is gently confronted, in Chekhov's theater, by the world of which she is a part: actual, alive, unfolding for an audience that approaches it under different terms and with decidedly different participation. Masha may absent herself into the realm of imaginative fiction, but she is acutely present within another realm, where the printed page is "translated" (to quote Peter Quince)[2] into the materials of impersonation, and where fiction is constituted within immediacy. In her private abstraction, Masha reading offers a visual counterpoint to the medium that, quite literally, embodies her.

It is this difference that the present study has sought to explore, as well as its implications for audience response and narrative form. As Masha sits on stage, she and the other figures inhabit a medium complex in its signals and nonliterary in many of its effects, a medium characterized by multiple channels of address. As a means of understanding this medium and the responses it occasions, this study has investigated dramatic narrative, grounding itself in the belief that narrative constitutes not only a feature of dramatic form, but one of the basic orientations of audience to play and one of the most fundamental activities by which audience appropriates *mise-en-scène*. Our approach has highlighted cognitive process because the audience's intellectual effort to endow performance with narrative structure constitutes one of its most acute forms of participation. Drama explores the range and boundaries of cognition, engaging the most fundamental activities by which the human subject generates coherence. That such activities are often taxed in the theater, pressured by a medium that eludes formulation, does not diminish their rewards: in performance—with its relentless forward movement, its surprises and reversals—narrative comprehension becomes a form of cognitive play, rife with anxieties and triumphs, a kind of jeu d'esprit. To explore this dimension of dramatic narrative is, as we have seen, to abandon for good the notion of a passive spectator and to relocate the audience at a formidable nexus of creativity, where it meets the patterns of performance with structures and formulations of its own.

At the same time, as we have seen, dramatic narrative continually reveals the performance dimensions outside its structures, from which it derives and to which it is bound in one of dramatic performance's central dualities. For narrative in the theater is not the thing itself, and it represents only one way in which the performance artifact addresses the perceiving subject. Dramatic narrative always risks surrender: to the moment, to the stage, to a world that reaches outside the realm of fiction. In the preceding plays, we have watched narrative yield, at various points and in varying degrees, to performance itself, which asserts its claim to actuality against the mediations of fiction. Guided by the fortunes of comprehension, we have glimpsed a range of meanings this performance moment has been accorded at different points in dramatic history. In the moralities, the unmediated stage was a problematically ethical arena, the source of a power to distract at once entertaining and morally disruptive. In the silences of *The Winter's Tale,* its moments freed from the lines of time, this presence was a redeeming one, a physical embodiment of grace's power to transform. In Jonson's exacting dramaturgy, the moment of performance asserted itself less benignly, reflecting in its bareness the devastating vulnerability of the self confronting its cognitive and perceptual limits; while in Shaw it embodied not only the intoxication of self-liberation, but also the frightening stasis of disillusionment. In *Not I* and *Footfalls,* we discovered powerful yet elusive revelations of presence, discerning within the distillations of Beckett's theatrical art both the emptiness of the self beneath its linguistic masks and the paradoxical fullness of an absence finally confronted.

Walter Benjamin has observed that "there is no story for which the question as to how it continued would not be legitimate,"[3] and his words are equally true for the story that this study has attempted to tell. There are other plays to consider, other explorations of the interface between narrative and the stage yet to be undertaken. There is also more that needs to be known about the specific features of audience response manipulated by theatrical narration. We need to know more about the processes of comprehension by which audience approaches play—both how they are structured and how they are subverted—and the ways in which these processes mediate between audience and play. As a corollary to this, we need to pursue the connections between cognitive and other, more directly physiological responses to the stage: the realm of images, sounds, traces beneath discursive memory that the theater, so demanding on linear temporal integration, clearly engages. For all the insights of dramatic and performance theory, aesthetics, and theater arts, the psychology of reception, and its implications for dramatic form, are still far too little understood.

In the meantime, we must continue the peculiar discipline that the study of drama requires of us, a discipline from which Masha, in her poetic reverie, is free: learning more fully how to approach the text of a play with an awareness of theatrical experience in its nonliterary modes of actuality. Only in this way will dramatic narrative escape its Aristotelian box and reassume its place within the phenomenological field of performance. In the theater, "story" is vastly more than an encumbrance, an element for parody and distortion, or a recourse (in Winnie's words) "when all else fails." As we have seen, the operations occasioned by dramatic narrative are complex, and its tensions are richly theatrical ones. To speak of dramatic narrativity apart from performance is to rob spectacle of fiction, and plot of its theatrical body. As with all dualities, each is a means to the other. Narrative is a mask of presence, and (as Pirandello reminds us) the theater's masks are naked ones.

Notes

Introduction

1. William Gillette, Introduction (1916) to "How to Write a Play," in *Papers on Playmaking*, ed. Brander Matthews (New York: Hill and Wang, 1957), p. 80.
2. Antonin Artaud, *The Theater and Its Double*, trans. Mary Caroline Richards (New York: Grove Press, 1958), pp. 76, 82.
3. Aristotle, *Poetics*, XXVI. *Aristotle's Poetics: A Translation and Commentary for Students of Literature*, translated by Leon Golden, commentary by O. B. Hardison, Jr. (Englewood Cliffs, N.J.: Prentice-Hall, 1968; Tallahassee: University Presses of Florida, 1981), p. 51. Unless otherwise noted, quotations from the *Poetics* are taken from this edition.
4. Quoted in Eric Bentley, *The Life of the Drama* (New York: Atheneum, 1964), p. 18. Bentley discusses the prejudice against plot on pp. 18–25.
5. Bernard Beckerman, "Theatrical Perception," *Theatre Research International*, n.s., 4 (1978–79), p. 163.
6. I have adapted the concept of "standing in" from Bruce Wilshire, *Role Playing and Identity: The Limits of Theatre as Metaphor* (Bloomington: Indiana University Press, 1982).
7. Bert O. States, *Great Reckonings in Little Rooms: On the Phenomenology of Theater* (Berkeley and Los Angeles: University of California Press, 1985), p. 20.
8. Émile Zola, letter; rpt. (without date) in *Papers on Playmaking*, p. 92.
9. Shaw, Preface to *Plays Unpleasant* (1898), in *Collected Plays with Their Prefaces* (London: Bodley Head, 1970–74), I: 28.
10. Thornton Wilder, "Some Thoughts on Playwriting," in *The Intent of the Artist*, ed. Augusto Centeno (Princeton: Princeton University Press, 1941), pp. 83–98; rpt. in *Playwrights on Playwriting*, ed. Toby Cole (New York: Hill and Wang, 1961), p. 114.

11. Malcolm Bradbury, "Towards a Poetics of Fiction: 1) An Approach through Structure," *Novel,* 1 (1967–68), p. 52. Susanne K. Langer states that "literature need not be made out of the author's memories (though it may be), nor does it necessarily present events explicitly *as* somebody's memories (though it may do so), but the *mode* in which events appear is the mode of completed experience, i. e. of the past" (*Feeling and Form* [New York: Charles Scribner's Sons, 1953], p. 264).

12. Tzvetan Todorov, *The Poetics of Prose,* trans. Richard Howard (Ithaca, N.Y.: Cornell University Press, 1977), p. 26. Gérard Genette correlates the presence of a narrator in his or her narrative with that of "every subject of an enuciating in his [or her] enunciated statement" (*Narrative Discourse: An Essay in Method,* trans. Jane E. Lewin [Ithaca: Cornell University Press, 1980], p. 244).

13. An additional word about this study's protagonist: the audience. Of all those involved in performance, none presents more problems for the theorist of drama. Elusive in its activities, idiosyncratic in its responses, comprised of countless variables—cultural, historical, economic, and personal, what we call "an audience" stands as divided within itself as it does from its counterparts in other times and places. To address questions of audience response, therefore, is to enter a complex territory equally the domain of psychology, physiology, and sociology, and to seek to describe a formidable nexus of elements and activities. It is also to employ a figure whose literary counterpart has been assaulted on a number of theoretical grounds in discussions of reader response (for a discussion of the theoretical and methodological issues raised by audience-response criticism, see Una Chaudhuri, "The Spectator in Drama/Drama in the Spectator," *Modern Drama,* 27 [1984], 281–98). But the problematic dimension of audience response, and its numerous variables, does not diminish its centrality to the theatrical interaction, or its often remarkable stability, especially on the level of cognition. The history of theatrical response, as we have been able to reconstruct it, suggests that basic mental operations, as well as specific conflicts between conceptual and nonconceptual features of audience response, retain a surprising consistency across ages and cultures: Ben Jonson, as we shall see, attacks his audience for the same cognitive difficulties that confront modern audiences of his plays. Borrowing Roger Gross' distinction between *hypothetical* audience response ("what an interpreter believes an ideal audience would experience") and *functional* audience meaning ("what actual individuals *do* experience in particular exposures to the play/script, a

'private' meaning which can never be fully known by an interpreter *or* the person experiencing it"), this study will theorize a representative audience in order to suggest the mental parameters within which dramatic narrative achieves its cognitive manipulations (see Roger Gross, *Understanding Playscripts: Theory and Method* [Bowling Green, Ohio: Bowling Green University Press, 1974], p. 82). Variables of history and culture are necessarily minimized, but they are by no means precluded by this study's stress on the more immediately cognitive dimensions of response; modification of its propositions in light of specific variation will, I hope, strengthen their broader outlines. For a discussion of the "model spectator" as a function of "the strategies within the [theatrical] text, the manner of interpretation anticipated by the text and written into it," see Marco De Marinis, "Dramaturgy of the Spectator," trans. Paul Dwyer, *The Drama Review,* 31 (1987), pp. 102–6.

14. Peter Brook, *The Empty Space* (Middlesex: Penguin Books, 1968), p. 11.

15. The centrality of cognition to narrative is etymologically grounded, since the word *narrative* derives from the Latin *gnarus,* or "knowing."

16. States, *Great Reckonings in Little Rooms,* p. 46. While the present study is not strictly phenomenological in method, its exploration of the audience-stage relationship raises issues of phenomenological pertinence.

17. George Meredith, "On the Idea of Comedy and of the Uses of the Comic Spirit: An Essay on Comedy" (1877), in *The Idea of Comedy: Ben Jonson to George Meredith,* ed. W. K. Wimsatt (Englewood Cliffs, N.J.: Prentice-Hall, 1969), p. 275; Francis Fergusson, *The Idea of a Theater* (Princeton: Princeton University Press), p. 178.

18. For a semiological discussion of dramatic time, see Anne Ubersfeld, *Lire le théâtre* (Paris: Éditions sociales, 1977), pp. 203–45 ("Le Théâtre et le Temps").

19. Bernard Beckerman, Foreword to *The Dynamics of Drama: Theory and Method of Analysis* (New York: Drama Book Specialists, 1979).

20. References to Shakespeare throughout this study are taken from *The Riverside Shakespeare,* textual ed. G. Blakemore Evans (Boston: Houghton Mifflin, 1974).

Chapter One

1. Langer, *Feeling and Form*, p. 264.
2. Samuel Johnson, "Preface to Shakespeare" (1765), in *Samuel Johnson's Literary Criticism*, ed. R. D. Stock (Lincoln: University of Nebraska Press, 1974), p. 152. Johnson, interestingly enough, based his defense of dramatic illusion on an essentially literary conception of drama: "A play read, affects the mind like a play acted. It is therefore evident, that the action is not supposed to be real, and it follows that between the acts a longer or shorter time may be allowed to pass, and that no more account of space or duration is to be taken by the author of a drama, than by the reader of a narrative, before whom may pass in an hour the life of a hero, or the revolutions of an empire" (pp. 154–55).
3. In his study of the formal development of modern drama, Peter Szondi offers useful observations on the strategies by which modern playwrights have sought to escape the chronological confines of traditional dramatic temporality. Though the plays he discusses reveal complex interpenetrations of past and present, and movements back through time, they achieve these effects against a sequentially developing stage present. See *Theory of the Modern Drama*, trans. Michael Hays (Minneapolis: University of Minnesota Press, 1987), esp. pp. 87–95.
4. Anton Chekhov, *The Major Plays*, trans. Ann Dunnigan (New York: New American Library, 1964), p. 235.
5. Elder Olson, *Tragedy and the Theory of Drama* (Detroit: Wayne State University Press, 1961), p. 13.
6. Richard Southern, *The Seven Ages of the Theatre* (New York: Hill and Wang, 1961), p. 26.
7. J. L. Styan, *The Elements of Drama* (Cambridge: Cambridge University Press, 1960), esp. pp. 48–140; *Drama, Stage and Audience* (Cambridge University Press, 1975), esp. pp. 31–67.
8. Keir Elam, *The Semiotics of Theatre and Drama* (London and New York: Methuen, 1980), p. 112.
9. D. E. Berlyne, *Aesthetics and Psychobiology* (New York: Meredith Corporation, 1971), p. 112.
10. Stephen Booth, "On the Value of *Hamlet*," in *Reinterpretations of Elizabethan Drama*, ed. Norman Rabkin, Selected Papers from the English Institute (New York and London: Columbia University Press, 1969), pp. 137–76; rpt. in *Literary Criticism: Idea and Act*, ed. William K. Wimsatt (Berkeley: University of California Press, 1974), pp. 285, 291.

11. H. R. Jauss, *Literaturgeschichte als Provokation* (Frankfurt: Suhrkamp, 1970); translated and quoted in Patrice Pavis, *Languages of the Stage: Essays in the Semiology of the Theater* (New York: Performing Arts Journal Publications, 1982), p. 74. Discussing the "horizon of expectation," Pavis cautions that such analysis must leave room for expectations generated within the work itself (p. 75).

12. Erving Goffman, *Frame Analysis: An Essay on the Organization of Experience* (New York: Harper & Row, 1974), p. 135. Bentley says of the Greeks and their awareness of a play's story: "They knew it, and their knowing it made a difference. Yet this difference was not a reversal of the psychological situation, it was a complication of it. An unstable equilibrium is established in the mind between certainty and uncertainty" (*The Life of the Drama*, p. 29).

13. One should also avoid overestimating a story's actual familiarity in accounts of theatrical reception. In response to claims that the Greeks arrived at the theater with a play's story clearly in mind, and the more detailed assumptions of many source scholars that a given historical audience shared their own familiarity with a source, one can note a little-cited passage in the *Poetics* where Aristotle mentions the drama of his time: "In some tragedies one or two of the names are well known and the rest have been invented for the occasion; in others not even one is well-known, for example, Agathon's *Antheus*, since in this play both the incidents and the names have been invented, and nonetheless they please us. Thus we must not seek to cling exclusively to the stories that have been handed down and about which our tragedies are usually written. It would be absurd, indeed, to do this since the well-known plots are known only to a few, but nevertheless please everyone" (*Poetics*, IX, p. 17).

14. Jackson Barry, *Dramatic Structure: The Shaping of Experience* (Berkeley: University of California Press, 1970), p. 81.

15. "No sensory imput is ever understood except as a 'version' of the perceiver's established meaning-structure; on the other hand, every understanding involves some modification of the perceiver's *system* of perceptual structures as a response to new input" (Gross, *Understanding Playscripts*, pp. 156–57).

16. L. S. Hearnshaw, "Temporal Integration and Behavior," *Bulletin of the British Psychological Society*, 30 (Sept. 1956), p. 8. The concept of "temporal integration" makes a transition to art criticism in the work of E. H. Gombrich, esp. "Moment and Movement in Art,"

Journal of the Warburg and Courtland Institutes, 27 (1964), pp. 293–306, and to literary studies in Frank Kermode, *The Sense of an Ending: Studies in the Theory of Fiction* (New York: Oxford University Press, 1967), esp. p. 46. Mari Reiss Jones discusses the attentional "trajectories" constituting mental time in "Only Time Can Tell: On the Topology of Mental Space and Time," *Critical Inquiry,* 7 (1980–81), pp. 557–76.

17. *St. Augustine's Confessions,* with an English translation by William Watts (1631), Loeb Classical Library (London: William Heinemann, 1912), II: 277–79; quoted in Hearnshaw, "Temporal Integration and Behavior," p. 3.

18. *Poetics,* VII, p. 14

19. Wilder, "Some Thoughts on Playwriting," p. 108.

20. William Archer, *Play-Making: A Manual of Craftsmanship* (New York: Dodd, Mead, and Co., 1912), p. 317.

21. Ibid., p. 316.

22. Clayton Hamilton, *So You're Writing a Play!* (Boston: Little, Brown, and Co., 1935), p. 178. Archer also employs the Olympian figure: "We are, in fact, in the position of superior intelligences contemplating, with miraculous clairvoyance, the stumblings and fumblings of poor blind mortals straying through the labyrinth of life. Our seat in the theater is like the throne on the Epicurean Olympus, whence we can view with perfect intelligence, but without participation or responsibility, the intricate reactions of human destiny" (*Play-Making,* p. 171).

23. Richard Levin, *The Multiple Plot in English Renaissance Drama* (Chicago and London: University of Chicago Press, 1971).

24. William James, *The Principles of Psychology* (1890; New York: Dover, 1950), I: 298.

25. Styan, *Drama, Stage, and Audience,* p. 27.

26. Elam notes "the necessary *projection* by the spectator of possible future developments in the action, his inferring of probable causes and effects, his filling of gaps in information, etc." and argues that "the drama is structured on the clashing of different and often opposing possibilities, i.e. conflicting possible states of affairs, and cannot be understood unless some notion of hypothetical worlds— realized or abandoned in the course of the drama—is applied" (*The Semiotics of Theatre and Drama,* pp. 101–2). Experimental aesthetics has explored the more general construction of hypotheses ("expectations of several mutually exclusive events . . . at once") in aesthetic response; see Berlyne, *Aesthetics and Psychobiology,* pp. 143–49.

27. Langer, *Feeling and Form*, p. 306.
28. Henrik Ibsen, *The Complete Major Prose Plays*, trans. Rolf Fjelde (New York: New American Library, 1965), pp. 232, 250.
29. For general discussions of memory, describing different models and the empirical research that they seek to explain, see John W. Donahoe and Michael G. Wessells, *Learning, Language, and Memory* (New York: Harper & Row, 1980), esp. pp. 409–513; Michael G. Wessells, *Cognitive Psychology* (New York: Harper & Row, 1982); Donald A. Norman, *Memory and Attention: An Introduction to Human Information Processing*, 2d ed. (New York: John Wiley & Sons, 1976); and Roy Lachman, Janet L. Lachman, and Earl C. Butterfield, *Cognitive Psychology and Information Processing: An Introduction* (Hillsdale, N.J.: Lawrence Erlbaum Associates, 1979). William James posited the distinction between "primary" and "secondary" memory in 1890; see *The Principles of Psychology*, I: 643–89. On the opportunities (and problems) presented by the use of cognitive psychology in the study of audience response, see Ed Tan, "Cognitive Processes in Reception," in *Multimedial Communication, vol. II: Theatre Semiotics*, ed. Ernest W. B. Hess-Lüttich, *Kodikas/Code*, 8 suppl. (1982), pp. 156–203; and Henry Schoenmakers, "The Tacit Majority in the Theatre," in Ibid., pp. 108–55.
30. George A. Miller, "The Magical Number Seven, Plus or Minus Two: Some Limits on Our Capacity for Processing Information," *The Psychological Review*, 63 (1956), p. 95.
31. De Marinis discusses the nature of theatrical attention in "Dramaturgy of the Spectator," pp. 106–12.
32. Martin Esslin writes, "We are conditioned to think of the stage (or a television or cinema screen) as spaces within which significant things are being shown; they therefore concentrate our attention and compel us to try and arrange everything that happens into a significant pattern, to make sense of it as a pattern" (*An Anatomy of Drama* [New York: Hill and Wang, 1976], p. 52).
33. Stanley E. Fish, *Surprised by Sin: The Reader in Paradise Lost* (Berkeley: University of California Press, 1971), p. 23.
34. Beckerman, "Theatrical Perception," p. 163.
35. Pavis, *Languages of the Stage*, p. 80. Pavis outlines some of the features of the enactment that "interrupt" dramatic fiction: "the event, the spectator's material reality, the actor's presence." On the power of the theater's sensory address alone, De Marinis writes: "In the case of theatrical performance, there is no doubt that the sensory faculties of the perceiving subject are called upon to sustain

an effort to which, for both quantity and quality, there is no equivalent in any other artistic field" ("Dramaturgy of the Spectator,"
p. 107).

36. Harold Pinter, *Betrayal* (New York: Grove Press, 1978), pp. 136–
37. Pinter's reverse chronology in this play has the effect of further
heightening the dramatic and theatrical present by denying
the spectator the contextualizing assurances of time's forward
movement.

37. Jean-Louis Barrault, "The Theatrical Phenomenon," trans. Thomas
B. Markus, *Educational Theatre Journal*, 17 (1965), p. 99. Noting
the physiological component of audience response, Marvin Rosen-
berg writes: "So tangible is this vicarious reaction in the presence
of drama that it is measured, in terms of skin reaction and pulse
beat, in a laboratory" ("The Languages of Drama," *Educational
Theatre Journal*, 15 [1963], p. 2).

38. Sir George Etherege, *The Man of Mode*, ed. W. B. Carnochan (Lincoln: University of Nebraska Press, 1966), p. 66.

39. Michael Goldman, *The Actor's Freedom* (New York: Viking Press,
1975), p. 87. Elsewhere, Goldman writes: "We relate to each of the
figures on stage in a number of ways simultaneously. We relate to
them as characters in a fiction, as real people moving and talking
close to us, and as actors, who are at once both real and fictitious,
and neither. Also we relate to them as parts of the entire stage activity, which likewise affects us bodily and directly" (*Shakespeare
and the Energies of Drama* [Princeton: Princeton University Press,
1972], p. 6). William B. Worthen writes: "In performance, the actor is engaged in two performances, a 'double-effect' that reveals
him as actor while it conceals him within his dramatic role." *The
Idea of the Actor: Drama and the Ethics of Performance* (Princeton: Princeton University Press, 1984), p. 3.

40. T. W. Baldwin, *The Organization and Personnel of the Shakespearean Company* (Princeton: Princeton University Press, 1927).

41. Thomas Kyd, *The First Part of Hieronimo and The Spanish Tragedy*, ed. Andrew S. Cairncross (Lincoln: University of Nebraska
Press, 1967), p. 62.

42. Barrault, "The Theatrical Phenomenon," p. 99; and Artaud, *The
Theater and Its Double*, p. 82. Brook writes: "When a performance
is over, what remains? . . . When emotions and arguments are harnessed to a wish from the audience to see more clearly into itself—
then something in the mind burns. The event scorches on to the
memory an outline, a trace, a smell—a picture" (*The Empty Space*,
p. 152).

Chapter Two

1. Pavis, *Languages of the Stage,* p. 81.
2. Ibid., p. 70.
3. Richard Hornby, *Script Into Performance: A Structuralist View of Play Production* (Austin: University of Texas Press, 1977), p. 91.
4. Bernard Beckerman, "Dramatic Theory and Stage Practice," in *Papers in Dramatic Theory and Criticism,* ed. David M. Knauf (Iowa City: University of Iowa Press, 1969), p. 36.
5. August Strindberg, *Six Plays by Strindberg,* trans. Elizabeth Sprigge (Garden City, N.Y.: Doubleday, 1955), p. 109 (ellipsis my own); John Millington Synge, *The Complete Plays of John M. Synge* (New York: Random House, 1935), p. 83.
6. Any way by which a play calls attention to its unreality, to its status as fictional construct, highlights the audience's expectation of narrative form. As Barry suggests, "even before art takes over, we are accustomed to order the events we observe into patterns; the events of a day, a career, an adventure, a voyage, etc. Stories enforce this kind of patterning in us" (*Dramatic Structure,* p. 164).
7. Arthur Wing Pinero, *Robert Louis Stevenson as a Dramatist,* Publications of the Dramatic Museum of Columbia University, ser. 1, vol. 4 (New York: Dramatic Museum of Columbia University, 1914), p. 43; discussed and applied by Barbara A. Mowat, *The Dramaturgy of Shakespeare's Romances* (Athens, Georgia: University of Georgia Press, 1976), pp. 35–94.
8. Eugene O'Neill, *Long Day's Journey Into Night* (New Haven: Yale University Press, 1956), p. 176. The sense of closure generated by such conclusions suggests that a play's resolution consists, in part, of the cessation of narrative uncertainty and in the final merging of story and stage, now linked in retrospective completeness. This feature of dramatic endings sheds interesting light on Hardison's discussion of Aristotelian *catharsis* as a "clarification of incidents" (*Aristotle's Poetics,* p. 116). Catharsis may occur, in part, through the final vindication of comprehension's attempts to order a dramatic world threatened by incompleteness and the unknown.
9. Bertolt Brecht, *Baal,* trans William E. Smith and Ralph Manheim, in *Collected Plays,* I (1971), p. 42. Brecht's theory and dramaturgy stand at an important juncture in terms of the dual modes of narrative manipulation explored in this study. On one hand, so pronounced was Brecht's interest in narrative comprehension and the possibilities of its command over the unmediated stage moment, so strong his insistence that performance must be kept "subordinate

to the story" (Foreword to *Antigone* [1948], in *Brecht on Theatre: The Development of an Aesthetic,* ed. and trans. John Willett [New York: Hill and Wang, 1957], p. 213), that his dramaturgy constitutes a catalogue of devices used to heighten cognitive formulation, including historicized dramatic settings, extradramatic commentary, summaries presented before scenes, and a philosophy of acting that stressed the clarification of incident. On the other hand, Brecht's "epic theater" cannot be adequately understood unless one recognizes that Brechtian dramaturgy depends equally on efforts to subvert the processes of narrative comprehension, to undercut the spectator's attempts to integrate stage events into coherent temporal pattern. Advocating a more "scientific" drama, Brecht practiced a dramatic art intended to break down conceptual wholes into clearly distinguishable segments, an art that would demand a perception at once alert, provisional, and critical, able to maneuver amid narrative discontinuity and the sociopolitical complexities Brechtian drama sought to represent: "As we cannot invite the audience to fling itself into the story as if it were a river and let itself be carried vaguely hither and thither, the individual episodes have to be knotted together in such a way that the knots are easily noticed. The episodes must not succeed one another indistinguishably but must give us a chance to interpose our judgment" ("A Short Organum for the Theatre" [1949], in Ibid., p. 201). Rejecting the closed system of classical irony with its hypnotizing inevitabilities and its unreflective empathy, Brecht manipulated an irony of discrepancy and disjunction that frustrated cognition so that it might recuperate its operations within a more sophisticated and engaged rationality. As a result of this commitment to a certain mode of audience response, this dramatist who agreed with Aristotle that "narrative is the soul of drama" (Ibid., p. 183) combined a heightening of narrativity with strategic cognitive disruption.

10. Kenneth Burke, *Counter-Statement,* 2d ed. (Los Altos, Calif.: Hermes, 1953), p. 31. Burke's remark forms part of a discussion entitled "Psychology and Form" (pp. 29–44).

11. Alvin Kernan, *The Cankered Muse: Satire of the English Renaissance* (New Haven: Yale University Press, 1959). Speaking of the satirist figure, Kernan writes: "As a result of his violent attacks on vice he acquires a number of unpleasant characteristics which make suspect his pose of a simple lover of plain truth" (p. 22).

12. For a discussion of the medieval *platea,* and its relationship to the more restricted acting area (*locus*), see Robert Weimann, *Shakespeare and the Popular Tradition in the Theater: Studies in the So-*

cial Dimension of Dramatic Form and Function, ed. Robert Schwartz (Baltimore and London: Johns Hopkins University Press, 1978), pp. 73–85. Weimann describes the incorporation of the *platea*'s extradramatic dimensions into English Renaissance dramaturgy: see pp. 237 ff.

13. Tom Stoppard, *Rosencrantz and Guildenstern Are Dead* (New York: Grove Press, 1967), p. 11.

14. Peter Handke, *Offending the Audience,* in *Kaspar and Other Plays,* trans. Michael Roloff (New York: Farrar, Straus and Giroux, 1969), p. 15.

15. John Webster, *The Duchess of Malfi,* ed. John Russell Brown (London: Methuen & Co., 1964), p. xli.

16. William Butler Yeats, *Collected Plays,* rev. ed. (New York: Macmillan, 1953), p. 436.

17. Shaw, *Collected Plays with their Prefaces,* II: 631.

18. David Bevington, *Medieval Drama* (Boston: Houghton Mifflin, 1975), p. 405.

19. Strindberg, *Six Plays,* p. 274

20. Artaud, *The Theater and Its Double,* pp. 76, 123, 93.

21. Tristan Tzara, *The Gas Heart* (1920), in *Modern French Theatre,* ed. and trans. by Michael Benedikt and George E. Wellwarth (New York: E. P. Dutton, 1964), p. 135.

22. Robert L. Caserio, *Plot, Story, and the Novel: From Dickens and Poe to the Modern Period* (Princeton: Princeton University Press, 1979), p. 282.

23. Christopher Marlowe, *Doctor Faustus,* ed. Sylvan Barnet (New York: New American Library, 1969). Unless otherwise indicated, subsequent references to the play are taken from this text.

24. The stage direction *"Thunder. Enter Lucifer and 4 deuils"* appears in the "B-text" (1616) of *Doctor Faustus* at the beginning of I.iii. For a discussion of this and other discrepancies between the extant texts of the play, see Marlowe, *Doctor Faustus,* parallel texts edited by W. W. Greg (Oxford: Oxford University Press, 1950). esp. p. 310.

25. Synge, *The Complete Plays of John M. Synge,* p. 37. Subsequent references to the play are taken from this text.

26. Edward Hirsch, "The Gallous Story and the Dirty Deed: The Two Playboys," *Modern Drama,* 26 (1983), p. 97.

27. Gross, *Understanding Playscripts,* pp. 134–36.

28. Such connections link the theatrical exploration of narrative with a number of recent studies that also explore the relationship between drama's thematic dimension and phenomenological aspects of au-

dience response: Thomas R. Whitaker, *Fields of Play in Modern Drama* (Princeton: Princeton University Press, 1977); Stephen Booth, *King Lear, Macbeth, Indefinition, and Tragedy* (New Haven and London: Yale University Press, 1983); Austin E. Quigley, *The Modern Stage and Other Worlds* (New York: Methuen, 1985); and States, *Great Reckonings in Little Rooms* (1985).

29. Barbara Hardy, "Towards a Poetics of Fiction: 3) An Approach through Narrative," *Novel*, 2 (1968–69), p. 5. Hardy's *Tellers and Listeners: The Narrative Imagination* (London: Athlone Press, University of London, 1975) provides a more extensive discussion of the narrator/audience relationship within fiction. For an approach to narrative activity within drama, see Kristin Morrison, *Canters and Chronicles: The Use of Narrative in the Plays of Samuel Beckett and Harold Pinter* (Chicago: University of Chicago Press, 1983).

30. Ben Jonson, *The Alchemist*, ed. Alvin B. Kernan (New York: Yale University Press, 1974), pp. 27–28.

31. During the lengthy Man of the Hill story in *Tom Jones*, by contrast, Tom and Partridge occasionally interrupt, but their presence is otherwise forgotten, for the storytelling situation is relegated to the background by the storyteller's narrative voice, always privileged in the linguistically conditioned world of the printed text. Interruptions revolve around incidental points (such as Partridge's own tale of the ghost), and the relative noninteraction between the narrator and his audience is several times rendered explicit: "Here *Jones* smiled at some Conceit which intruded itself into his imagination, but the Stranger, I believe, perceived it not, and proceeded thus" (Henry Fielding, *The History of Tom Jones, a Foundling*, introduction and commentary by Martin C. Battestin, text edited by Fredson Bowers [Middleton, Conn.: Wesleyan University Press, 1975], p. 472).

32. Bertrand Evans, *Shakespeare's Comedies* (Oxford: Oxford University Press, 1960), p. viii.

33. Artaud, *The Theater and Its Double*, p. 106.

34. Marjorie Garber analyzes the levels of irony and complicity, and the complications of temporal perspective, that result from Shakespeare's use of prophesy in the history plays; see "'What's Past is Prologue': Temporality and Prophesy in Shakespeare's History Plays," in *Renaissance Genres: Essays in Theory, History, and Interpretation*, ed. Barbara Kiefer Lewalski (Cambridge, Mass.: Harvard University Press, 1986), pp. 301–31.

Chapter Three

1. Robert A. Potter, *The English Morality Play: Origins, History, and Influence of a Dramatic Tradition* (London: Routledge & Kegan Paul, 1975), p. 244.

2. Anne Righter, *Shakespeare and the Idea of the Play* (London: Chatto and Windus, 1962; Middlesex: Penguin Books, 1967), p. 25.

3. The case of *Everyman* is more problematic, since the text of the play contains no explicit stage directions, and since the play is called a "treatise . . . in the manner of a moral play" in one of its early printings as though, Arnold Williams notes, its original publisher did not consider it a stage play at all (*The Drama of Medieval England* [East Lansing: Michigan State University Press, 1961], p. 160). Whether or not this is true, its dramatic text reveals a consistent mode of theatrical address, and a stage sophistication borne out by its subsequent production history.

4. For a version of this chapter that deals more directly with the issue of theatricality, see Stanton B. Garner, Jr., "Theatricality in *Mankind* and *Everyman*," *Studies in Philology*, 84 (1987), pp. 272–86.

5. Quotations from *Everyman* and *Mankind* are taken from Bevington, *Medieval Drama*.

6. King James Version (1611).

7. A. C. Cawley, ed., *Everyman and Medieval Miracle Plays* (New York: E. P. Dutton, 1959), p. xvii.

8. Thomas F. Van Laan, "*Everyman*: A Structural Analysis," *PMLA*, 78 (1963), p. 465. Van Laan extends this verdict to the Epilogue, as well.

9. V. A. Kolve, "*Everyman* and the Parable of the Talents," in *The Medieval Drama*, ed. Sandro Sticca (Albany: State University of New York Press, 1972), pp. 69–98, rpt. in *Medieval English Drama: Essays Critical and Contextual*, ed. Jerome Taylor and Alan H. Nelson (Chicago: University of Chicago Press, 1972), p. 321. The possible exception to the dramaturgical principle that no character returns to the stage is Everyman himself, who moves away from the others to receive extreme unction after line 749. Both Bevington and Cawley regard this as an exit and reentrance, but even though Five Wittes says "Peas, for yonder I se Everyman come" (l. 769), there is no textual necessity for Everyman actually to go offstage.

10. Potter, *The English Morality Play*, p. 53.

11. In Potter's words, the play's "solution" to death "leads, by way of repentance, toward putting the sequence of one's life and death in consonance with the redeeming life and death of Christ, and hence with the pattern of salvation" (Ibid., p. 53).

12. Comparison with the Japanese Noh is more than fanciful, since the play's story, like those of the Noh, derives from a Buddhist source; see Genji Takahashi, *A Study of Everyman* [Tokyo:] Ai-iku-sha, [1953?], pp. 19–38. The play bears striking dramaturgical similarity with Noh drama, from the explicit narrative openings and ritualistically patterned exits and entrances to the stylized evocation of a past splendor against the starkness of the stage present. Its thematic concern with mutability and abandonment finds parallels within the Noh. Cf. this passage from *Kantan*, a play roughly contemporary with *Everyman*: "ROSEI: Yet when I well consider / Man's life in the world of men . . . / CHORUS: Then shall you find that a hundred years of gladness / Fade as a dream when Death their sequence closes" (Arthur Waley, *The No Plays of Japan* [New York: Grove Press, 1957], p. 204 [ellipsis within the text]).

13. There have been elaborate modern productions of *Everyman*, such as that staged in Rockefeller Chapel at the University of Chicago (1973), but such efforts, while they highlight certain strains of realism within the play, risk working against its more fundamental theatrical asceticism.

14. Sr. Mary Philippe Cogan, *An Interpretation of the Moral Play, Mankind* (Washington, D.C.: The Catholic University of America Press, 1947), pp. 57–91.

15. Like Mischeff at the play's beginning, the three rogues generally arrive uninvited and unannounced, and although Titivillus is a celebrated exception to this rule, he is heralded as much for his entertainment promise as for his role in the developing allegory. But this randomness of entrance and exit characterizes the other characters as well: unlike his counterpart in *Everyman*, Mankinde enters unannounced, and even Mercy's final entrance is unexpected, throwing the stage into momentary confusion as he scatters Mischeff and his accomplices: "Lo, Mercy is here!" (l. 806). Instead of providing continuity, such entrances and exits disrupt pattern, diverting events onto unexpected courses.

16. Kathleen M. Ashley, "Titivillus and the Battle of Words in *Mankind*," *Annuale Medievale*, 16 (1975), p. 130.

17. Weimann, *Shakespeare and the Popular Tradition*, p. 151.

18. Williams, *The Drama of Medieval England*, p. 154 (for an opinion of the play's "degeneracy"); A. P. Rossiter, *English Drama from*

Early Times to the Elizabethans (London: Hutchinson's & Co., 1950; New York: Barnes and Noble, 1967), p. 107. Righter considers the play an example of "religious decadence" (*Shakespeare and the Idea of the Play,* p. 29).

19. Richard Axton, "Popular Modes in the Earliest Plays," in *Medieval Drama,* ed. Neville Denny, Stratford-Upon-Avon Studies 16 (London: Edward Arnold, 1973), p. 37.

20. Glynn Wickham, "Medieval Comic Traditions and the Beginnings of English Comedy," in *Comic Drama: The European Heritage,* ed. W. D. Howarth (New York: St. Martin's Press, 1978), p. 51; see also G. R. Owst, *Literature and the Pulpit in Medieval England* (Cambridge: Cambridge University Press, 1933). Michael R. Kelley has made an intriguing study of the Macro plays in terms of fifteenth-century "flamboyant style": see *Flamboyant Drama: A Study of the Castle of Perseverance, Mankind, and Wisdom* (Carbondale: Southern Illinois University Press, 1979), esp. pp. 1–28, 64–93.

Chapter Four

1. Sonnet 73, ll. 1–2.
2. Inga-Stina Ewbank, "The Triumph of Time in 'The Winter's Tale,'" *Review of English Literature,* vol. 5, no. 2 (April, 1964), p. 84.
3. Sonnet 15, ll. 1–2.
4. "It was Shakespeare's usual practice, histories apart, to bring the whole action of his plays within the frame of the picture, leaving little or nothing to narrative exposition" (Archer, *Play-Making,* p. 98).
5. T'ao Ch'ien (A.D. 365–427). Arthur Waley, trans., *A Hundred and Seventy Chinese Poems* (New York: Alfred A. Knopf, 1919; popular ed. 1923), p. 116; quoted (with slight inaccuracy) and discussed in William Empson, *Seven Types of Ambiguity* (London: Chatto and Windus, 1930), pp. 30–32. This thematic duality of the temporal and the atemporal no doubt drew upon the opposition present in the Elizabethan/Jacobean conception of temporality, in which time was viewed both as an unchanging realm of universal abstraction and as the more familiar realm of contingency and temporal change. Bernard Beckerman terms these two notions of time *iconic* and *historic,* and suggests that the development of Tudor drama saw a general movement from the former conception of time to the latter; see "Historic and Iconic Time in Late Tudor Drama," in *Shakespeare: Man of the Theater,* ed. Kenneth Muir, Jay L. Halio, and D. J. Palmer (Newark: University of Delaware Press,

1983), pp. 47–54. While the thematic celebration of unchanging ideals may have been relatively muted by the reign of James, *The Winter's Tale* demonstrates that the theatrical manifestation of iconic time in the stage's immediacy was being explored with unabated dramatic interest.

6. Investigating this connection brings us into the company of those critics who have approached this play's dramaturgy and stagecraft: Nevill Coghill, "Six Points of Stage-Craft in *The Winter's Tale*," *Shakespeare Survey*, 11 (1958), pp. 31–41; William H. Matchett, "Some Dramatic Techniques in 'The Winter's Tale,'" *Shakespeare Survey*, 22 (1969), pp. 93–107; Barbara A. Mowat, *The Dramaturgy of Shakespeare's Romances* (1976); and Charles Frey, *Shakespeare's Vast Romance: A Study of The Winter's Tale* (Columbia: University of Missouri Press, 1980). *The Winter's Tale* has made itself available to some of the finest "theatrical" readings in Shakespearean criticism, perhaps because (as we have long sensed) its dramatic effects depend more than any other play on its realization in performance. The statue scene alone has been an important school for such readings.

7. Matchett, "Some Dramatic Techniques," pp. 94–98. Shakespeare, after all, makes the relationship between Hermione and Polixenes much less "ambiguous" than Greene did in *Pandosto*, where Bellaria, "willing to shew how unfainedly she loved her husband, by his friends entertainment, used him likewise so familiarly, that her countenance bewrayed how her mind was affected towards him: oftentimes comming her selfe into his bedchamber, to see that nothing shuld be amisse to mislike him." James Winny, ed., *The Descent of Euphues: Three Elizabethan Romance Stories* (Cambridge: Cambridge University Press, 1957), p. 69. For ways in which this question has been addressed in productions of *The Winter's Tale*, see Dennis Bartholomeusz, *The Winter's Tale in Performance in England and America, 1611–1976* (Cambridge: Cambridge University Press, 1982), esp. pp. 229–32.

8. Frey, *Shakespeare's Vast Romance*, pp. 134–38.

9. See Stanley Wells, "Shakespeare and Romance," in *Later Shakespeare*, Stratford-upon-Avon Studies 8 (London: Edward Arnold, 1966), pp. 66–67, and J. H. P. Pafford, ed., *The Winter's Tale*, The Arden Shakespeare (London: Methuen, 1963), pp. lxiii–lxvii.

10. Ibid., p. lv. Though Mowat disputes the claim of critics such as E. M. W. Tillyard that Acts I through III constitute the equivalent of Shakespearean tragedy (*The Dramaturgy of Shakespeare's Romances*, pp. 5–21), it is nonetheless striking how dramaturgically

similar this concluding scene is to the tragedies and how many devices it borrows from them: the stage configuration of assembled characters grouped around a locus of suffering, commemoration of the tragic events in the form of narrative, the ironic counterpointing of knowledge and loss.

11. Evans, *Shakespeare's Comedies* (1960) and *Shakespeare's Tragic Practice* (Oxford: Oxford University Press, 1979).

12. Daniel Seltzer, "The Staging of the Last Plays," in *Later Shakespeare*, pp. 137–38.

13. Matchett, "Some Dramatic Techniques," p. 101.

14. One of the most extensive thematic studies of Autolycus' role within the play is Lee Sheridan Cox, "The Role of Autolycus in *The Winter's Tale*," *Studies in English Literature*, 9 (1969), pp. 283–301.

15. Francis Berry, "Word and Picture in the Final Plays," in *Later Shakespeare*, pp. 93–94.

16. Coghill, "Six Points of Stage-Craft," pp. 38–39. "In practice this scene is among the most gripping and memorable in the play" (p. 39).

17. To a much lesser extent, the reunions between Leontes and Polixenes and between Leontes and Camillo are also "obligatory," and these too are merely reported. The Messenger speeches do contribute something important to the play's conclusion, in part through their narrative activity. The Messengers present the offstage events in the terms of story and fable—"like an old tale" (V.ii.28); "like an old tale still" (l. 61)—contributing to the almost formal narrativity of the play's final scenes. But the scene itself underscores the limits of such narrativity, for the burden of these reports is to suggest how fully the offstage reconciliations *exceed* the bounds of story—"Such a deal of wonder is broken out within this hour that ballad-makers cannot be able to express it" (ll. 23–25); "I never heard of such another encounter, which lames report to follow it, and undoes decription to do it" (ll. 56–58)—and to make the conventions of narrative feel inadequate to the "wonder" recounted and (unknown to the audience) soon to be staged. Marjorie Garber discusses the messenger scene in terms of the "inexpressibility topos"; see "'The Rest is Silence': Ineffability and the 'Unscene' in Shakespeare's Plays," in *Ineffability: Naming the Unnamable from Dante to Beckett*, ed. Peter S. Hawkins and Anne Howland Schotter (New York: AMS Press, 1984), pp. 47–48.

18. In this role, she anticipates Ariel, who likewise scourges memory in his "ministers of Fate" speech to Alonso, Antonio, and Sebastian:

"But remember / (For that's my business to you) that you three /
From Milan did supplant good Prospero, / Expos'd unto the sea
(which hath requit it) / Him, and his innocent child" (*The Tempest,*
III.iii.68–72).

19. Aristotle, *On Poetry and Style,* trans. G. M. A. Grube (Indianapo-
lis: Bobbs-Merrill, 1958), p. 33. For Grube's "Antinous," I have
substituted the more familiar "Alcinous." See *Aristotle's Poetics,*
p. 28.

20. For a discussion of the ways in which Shakespeare uses specific
notations in the text to control the theatrical realization of the
statue scene, see Jörg Hasler, "Romance in the Theater: The Stagecraft of the 'Statue Scene' in *The Winter's Tale,*" in *Shakespeare:
Man of the Theater,* pp. 203–11.

21. Ewbank, "The Triumph of Time," p. 97. On the importance of ges-
ture within Shakespearean drama, see David Bevington, *Action is
Eloquence: Shakespeare's Language of Gesture* (Cambridge,
Mass.: Harvard University Press, 1984), esp. pp. 67–98.

22. See S. L. Bethell, *The Winter's Tale: A Study* (London: Staples Press,
[1947]), and Roy Battenhouse, "Theme and Structure in 'The Winter's Tale,'" *Shakespeare Survey,* 33 (1980), pp. 123–38.

23. Matchett, "Some Dramatic Techniques," p. 106.

Chapter Five

1. T. S. Eliot, "Ben Jonson" (1919), in *Essays on Elizabethan Drama*
(New York: Harcourt, Brace & World, 1932), p. 65.

2. *Volpone,* Prologue, ll. 34–35. References to *Volpone* and *The
Alchemist* are from *Volpone,* ed. Alvin B. Kernan (New Haven:
Yale University Press, 1962) and *The Alchemist,* ed. Alvin B. Kernan (New Haven: Yale University Press, 1974). References to Jonson's other plays are from *Ben Jonson,* ed. C. H. Herford and Percy
and Evelyn Simpson, 11 vols. (Oxford: Oxford University Press,
1925–52), spelling and punctuation modernized, volume and page
numbers omitted.

3. Jonas A. Barish, *Ben Jonson and the Language of Prose Comedy*
(New York: W. W. Norton & Co., 1960), p. 80. For an intelligent
discussion of Jonsonian plotting, see Gabriele Bernhard Jackson's
Introduction to *Every Man in His Humor* (New Haven and London: Yale University Press, 1969). William E. Gruber offers a compelling reading of Jonson's plotting and its subversions of audience
expectation in *Bartholomew Fair,* in *Comic Theaters: Studies of
Performance and Audience Response* (Athens: University of Georgia Press, 1986), pp. 71–99. Gruber writes of this play: "Jonson's

audience is forced to sympathize, to judge, to plot sequences of action, and then is mocked for its folly" (p. 82).

4. Samuel Taylor Coleridge, July 5, 1834. *Table Talk and Omniana* (2d ed., rev. 1836; Oxford: Oxford University Press, 1917), p. 311. In an article entitled "How to Read *The Alchemist*" (*College English,* 21 [1959–60], pp. 456–60), Robert E. Knoll challenges the view that the play's narrative is demanding. Claiming that Jonson structures his play according to five versions of a common pattern—introduction, an interval of neglect, then a gulling—Knoll argues that this structure makes only minor demands on comprehension: "A simple situation is repeated five times. One must not mistake quantity for complexity." Again: "The action of the play is not complicated; it is only multiplied" (p. 458). Knoll's claim, though, not only misrepresents Jonson's dramaturgy (Jonson rarely structured his plays according to systematic parallels), it more seriously mistakes the cognitive dimension of audience response. Given memory's limitations, qualtity is complexity, multiplicity is complication, and the play's intricacy places severe pressure on faculties limited in their ability to order and retain incoming impressions. If Knoll's claim constitutes an inadequate response to those who find *The Alchemist* taxing to read, its assumptions are even more inappropriate when applied to performance, where the "multitude of details" (p. 458) becomes physical activity unfolding on its own terms, implicated within the sensory immediacies of performance.

5. Aristotle betrays this spatial conception in his remarks on the primacy of plot over character: "A closely corresponding situation exists in painting. For if someone should paint by applying the most beautiful colors, but without reference to an over-all plan, he would not please us as much as if he had outlined the figure in black and white" (*Poetics,* VI, p. 13).

6. Etymological material in these paragraphs, including the Shakespearean example, are taken from *The Compact Edition of the Oxford English Dictionary* (New York: Oxford University Press, 1971).

7. This sense of struggle, as characters cluster around one another, jockey for predominance, and tug the plot in their own direction, is noticeably absent from the Politic/Peregrine subplot and helps explain why this narrative line, if it has not always bothered the critic, often remains limp and unsatisfying to reader and spectator. Politic Would-be, as his name suggests, wants to become something he is not, and he hints at the secret details of a plot that he is wait-

ing to act upon: "certain projects that I have, / Which I may not discover" (IV.i.46–47). However, he never translates this intrigue into action, never extends his fascination with the minutiae of politics to the point at which he exerts any significant pressure on the play's events. While the suitors impel themselves into action, Sir Politic remains largely passive in his delusions, and Peregrine's counterplot, like the gulling of Puntarvolo in *Every Man out of His Humor,* is designed primarily for ridicule. The Would-be subplot is different from the rest of *Volpone* not simply because of the separateness of its action, but also through its more fundamental difference in mode, a looseness of action and activity far more reminiscent of the Humors comedies.

8. Stephen J. Greenblatt notes the "deadness," revealed in V.i that has lurked beneath the brilliance of Volpone's histrionic and linguistic performance—an emptiness that propels him into further activity, and the play, seemingly over, into further action. See "The False Ending of *Volpone,*" *JEGP,* 75 (1976), p. 93.

9. Jackson, ed., *Every Man In His Humor,* p. 26.

10. Alexander Leggatt, "The Suicide of Volpone," *University of Toronto Quarterly,* 39 (1969–70), pp. 19–32.

11. John Sweeney, "*Volpone* and the Theater of Self-Interest," *ELR,* 12 (1982), p. 221.

12. Focusing on the play's morality elements, Robert Potter considers *Volpone* "A Jacobean *Everyman*" (*The English Morality Play,* pp. 144–52).

13. See Harry Levin, "Jonson's Metempsychosis," *PQ,* 22 (1943), pp. 231–39.

14. Gabriele Bernhard Jackson, *Vision and Judgment in Ben Jonson's Drama* (New Haven and London: Yale University Press, 1968), p. 66.

15. Anne Barton discusses Jonson's varying use of names in *Ben Jonson, Dramatist* (Cambridge: Cambridge University Press, 1984), esp. pp. 170–93.

16. Edward B. Partridge, *The Broken Compass: A Study of the Major Comedies of Ben Jonson* (London: Chatto and Windus, 1958), p. 86. Though Partridge asserts that "the names of the characters obviously identify them" (p. 83), he notes (p. 84) confusion in the identification of *Corbaccio* and *Corvino,* since the former derives from the Italian for "crow" and the latter from the Italian for "raven," and since the word *crow* generally refers to the genus *Corvus,* which includes ravens. The point is slight, but were his aim genuinely to identify these characters with animal counterparts, Jonson was too accomplished a linguist not to distinguish more clearly.

17. Kernan writes of the Pythagorean scene: "In the body of the play itself the characters pass through a variety of assumed shapes, ending in the forms of ridicule and sickness which the court forces them into at the end of the play" (*Volpone*, p. 210).

18. The interaction of Peregrine and Sir Pol in the mountebank scene suggests a characteristically Jonsonian subversion of a device generally employed by his contemporaries for narrative heightening. As a rule, outside observers provide distancing perspective on dramatic action, often—as in the case of the four lovers in *Love's Labour's Lost,* or of Troilus and Thersites—pointing a dramatic sequence's shape and its relationships (often ironic) to other sequences and to the action as a whole. Peregrine and Sir Pol, on the other hand, refuse this subordinate function, claiming attention for their own interaction; in the theater, their dialogue constitutes a performance of its own, rivalling that of Volpone. A potentially simplifying device, in other words, ends by complicating the multiplicity of events and issues it would otherwise streamline. Jonson occasionally dramatizes onstage audiences within separate inductions constituting small plays in their own right.

19. Barish, *Ben Jonson and the Language of Prose Comedy,* p. 187.

20. Eliot, "Ben Jonson," p. 66. In an observation that bears upon Jonsonian drama and the particular difficulty it presents in the theater, Eliot writes: "Poetry of the surface cannot be understood without study; for to deal with the surface of life, as Jonson dealt with it, is to deal so deliberately that we too must deliberate, in order to understand." It is precisely this kind of deliberation that the theater renders so difficult.

21. Jonas A. Barish, "The Double Plot in *Volpone,*" *Modern Philology,* 51 (1953–54), pp. 83–92.

22. Thomas M. Greene discusses this Jonsonian symbol in "Ben Jonson and the Centered Self" *SEL,* 10 (1970), 325–48.

23. For more extensive discussion of Jonson's turbulent relationship with his audience, see Jonas A. Barish, "Jonson and the Loathèd Stage," in *A Celebration of Ben Jonson,* ed. William F. Blissett (Toronto: University of Toronto Press, 1973), pp. 27–53; rpt. (with modifications) in Jonas Barish, *The Antitheatrical Prejudice* (Berkeley: University of California Press, 1981), pp. 132–54; see also Peter Carlson, "Judging Spectators," *ELH,* 44 (1977), pp. 443–57.

Chapter Six

1. Langer, *Feeling and Form,* p. 307.

2. See Stephen S. Stanton, ed., *Camille and Other Plays* (New York: Hill and Wang, 1957).

3. Shaw, *The Perfect Wagnerite* (Chicago: Herbert S. Stone, 1898), p. 36.

4. References to Shaw's plays (and prefaces) are taken from *Collected Plays with their Prefaces*. With the exception of *Major Barbara* and *Heartbreak House*, which form the main texts of this chapter and which appear in volumes III and V respectively, references will include volume number and page. Shaw's peculiarities of spelling and punctuation have been preserved.

5. Shaw, *Our Theatres in the Nineties*, rev. ed. (London: Constable and Co., 1932), III: 85.

6. Shaw, *The Quintessence of Ibsenism*, rev. ed. (New York: Brentano's, 1913), p. 232.

7. On Shaw's inversions of dramatic convention, see Martin Meisel, *Shaw and the Nineteenth-Century Theater* (Princeton: Princeton University Press, 1963), p. 122. For a more general discussion of how Shaw subverts plot expectations, see J. L. Wisenthal, "Having the Last Word: Plot and Counterplot in Bernard Shaw," *ELH*, 50 (1983), 175–96.

8. Shaw, Preface to *Plays Pleasant* [1898], I: 378.

9. Shaw, "To Audiences at *Major Barbara*," prefatory note circulated to the press for Grace George's American production of *Major Barbara* in 1915 and 1916; rpt. in *Shaw on Theatre*, p. 118.

10. Fergusson, *The Idea of a Theater*, p. 180.

11. Robert F. Whitman, *Shaw and the Play of Ideas* (Ithaca and London: Cornell University Press, 1977), p. 227.

12. Shaw, "To Audiences at *Major Barbara*," p. 118.

13. Shaw used *heartbreak* as a term for disillusionment in *Major Barbara,* both in the account of Todger Fairmile's conversion—"He gave in to the Jap when his arm was going to break. But he didnt give in to his salvation until his heart was going to break" (p. 113)—and in the scene of Barbara's desolation: "Dolly: you are breaking my heart" (p. 135). One might also recall the boast of self-sufficiency in Tanner's remark to Mendoza: "[The mountains] will not make me dream of women, my friend: I am heartwhole" (*Man and Superman*, II: 629).

14. The exception to this rule is the conversion of Bill Walker, which operates at a personal level forced, perhaps, by his otherwise frightening lack of emotional sensitivity. It is a striking feature of *Major Barbara*'s central act, and a complicating element of Barbara's character, that Shaw's protagonist engineers a seduction as ruthlessly attuned to male vulnerability as that of Lady Macbeth and the "demon daughters" (p. 156) of *Heartbreak House*.

15. Meisel, *Shaw and the Nineteenth-Century Theater,* p. 321.

16. V. S. Pritchett, in a 1950 memorial essay on Shaw, wrote that *Heartbreak House* "appeared to many as a confusion." See "G. B. S.: 1856–1950," *Time,* 56 (13 November 1950), pp. 30–31; rpt. in *George Bernard Shaw: A Critical Survey,* ed. Louis Kronenberger (Cleveland: World Publishing, 1953), p. 244.

17. On this and other features of the play's dramaturgy, see Frederick P. W. McDowell, "Technique, Symbol, and Theme in *Heartbreak House,*" *PMLA,* 68 (1953), p. 337.

18. Charles A. Berst, *Bernard Shaw and the Art of Drama* (Urbana: University of Illinois Press, 1973), p. 231.

19. One might speculate that in the theater, as in life, a mistaken structure of comprehension is never fully abandoned, but persists even after it has been discredited. Such traces account for the double and multiple vision so often occasioned by Shavian drama and for the dreamlike haziness characteristic of *Heartbreak House.* For a discussion of this phenomenon in literary narrative, see Menackhem Perry, "Literary Dynamics: How the Order of a Text Creates Its Meaning," *Poetics Today,* 1 (1979), esp. pp. 355–356.

20. Fergusson, *The Idea of a Theater,* p. 183.

21. Eric Bentley, *Bernard Shaw: A Reconsideration* (New York: New Directions, 1947; W. W. Norton, 1976), p. 140.

22. Shaw, Preface to *Three Plays by Brieux* (New York: Brentano's, 1912), p. xv. Compare his remark on dramatic endings in 1898: "The end may be reconciliation or destruction; or, as in life itself, there may be no end" (Preface to *Plays Pleasant,* I: 373).

23. Friedrich Nietzsche, *The Birth of Tragedy and the Genealogy of Morals,* trans. Francis Golffing (Garden City, N.Y.: Doubleday and Co., 1956), p. 22; quoted (in different translation) in Margery M. Morgan, "*Major Barbara,*" in *Twentieth Century Interpretations of Major Barbara,* ed. Rose Zimbardo (Englewood Cliffs, N.J.: Prentice-Hall, 1970), p. 75. Michael Goldman discusses the Dionysiac foundations of *Major Barbara* (and of Shaw's drama in general) in "Shaw and the Marriage in Dionysus," in *The Play and Its Critic: Essays for Eric Bentley,* ed. Michael Bertin (New York: University Press of America, 1986), pp. 97–111.

24. Shaw, in Archibald Henderson, *George Bernard Shaw: Man of the Century* (New York: Appleton-Century-Crofts, 1956), p. 628.

25. For a provocative discussion of Shaw's flight from the darker implications of his dramatic art, a discussion not always fair to the willingness with which he often engaged these implications in his

plays, see Robert Brustein, *The Theatre of Revolt* (Boston: Little, Brown, 1962), pp. 181–227.

26. Stark Young, *Immortal Shadows: A Book of Dramatic Criticism* (New York: Charles Scribner's Sons, 1948), p. 207.

27. Shaw, "The Play of Ideas," *The New Statesman and Nation,* 39 (May 6, 1950); rpt. in *Shaw on Theatre,* p. 290.

Chapter Seven

1. Dates of Beckett's plays refer to year of first performance. References to these plays are taken from the following texts: *Waiting for Godot* (New York: Grove Press, 1954; verso and recto indicated with the letters *a* and *b*), *Endgame* (New York: Grove Press, 1958), and *Happy Days* (New York: Grove Press, 1961).

2. Alain Robbe-Grillet, himself no stranger to the edges of narrative, wrote of Beckett's drama precisely in terms of this "presence." Alain Robbe-Grillet, "Samuel Beckett, or 'Presence' in the Theater," trans. Barbara Bray, in *Samuel Beckett: A Collection of Critical Essays,* ed. Martin Esslin (Englewood Cliffs, N.J.: Prentice-Hall, 1965), pp. 108–16.

3. References to these plays, and to Beckett's plays for radio and television, are taken from Samuel Beckett, *Collected Shorter Plays* (New York: Grove Press, 1984). Because of textual discrepancies between this and earlier editions, references to *Not I* and *Footfalls* are from *Ends and Odds* (New York: Grove Press, 1976), and the two references to *Cascando* and *Rockaby* are taken from *Cascando and Other Short Dramatic Pieces* (New York: Grove Press, 1977) and *Rockaby and Other Short Pieces* (New York: Grove Press, 1981).

4. Holograph note written during the composition (1974–75) of *That Time*. Reading University Library, ms. 1639; quoted in James Knowlson and John Pilling, *Frescoes of the Skull: The Later Prose and Drama of Samuel Beckett* (London: John Calder, 1979), p. 219.

5. For a discussion of the visual dimensions of Beckett's performance image in the plays from *Not I* through *What Where,* see Stanton B. Garner, Jr., "Visual Field in Beckett's Late Plays," *Comparative Drama,* 21 (1987–88), 349–73.

6. Enoch Brater discusses Beckett's late plays as "theater poems" in *Beyond Minimalism: Beckett's Late Style in the Theater* (Oxford: Oxford University Press, 1987), esp. pp. 3–17.

7. On the fictionalizing activities of Beckett's dramatic characters (activities that align them with the playwright's prose characters), see

Elin Diamond, "The Fictionalizers in Beckett's Plays," in *Samuel Beckett: A Collection of Criticism,* ed. Ruby Cohn (New York: McGraw-Hill, 1975, pp. 111–19; and Kristin Morrison, *Canters and Chronicles.*

8. Among studies that consider Beckett's late plays as performance pieces, especially *Not I* and *Footfalls,* the following are particularly illuminating: Knowlson and Pilling, *Frescoes of the Skull* (1979); Enoch Brater, *Beyond Minimalism* (1987); Ruby Cohn, *Just Play: Beckett's Theater* (Princeton: Princeton University Press, 1980); Paul Lawley, "Counterpoint, Absence, and the Medium in Beckett's *Not I," Modern Drama,* 26 (1983), pp. 407–14; William B. Worthen, "Beckett's Actor," *Modern Drama,* 26 (1983), pp. 415–24; R. Thomas Simone, "A Commentary on Beckett's *Footfalls," Modern Drama,* 26 (1983), pp. 435–46; and S. E. Gontarski, *The Intent of* Undoing *in Samuel Beckett's Dramatic Texts* (Bloomington: Indiana University Press, 1985).

9. Paul Lawley discusses this kind of dismemberment in the text of *Not I;* see "Counterpoint, Absence, and the Medium," pp. 410–12.

10. Beckett has said: "Somewhere [man] must know that self-perception is the most frightening of all human observations. He must know that when man faces himself, he is looking into the abyss." John Gruen, "Samuel Beckett Talks about Beckett," *Vogue,* vol. 154, no. 10 (December 1969), pp. 210–11; quoted in Hersh Zeifman, "Being and Non-Being: Samuel Beckett's *Not I," Modern Drama,* 19 (1976), p. 42.

11. On the roles of Beckett's dramatic listeners, especially those in the late plays, see Bernard Beckerman, "Beckett and the Act of Listening," in *Beckett at 80/Beckett in Context,* ed. Enoch Brater (New York: Oxford University Press, 1986), pp. 149–67; and Katharine Worth, "Beckett's Auditors: *Not I* to *Ohio Impromptu,"* in Ibid., pp. 168–92.

12. Quoted in Brater, *Beyond Minimalism,* p. 23.

13. Ibid., p. 40. Beckett's remark on *That Time* is from a letter to J. Knowlson (September 24, 1974), quoted in Knowlson and Pilling, *Frescoes of the Skull,* p. 206.

14. Recounted by Walter D. Asmus in "Practical Aspects of Theatre, Radio, and Television: Rehearsal Notes for the German Premiere of Beckett's 'That Time' and 'Footfalls' at the Schiller-Theater Werkstatt, Berlin (directed by Beckett)," trans. Helen Watanabe, *Journal of Beckett Studies,* no. 2 (Summer 1977), p. 83 (quotations of Beckett within Asmus' invaluable production notes are indirect). Martin Esslin has applied the term *moving image* to Beckett's late

plays as a group; see "A Poetry of Moving Images," in *Beckett Translating/Translating Beckett*, eds. Alan Warren Friedman, Charles Rossman, and Dina Sherzer, (University Park: Pennsylvania State University Press, 1987).

15. Beckett's characterization of the piece as "chamber music" was made at the rehearsals of the original production (Royal Court Theatre, Spring 1976), quoted in S. E. Gontarski, "Texts and Pretexts of Samuel Beckett's *Footfalls*," *Papers of the Bibliographical Society of America*, 77 (1983), p. 191.

16. Ibid., p. 194. For the Grove Press edition of *Ends and Odds* (1976), Beckett removed the lines "My voice is in her mind. (*Pause.*)" from page 45, line 5, and "She hears in her poor mind, She has not been out since girlhood. (*Pause.*)" from line 8 (revising the earlier Faber edition [1976]). For Beckett's specifications concerning the duration of the breaks between movements (seven seconds each for the light fade out, the chime sound, and the light fade up), and for his instructions concerning the actress' lip movements during the monologue of the second movement, "as though she were murmuring something to herself," see Asmus, "Practical Aspects," pp. 83, 87.

17. This concern with the ambiguous status (and unclear origin) of stage voice has characterized Beckett's drama from its start: witness the indeterminate "voices" mentioned in *Godot* and the abrupt shifts in *Endgame* and *Happy Days* between "normal" and "narrative" voice, shifts that have the Brechtian effect of fragmenting utterance into discontinuous vocal gestures. Beckett's work with the disembodied voices of radio and television allowed him to explore the performance phenomenon of "internal" voice, and its potentially indeterminate origins (Opener alludes to this question of status in the radio play *Cascando* [1963], referring to the Voice he commands: "They say, It's in his head. / It's not," p. 12). In the late plays, voices fill the stage in a space often ambiguously placed between internal and external, probing consciousness while maintaining a carefully objectified stage presence. Even the monologue of *Not I*, seemingly bound to the illuminated Mouth, has a vaguely problematic source (the voice in the tale, after all, rambles on unbidden and unstoppable: "something in her begging . . . begging it all to stop . . . unanswered," (p. 23); more than one critic has been tempted to view Mouth as the conduit of an independent narrative stream.

18. Asmus, "Practical Aspects," p. 84.

19. Asmus, "Practical Aspects," p. 85. On the "ghost" dimensions of this this play, see Worth, "Beckett's Auditors," pp. 189–90. Worth

characterizes *Footfalls* as "a structure of echoes, so artful that we are never able to know for certain who is listening to whom and in what dimension of reality" (p. 183). Not only does *Footfalls* share the otherworldliness of Beckett's later works for television—*Ghost Trio* (1977), *but the clouds,* and *Nacht und Träume* (1983)—it recalls the gothic image of the woman "all alone in that ruinous old house" (p. 12) whose music ("Death and the Maiden") frames Beckett's radio play *All that Fall* (1957). The echo of titles and the rhythmic footsteps in the former suggest a connection between *Footfalls* and this earlier play.

Afterword

1. O'Neill, *Long Day's Journey Into Night,* p. 11.
2. *A Midsummer Night's Dream,* III.i.119.
3. Walter Benjamin, *Illuminations,* ed. Hannah Arendt, trans. Harry Zohn (New York: Schocken Books, 1969), p. 100.

Index

Note on the Author

Stanton B. Garner, Jr., who received his Ph.D. in English from
Princeton University, has published on medieval, Renaissance,
and modern drama. He is currently an assistant professor at
the University of Michigan.